SHAKESPEARE'S WIDE AND UNIVERSAL STAGE

edited by C. B. COX and D. J. PALMER

Shakespeare's wide and universal stage

Manchester University Press

© Manchester University Press 1984

Published by Manchester University Press
Oxford Road, Manchester M13 9PL
and 51 Washington Street, Dover, New Hampshire 03820, USA

British Library cataloguing in publication data

Shakespeare's wide and universal stage.
  1. Shakespeare, William – Criticism and
  interpretation
  I. Cox, C. B.   II. Palmer, D. J.
  822.3'3   PR2976
ISBN 0-7190-1075-6

Library of Congress cataloguing in publication data
  applied for

Printed in Great Britain
by Butler & Tanner Ltd, Frome and London

Photoset by Elliott Brothers & Yeoman Ltd, Liverpool

Contents

Foreword

These essays first appeared separately in *The Critical Quarterly* and we are grateful to the authors for permission to reprint them in collected form. During the course of twenty-five years *The Critical Quarterly* has published a substantial amount of Shakespeare criticism, including discussions of recent major productions and surveys of critical approaches to particular plays. This volume represents the range of such work and offers a broad and balanced selection of essays on the comedies, histories and tragedies. It is not an introductory guide to Shakespeare, but it reflects a spectrum of modern critical interest in the plays, addressed to that 'great variety of readers' invoked by the First Folio itself. Originating as they did in a journal of wide literary appeal, these essays counter the notion that modern Shakespearians write only for other Shakespearians. Each is strongly individual in its point of view, but neither rigidly schematic nor perversely ingenious, sharing durable qualities of insight and illumination which merit their re-issue.

C. B. COX
D. J. PALMER

JOHN RUSSELL BROWN

Mr Beckett's Shakespeare

I

Shakespeare's plays are often described as extended symbols, more or less elaborate presentations of figures in significant patterns. Two schools of criticism have been responsible for this. The first was an 'Imagist' school, starting around 1930 and applying verbal analysis to a play as if it were a poem. Wilson Knight can be its spokesman:

> While we view the plays primarily as studies in character, abstracting the literary person from the close mesh of that poetic fabric into which he is woven, we shall. . . end by creating a chaos. . . If, however, we give attention always to poetic colour and suggestion first, thinking primarily in terms of symbolism, not 'characters', we shall find each play in turn appear more and more amazing in the delicacy of its texture, and then, and not till then, will the whole of Shakespeare's work begin to reveal its richer significance, its harmony, its unity. *(The Shakespearian Tempest* (ed. 1953), pp. 3–4)

Professor Knight drew up a chart showing the 'real lines of force in Shakespeare' and how the 'basic symbols of tempest and music in vital opposition unify Shakespeare's world'. For him the plays are allegories, their incidents defined by poetic 'images'. Thus, in *The Merry Wives of Windsor*, Falstaff is 'bodily grossness personified', his ducking a punishment (with 'appropriate ignominy'), and the amateur theatricals of the conclusion a vindication of spiritual values:

> Excessive fleshiness is eventually punished by 'spirits' or 'fairies', that spiritual element that has been outraged by lust or any excessive bodily indulgence. (pp. 100–2)

Critics of the other symbolic school travel a more obviously arduous road, exploring an Elizabethan 'background' to the plays. So E. M. W. Tillyard reviewed Tudor attitudes to English history before deciding that Shakespeare presented an unambiguous doctrine:

> In the total sequence of his plays dealing with the subject matter of Hall [the Chronicler], he expressed successfully a universally held and still comprehensible scheme of history: a scheme fundamentally religious, by which events evolve under a law of justice and under the ruling of God's Providence, and of which Elizabeth's England was the acknowledged outcome. *(Shakespeare's History Plays* (1944), pp. 320–1)

In Tillyard's view the histories were no longer experiments for writing tragedies, but Shakespeare's reworking of the 'old Morality form' in which 'the personalities of his kings' were never allowed to 'trespass on the

1

fundamental Morality subject of Respublica'. These plays became 'fundamentally' comprehensible, as if they were allegories. Sixteen years later another 'historical' critic, Irving Ribner, could display *Patterns in Shakespearian Tragedy* (1960), so that its characters are viewed as symbols. According to him: 'Edgar becomes a *symbol* of divine justice triumphing over evil to reassert the harmony of God's natural order. The blast of his trumpet as he goes into combat is a *symbolic* echo of the last judgement', or again: 'Cordelia cannot be judged by any standard of psychological verisimilitude . . . She is not a real person . . . She serves, like the earlier Desdemona, as a *symbol* of love and self-sacrifice, a reflection of the love of God (p. 135).' In a footnote, the professor explained that Cordelia 'has been called, in fact, a symbol of Christ, who must die to make possible her father's redemption', and he summoned Marion Parker, S. L. Bethell and P. N. Seigel as witnesses. By studying Shakespeare's plays 'in the light' of beliefs supposed to be 'universally held', the critics have seen *Hamlet* as a study of regeneration, *Othello* and *Macbeth* as representations of damnation. Comedies and tragedies have been given 'symbolic significance' by finding in them the patterns of primitive rituals: C. L. Barber has said that Shakespeare's 'fundamental method' in his romantic comedies was 'to shape the loose narrative so that "events" put its persons in the position of festive celebrants' (*Shakespeare's Festive Comedy* (1959), p. 6).

In short, critics of both schools have found, everywhere in Shakespeare, a 'fundamental' idea, and they value individual plays as they present 'symbols' of that idea.

II

Judged by this measure our present generation of dramatists will seem feckless. Ionesco has renounced ideas:

> I have no ideas before I write a play . . . I believe that artistic creation is spontaneous. At least it is for me. Only spontaneity can guarantee a direct knowledge of reality. All ideology ends up with indirect knowledge which is only secondary, oblique and falsified.   ('Discovering the Theatre',
> tr. L. C. Pronko, *Tulane Drama Review*, iv (1959), 16)

He is content to define *after* he has written a play, or when he is not writing at all: 'Creation . . . is life, it is liberty, it can even be counter to the conscious desires (these are seldom fundamental desires) and to the prejudices of the creator' ('Reality in Depth', *Encore*, 5 (1958), 10). Such statements are taken up in chorus: Miss Jellicoe, for example: 'I did not know what the play was about. I wrote without thought and rewrote and rearranged intuitively' ('Something of Sport', *Encore*, 5 (1958), 26). For a closer description of such an activity we may turn to contemporary 'abstract' or 'action' painters who have had a longer experience in such endeavour; Jackson Pollock has explained:

> When I am *in* my painting, I'm not aware of what I'm doing. It is only after a sort of 'get acquainted' period that I see what I have been about. I have no fears about making changes, destroying the image, etc., because the painting has a life of its own. I try to let it come through. It is only when I lose contact with the painting that the result is a mess. Otherwise there is pure harmony, an easy give and take, and the painting comes out well.
>
> ('My Painting', *Possibilities*, 1 (1947), 79)

The new 'harmony' or unity is not easily defined in ideological terms. Harold Pinter confesses himself much interested in 'form', but careless of 'meaning':

> I start off with people, who come into a particular situation. I certainly don't write from any kind of abstract idea. And I wouldn't know a symbol if I saw one. ('Writing for Myself' [an interview], *Twentieth Century* (February 1961), p. 174)

New dramatists reject thematic development and symbolic situation: they claim that ideology plays no part in the conception of their work.

But we must not be overpersuaded: ideas are not easily banished from anyone's mind. Professor Clifford Leech in *Stratford-upon-Avon Studies, IV* (1962), described the characters of *The Caretaker* in morality terms, almost as if Dr Tillyard were speaking of Shakespeare's history plays: Davies is 'Everyman', Mick 'Affairs of the World' and Aston 'Charity'. In *Tulane Drama Review* (1962) Bernard Dukore has stated that in Davies 'we recognize not only the old man whose powers have failed, but also the Old England whose powers have failed', and, in contrast to Pinter himself, claims roundly that 'Pinter's plays are obviously symbolic'. The same might be said of Ionesco: in his *Killer*, the Architect is a representative, almost a symbol, of Bureaucracy, and Mother Peep another Boanerges, a symbol of Political Enthusiasm. As Jackson Pollock's paintings were entitled 'War' or 'The She-Wolf', so these new plays are not unnameable 'Compositions'.

The artist lives in a human context which includes ideologies, and he creates his artefacts to satisfy his mind which is consciously and unconsciously formed by that context. He may not intend to write with reference to ideologies, but he inevitably will, unconsciously at least. No element is new in such activity, except priorities: perhaps all that we should say is that the new dramatist, like the contemporary painter, does not place clearly articulated ideas high among his conscious artistic concerns.

Yet even this is saying a great deal. The language of much Shakespearean criticism is inappropriate to the new drama because of the different priorities. As we would severely limit our response to a Kandinsky or Pollock painting by fastening on a recognisable image within its composition, so we should not be content with the symbols that can be discerned in the plays of Ionesco, Pinter and their fellows. Their *dramatis personae* may sometimes appear as ideograms, but if we describe the plays according to such identifications we must judge them to be over-elaborate and clumsy. The manner of presentation and the complexity of an audience's involvement must also be described.

And, on the other hand, the relevance of the new drama to our understanding of Shakespeare should be obvious: it is a presumption to believe that dramatic experience can be fully described in terms of pattern and symbol. Shakespeare *may* have been more secure in his beliefs concerning the nature of man than we are, more confident of the efficacy of ideograms, but even if this could be proved we should remember that his imagination contained other elements, and that drama might have satisfied these as well. To speak of Shakespeare's plays in symbolic terms reveals a unity, but it does not necessarily follow that the plays are wholly harmonious, or that this unity is the only one. Such criticism may seem to clarify our appreciation, but it does not necessarily follow that the plays are without other aspects important to author and to audience: Falstaff may have been created to serve other purposes than the personification of 'bodily grossness', Cordelia to be something which in the dramatic context is more powerful than a 'symbol of Christ'.

I I I

The contrast between the new dramatists and many Shakespearean critics is most interestingly posed by *Waiting for Godot*. No new play makes more obvious and continual use of symbols, yet none of comparable success has so baffled understanding. It has been produced as an optimistic play and as a pessimistic, as a Christian and as an atheistic. Yet there are symbols, personifications and signposts which might be expected to control the audience's response: Cain and Abel, scapegoat and innocent, master and servant, night and day, isolation and community, suffering and will-power, blindness and sight, a tree without leaves and a tree with leaves, Christ and 'all mankind'. The paradox for Shakespearean critics is that these symbols do not reveal the play's unity – a unity attested by its power to hold attention in many different interpretations. They do not draw the action 'towards some overwhelming question', or pose a single dramatic issue. A Wilson Knight could readily discover a 'richer significance' in terms of *Godot*'s symbolism, but where he saw 'discord' a Ribner might find 'love', or where he saw an 'ignominious punishment' a Barber might discern a joyful 'celebration'. All critics would have to simplify the drama to make it conform to a single 'pattern'. (Here, perhaps, we may understand why Beckett has discouraged actors from discussing what their parts may *mean*.)

Flat contradictions arise on all sides. Estragon is a Christ-figure:

Vladimir	Your boots. What are you doing with your boots?
Estragon	*(turning to look at his boots)* I'm leaving them there. *(Pause)*. Another will come, just as . . . as . . . as me, but with smaller feet, and they'll make him happy.
Vladimir	But you can't go barefoot!
Estragon	Christ did.
Vladimir	Christ! What's Christ got to do with it? You're not going to compare yourself to Christ!
Estragon	All my life I've compared myself to him.
Vladimir	But where he was it was warm, it was dry!
Estragon	Yes. And they crucified quick.

Silence.

The comparison with Christ seems to give 'significance' to many of Estragon's actions: when Vladimir tells him to 'Do the tree', he tries to balance on one foot with arms spread out and asks 'Do you think God sees me?'; closing his eyes as he is instructed, he *'staggers worse'*; he stops, and then cries *'at the top of his voice'*: 'God have pity on me! . . . On me! Pity! On me;' Pozzo and Lucky enter immediately and Estragon believes that his prayer has been answered by the arrival of Godot; despite the commotion caused by the newcomers collapsing among their luggage and by cries for help, Estragon has become confident that he and Vladimir have finished with waiting. The outcast, through pain, mortification, struggle, prayer and the physical attitude of Christ on the tree of the cross, has found assurance. But the imitation of Christ is momentary: even in his prayer Estragon is selfish; he has tried to commit suicide before and will again, like Judas on a willow; he is cruel, spiteful, stupid, inconstant, deceitful, ungrateful. Besides, other characters are also, at certain moments, Christ-figures. Lucky is the suffering servant, or the fool, who is being taken to the fair to be sold. (In the French version this destination is named *'Saint-Sauveur'*.) Even Pozzo, when he re-enters blind and has to be held up between Estragon and Vladimir, is a helpless sufferer freed from a sense of time, dispossessed of the 'love of created things'. (Vladimir's story of the crucifixion early in the play, together with Pozzo's fears that they are highwaymen, may help to identify the two supporters as the two thieves.) We cannot say that any one character 'serves as a symbol of Christ', though several perform this function, in various ways and fragmentarily.

We may say that *Waiting for Godot* has a *momentary* symbolism; this awakes strong reactions, but inconsistently. The tree, the one dominant feature of the setting, serves as a simple indentification of place; it is simply a tree, a notable object in its surroundings which might have been a 'bush' or a 'shrub'. But this tree is also a willow on which men may hang themselves, and also, in direct contradiction to this, the 'Tree' by which men must wait patiently and behind which, as a last resort, they try to hide from unknown assailants. When it grows four or five leaves overnight, it seems to change again, to represent the 'Tree of Life', or 'Nature', or 'Spring'. Similarly the 'road' of the stage-setting is the 'Way' for human pilgrims, but also 'like nothing'; and, yet again, it is the road to 'the Fair'; and Pozzo wonders if it is the Board or the plank (the French is *'la planche'*) which he, being blinded, must walk to destruction. Or, to follow another series of momentary symbols, Estragon and Vladimir are 'all mankind' (but at another time two individuals isolated from society); and, in helplessness, Pozzo is likewise 'all mankind' (and elsewhere 'Landlord' and 'Keeper'). If we follow one character, Estragon is seen as a 'poet', awakening to his vision by a reminder of 'maps of the Holy Land', and forgetting most experiences except those he 'never forgets', and yet he is also a man without vision who tries to enjoy a dream-world in sleep. Lucky, too, is a poet whose first job was to supply Pozzo with 'Beauty, grace, truth of the first water', and he is also the dependent man who needs to be a 'slave'.

Godot, who never appears, may seem more secure as a symbol, especially to English audiences who will hear echoes of 'God' in his very name. He keeps goats and sheep, and sends messengers to say he will appear; and he probably has a white beard. (In the French version Vladimir asserts that *chez Godot*, *'Il fait encore jour'*.) Vladimir believes that Godot can both 'save' and 'punish', and hearing of his beard, prays (more generously than Estragon): 'Christ have mercy on us!' (the French version has *'Misericorde'*). But in the shifting consciousness awakened by other traditional symbols, Godot cannot 'serve as a symbol of God'. Certainly he cannot represent the Christian God, for, although he inspires fear and hope, he shows no sign that, like Lucky's hypothetical 'personal God', he 'loves us dearly'. Vladimir who is most assured of Godot's existence speaks of him consulting his family, agents and books before taking a decision, as if this were 'the normal thing' for Godot as for men of influence. Moreover, Vladimir has other gods: the 'Saviour' who forgives from the cross, the 'cruel fate' which consigns men among a 'foul brood' and, perhaps, the 'reinforcements' of other men which put an end to waiting for Godot. At certain moments Godot seems to symbolise aspects of the Christian God; at other moments he seems to represent the illusion of such a God; at still others he seems to be a man of influence, or the illusion of such a man.

When Vladimir says that the 'air is full of the cries' of men, he describes the momentary symbolism of the play: among many inaudible influences are Christian and aesthetic ones, and these are sometimes caught, or reflected, in words and action on the stage. So, for example, Vladimir's kidneys have taught him 'never neglect the little things of life' and cause him to think of the 'last moment': when he feels this moment coming he is 'relieved and at the same time ... appalled'. These reactions have certain common associations which encourage the audience to think, for an instant, of 'The Last Moment' or the day of doom. Certain 'cries in the air' have been reflected in Vladimir's words, but they are not his cries, nor is his action wholly represented by them: while he (like the audience, perhaps) proceeds to remember Christ crucified, he believes there is 'nothing to be done' for himself and, certainly, he has no thought of Godot. The traditional voice is insubstantial, like an echo, and heard only for a moment.

The play's obvious symbols do not, then, reveal the play's unity. That depends on the progressive revelation of the innermost natures of the four major characters through the apparently inconsequential repetitions and dialogue and stage-business. The audience progressively realises that Vladimir deliberates and Estragon feels, that Pozzo is frightened and lonely, while Lucky is secure; it will also come to recognise that each of these characters needs the mere presence of his fellow.[1] These revelations are presented in an unspecific manner beneath (or behind) the words, by means of unusual emphases, pauses, juxtapositions, by wordless or word-denying actions and by repetitions. Beckett has refused to choose and establish symbols to define this development; but rather, in Pollock's words, he prefers his play to have a 'life of its own' which he allows to 'come through'. In performance, in spite of apparent contradictions in symbolism, there 'is pure harmony', an instinctively conceived and indirectly perceived unity.

The manner of the Shakespearean critics would be too simple to describe this play. We might liken the stage to a radar screen, and say that, while much that it shows seems to signify nothing, occasionally an outward manifestation of character comes 'on beam', according to some traditional setting. But this screen is important for itself, and its apparently meaningless and repetitious 'nonsense' carries the main subject of the play. We might prefer to say that the dramatic action has been given a backcloth depicting a perspective according to Christian and other concepts, and that occasionally a figure seems to be 'placed' within its world; but this metaphor would have to be further complicated, because the backcloth is visible only when one of these momentary placings occurs. To catch the double life of *Waiting for Godot*, we might contend that the characters perform an apparently formless and repetitive drama, one without narrative line or explicit theme, and that this is accompanied by unheard music; occasionally an individual performance conforms to that music and then a character momentarily appears to sing or dance, to have 'significance'; but the apparently formless drama is the true drama in its progressive revelation of human characters in time, and in their conscious and unconscious life.

Lucky's tirade, his single speech, is an epitome of the play. It is bewilderingly complex and yields no consecutive 'sense'. Yet during its course there is a consistent development from his reluctance to speak to his determination to do so (from what the French version describes as a *'monotone'* to struggling and shouting), so that beneath the words by the manner of their delivery, the tirade reveals a will to think and speak in a human context, however imperfectly. Its words abundantly reflect cries which are in the 'air' of the whole play, traditional notions of a personal God and human activities, but, while each notion is heard several times, clarity is always lost after a moment. It is lost by habitual repetitions, as 'for reasons unknown', 'but not so fast', 'in spite of', 'I resume', 'in the light of', 'what is more', 'alas'. The play offers no direct comment on these repeated phrases, but if while reading the text we pause in an attempt to assemble the attitude of mind implicit in them it will have nothing in common with the ideas Lucky momentarily seems to define; it will be pessimistic, habitual and, perhaps, stoical.

Mr Beckett can recognise traditional symbols and he identifies them clearly for his audience. Nevertheless his *dramatis personae* are actuated by forces not represented by those symbols: they act according to physical and mental characteristics, their need for each other and the habit of performing in order to 'pass the time'. If we wish to understand their 'significance' we must wait until after a performance and then deduce it for ourselves. For example, we may say that the world of Schopenhauer, Bergson and some Existentialists is realised in the human figures of the foreground, that of Christianity occasionally suggested in the background; that a pragmatic world is presented over against one that is authoritarian, traditional and theoretical; continuous pessimism over against intermittent optimism; 'living' meaningless over against 'dead' meaning. Certainly the play evokes a double perception: that of the existence of the characters and that of Christian thought. The former depends on action and words that are frequently puzzling, especially if viewed out of context, and is slowly revealed without recourse to statement or symbol. The latter depends on the clear symbolic 'significance' of isolated moments, a significance which will seem to be greater, more stereotyped, or more irrelevant to life, according to the presuppositions of the audience.

In terms of dramatic experiment, Mr Beckett has shown that theatrical illusion can present men as instinctively perceived in relation to each other

8

in time and simultaneously suggest another world of thought by 'momentary' symbolism, a world independent of those men, unified in its own conceptual terms and not in their humanly realised ones. Other modern dramatists have tried to escape from symbols; he has proved that the theatre can invoke symbolism without being limited by it, can present human beings who are measured by an 'idea' but not restricted by it.

This theatrical possibility, drawn to our attention by the 'new' drama and, especially, by *Waiting for Godot*, is of utmost importance for our understanding of Shakespeare. He seldom perplexes so obviously as Mr Beckett, but he does perplex some men and frequently divides opinion; he might have discovered the same inherent quality of theatrical illusion.

IV

We have been so schooled by the critics who hunt for 'significance' that Beckett's momentary symbolism may appear thoroughly un-Elizabethan, a kind of drama that Shakespeare could not have attempted. Yet occasionally, even these critics seem to recognise something in Shakespeare's plays that is very similar. So Muriel Bradbrook has found fault with *All's Well That Ends Well*:

> the reason . . . it is not a successful play, is that a personal and an impersonal theme are here in conflict. It began by being a 'moral play', a grave discussion of the question of what constituted true nobility, and the relation of birth to merit . . . But in *All's Well* the 'social problem' – to give it the modern term – of high birth, exemplified in Bertram, and native merit, exemplified in Hellen, is bisected by a human problem of unrequited love.
>
> (*Shakespeare and Elizabethan Poetry* (1951), p. 162)

But suppose Shakespeare intended to suggest a patterned, 'exemplifying' drama in the background and in the foreground to present characters with a related but independent stage 'life': would *All's Well* then be a 'successful play'? We now know that this kind of double perspective is a theatrical possibility.

Or when Wilson Knight admonished us, in his *Crown of Life* (1947), to view the appearance of Jupiter in *Cymbeline* in a special way, might he have been encouraging us to neglect an important element in the play? 'The extraordinary event', he wrote, 'cannot be properly received without full appreciation of the more-than-personal significance of Posthumous' (p. 164). This is like Professor Ribner's: 'Cordelia cannot be judged by any standard of psychological verisimilitude . . . : she serves . . . as a symbol of love and self-sacrifice'. These critics recognise that the plays provoke a reaction that conflicts with 'symbolism': perhaps they are wrong in arguing that this 'no-more-than-personal' reaction must be relinquished in order to preserve the symbolic.

Sometimes a critic is less obviously Procrustian, and then we must re-examine the play and the records of performance in order to observe how much has been lopped away in favour of an exclusive 'symbolism'. Tillyard has written that Richard the Third 'melts from credible character into a combination of sheer melodrama villain and symbol of diabolism' (p. 211); he argued that the play changes from 'realism' to 'symbolism', and implied that Shakespeare had to choose one of two kinds of drama. But in performance *Richard III* has always been esteemed for its progressive revelation of the hero's character. The most realistic actors of their times – Garrick, Kean, Cooke, Mansfield and Irving among them – have been particularly memorable in Richard's awakening from his dream just before the conclusion. (Hogarth's portrait of Garrick as Richard III depicts this moment.) Moreover, Richard's words at this late moment are in a *new* style, more subtly representing the mind sustaining them than elsewhere in the play and revealing fears hitherto almost completely hidden. Both the stage-history and the text suggest that Tillyard, in emphasising the play's symbolic significance, has urged us to suppress a less ideological reaction for which Shakespeare has well provided.

Beckett can present men in relation to each other and at the same time suggest a symbolic pattern they do not wholly or consistently follow. This is a kind of dramatic illusion that Shakespeare might have discovered for himself. I believe he did, and that this accounts for divergent qualities that have been observed in his plays: we need not deny one of two conflicting reactions; symbolism can be established momentarily; a play can present issues which have little relevance to the pattern of its symbolism.

V

We may begin by considering *Richard III*, an early play and one comparatively easy to describe. Let us look at the conclusion where, as Tillyard teaches us, symbolism seems to conflict with the impression of Richard as a 'credible character'. The symbolism is obvious: the tents of Richard and Richmond are pitched at either side of the stage; the ghosts of those whom Richard has murdered move regularly from one to the other, cursing and then blessing; their words sum up many formal speeches of lamentation and prophecy throughout the play – Richard is 'devil', 'butcher', 'boar', and Richmond is associated with 'good angels', 'peace', 'offspring'. The opposing symbolic figures meet in combat, isolated from their armies, and then the crown is placed formally on Richmond's head as victor, king and pacifier. In the final scene, presumably with Richard's dead body before him, Richmond praises God, announces his marriage that will 'unite the white rose and the red', and relates the death of the 'bloody dog' to the purging of a nation that has been 'mad':

> The brother blindly shed the brother's blood,
> The father rashly slaughter'd his own son,
> The son, compell'd, been butcher to the sire.

Richard is destroyer and divider: Richmond, who dares to oppose him, is pacifier and unifier. They are conceptually opposed: devil and angel.

But the play is not so simple as this. If we take Richard's soliloquy after his dream as its full climax rather than the combat – in subtlety and range of reference it is certainly the verbal climax – we may say that the realisation of Death is the theme of the play. This is represented by a recurrent incident: Richard faces Death after all his victims have done so, similarly isolated, and after Edward IV, the two murderers, and, by report, Dighton and Forrest. Repetition enforces the importance of this 'action' and clarifies its terms. Moreover it is in newly-immediate utterance that Richard finds awakened, in himself as in the others, a consciousness called 'conscience'. Here is another clear thematic unity or pattern for the play: the figure of death, who repeatedly halts the narrative drive for reconsideration, is the unseen antagonist of Richard and of the other characters: the essential action is between Death and Man. Richmond, in this view, is a minor contrast only, for he looks to the future trusting in God, rather than to the past and present judging his own life; he remains unvisited by Death and is, therefore, less involved with this aspect of the play's significance.

Already we have seen a recurrent *and* a narrative symbolism: the characters are not limited by one theme or concept, but serve at least two, with different demands upon them. As in *Waiting for Godot*, the clearest symbols are animated momentarily rather than continuously, for only thus could confusion be avoided. They are, perhaps, cries in the air which are occasionally reflected by words and actions, and (as seldom in *Godot*) by character and narrative as well. And still we have left unexamined many elements of this play: Richard's death concludes a far less symbolic drama as well, one as unrelated to conceptual thought as the interplay of Estragon and Vladimir.

It is generally agreed that Richard dominates the first acts. He does so by a series of impersonations:

> – Dive, thoughts, down to my soul: here Clarence comes.
> – Cannot a plain man live and think no harm?
> – Come, cousin, canst thou quake, and change thy colour . . . ?
> – Come, let us to our holy task again.

John Russell Brown

Hastings judges that 'His Grace looks cheerfully and smooth today', when, in fact, Richard is about to have him beheaded. But Richard's performance is not always perfect. When he enters crowned with his court (IV.ii), he orders 'Stand all apart': the king, who should be the dependent centre, is isolated; he is seen to be 'angry' and to 'bite his lip'; soon he acknowledges the 'uncertainty' of gain in soliloquy. At the beginning of the play his impersonations were smooth and spirited; now they are uneasy. In the last act Richard himself realises:

> I have not that alacrity of spirit,
> Nor cheer of mind, that I was wont to have.

Now he repeatedly searches the faces of others:

> – My Lord of Surrey, why look you so sad?
> –Saw'st thou the melancholy Lord Northumberland?
> – What said Northumberland . . . and what said Surrey then?

He repeats his demands – to pitch his tent, to be given a bowl of wine, to be left alone. He can no longer boast 'I am determined to prove a villain' (I.i.30): he is a villain, *and* he is afraid. There are indirect signs of this from his coronation onwards: allusions to bad dreams, and a new forgetfulness and recklessness; and, in the last act, abrupt changes of mood, and the repetitions and questions we have already noticed. Then the soliloquy on wakening from his dream expresses his innermost thoughts in the release, the slackened control, of excitement and fear:

> Have mercy, Jesu! . . . O coward conscience . . . What do I fear? . . .
> I am a villain: yet I lie, I am not.
> Fool, of thy self speak well: fool, do not flatter.

The climax of the soliloquy reveals still more deeply: Richard's inner-antagonist is fear of isolation, of being unloved:

> I shall despair. There is no creature loves me;
> And if I die, no soul shall pity me.

When Ratcliff's familiar voice calls him, Richard is terrified: ' 'Zounds! who is there?'; and then, with reassurance, confesses:

> O Ratcliff, I have dream'd a fearful dream!
> What thinkest thou, *will our friends prove all true ?*
> – No doubt, my lord.
> –   O Ratcliff, I fear, I fear, –

He leaves the stage to 'play the eavesdropper, to see if any mean to shrink from me'.

The presentation of Richard's inward fear does not depend on symbolic identifications, and it is explicit only for a moment. But Shakespeare has provided many devices to ensure its effectiveness: it is progressively revealed; it speaks with gestures as well as words; it is emphasised by repetitions. This dramatic interest is sustained almost to the conclusion of the play: Richard's answer to fear is action, speed, exaggeration, and courage. At the last he is still questioning and has a new interest in omens, but he 'enacts more wonders than a man, daring an opposite to every danger'; turning his thoughts from his isolation he seeks Richmond 'in the throat of death'. His prowess and commital to the 'hazard of the die' are all a measure, and even a presentation of his loneliness.

As we have seen, Richmond's concluding speech sums up one of the explicit themes of the play, but, as he announces the 'bloody dog is dead', the audience will know better: the 'dog' was also an isolated and frightened man. The audience, which has seen what Richmond has not, may consider the final unhurried words of the victor as a conventional close to the play, a final curtain that will not be examined too curiously. There is a rapid widening of the dramatic focus; from the intensity of our knowledge of Richard we are required to consider other modes of existence and the continuing course of man. So the play ends enigmatically, for what hides beneath these continuing impersonations?

In an earlier play Shakespeare had already presented the death of a villain and defined three different responses. Cardinal Beaufort, in *Henry VI, Part II*, dies conscience-stricken for the murder of his brother, and speaks with something of the immediacy of Richard's last soliloquy (III.iii.11–8). The responses on stage are varied. Salisbury, for instance, piously wishes that the dying man's soul might 'pass peaceably'; this is the reaction of critics who see *Richard III* as a play about Death's judgement. In contrast, Warwick sternly recognises the justness of 'so bad a death' after a 'monstrous life'; this is the reaction of those who see *Richard III* as Right's struggle against a 'monster'. But the king rebukes Warwick with: 'forbear to judge, for we are sinners all'. This is a third response; he has entered into Beaufort's agony, as if it were his own. No one else speaks, and the king concludes the scene with:

> Close up his eyes and draw the curtain close;
> And let us all to meditation.

In *Richard III* Shakespeare has developed the presentation of the inner-drama of his hero, so that this third response is also appropriate. The symbolic or thematic values of the play speak clearly to the Warwicks and Salisburys in the audience; but the presentation of its central character is partly in other terms, less explicit and therefore more bewildering; Richard is realised in terms of a human being in action. Shakespeare has evoked a conceptual world without being limited by it.

To understand the importance of the unspecific, inward drama of *Richard III*, we have only to turn to the long history of success in the theatre. In performance the enigmatic 'star' part has always held attention: Richard is the man who cries 'A horse! a horse! my kingdom for a horse!' not a villain anatomised for our consideration.

VI

We can describe the 'themes', or symbolism, of *Richard III* more confidently than those of *Waiting for Godot*, for the concepts are represented by narrative as well as words and incidents, and individual characters bear a consistent, if not continuous, relation to them. But we should not allow this assurance to prevent us from looking further, to those elements which are not so readily defined; these might have had an equal, or greater, importance for Shakespeare, and certainly they reveal another shaping influence upon the drama.

The critics who tell us to reject a 'credible character' in order to recognise a 'symbol' have been ignoring the nature of theatrical illusion. They are like earlier 'neo-classical' critics who taught that the stage could represent only one place during any one performance. Today our new theatre proves that a play may be observed successively, or even simultaneously, in symbolic and realistic terms, according to thematic 'significance' *and* according to an apparently 'meaningless' illusion of life. We may have the Richard of Dr Tillyard *and* the Richard of countless actors and audiences.

'The artist creates to satisfy his conscious and unconscious mind'; 'Form is not always dependent on a recognisable ideology'; 'Explicit meanings can co-exist with implicit unspecific meanings'; 'Symbolism can be evoked momentarily': – if we accept these statements much of the criticism of Shakespeare's plays ceases to be controversial. Every opinion will not be right, of course; nor will the inter-relation of the kinds of dramatic illusion within a single play be easy to describe. But on these grounds, substantiated by the one-sided experiments of the new dramatists, we may found a criticism which is capable of comprehending a great range of the reactions recorded by critics and men of the theatre from many ages and with many differing sensibilities.

VII

Measure for Measure is another play with at least two faces. It has been called a Christian play: in this view, the duke represents the 'Incarnate Lord' or

14

'Providence'; Isabella might be called Virtuous Chastity.[2] Echoes are heard from the Bible and the Homilies, and words or actions sometimes have an obvious symbolic importance:

> I perceive your grace, like power divine,
> Hath look'd upon my passes.

> He who the sword of heaven will bear
> Should be as holy as severe.

> More than our brother is our chastity.

Lucio sticks 'like a burr', is no respecter of persons or occasions, and leaves with a grimace; in all this and more, as Nevill Coghill has shown, he is in the same tradition as the fiends of medieval drama.[3] Momentarily, 'meaning' is transmitted loud and clear. But there are other less explicit issues. The duke is easily confident and unnecessarily ingenious; he leaves his realm with mystifying drama; he speaks disdainfully of the 'dribbling dart of love' and yet presumes to judge the devoted responses of Juliet and Mariana; he is disguised as a Christian friar and yet tells Claudio that life is 'a thing that none but fools would keep'; while the happiness of many people is at stake, he has a soliloquy in which he considers how gossip is attracted to great men, like himself; he takes needless pains to praise Angelo when he is assured that his earlier suspicions were well-grounded. All this seems inappropriate to his symbolic role of 'Incarnate Lord' or 'Providence'. But the energetic craftiness has not arisen accidentally from the artifice of the plot; it is a consistent element of his presentation. Shakespeare has accentuated it by a contrast with the good sense and reliability of the Provost; even the ineffectual concern of Escalus acts as a dramatic foil to the duke's ready confidence, and Lucio gives the audience fit words for exaggerating these aspects of his character in his jibe at the 'fantastical duke of dark corners'.

Such responses are often dismissed as impertinent:

> We have two sharply-defined and widely-held views diametrically opposed to each other [wrote Nevill Coghill]; at least one of them must be wrong, and by 'wrong' I mean 'hostile or contrary to Shakespeare's understanding of [the play]'.

Symbolic significance usually wins; but despite Professor Coghill, the two views may both be right. Shakespeare may have shown a strangely and deeply motivated character over against a symbolic pattern of behaviour which he momentarily suggests, and a large part of his artistic concern may have been to explore such a character's inward nature instinctively.

So, too, Isabella is more than 'Virtuous Chastity'. She moves from a novitiate in a nunnery to a sustained denunciation of her brother which is violently self-defensive and alight with sexual imagery, and later to a willingness to exhibit herself as a deflowered virgin. Here there is a progressive character revelation as fear displays its power and sexual foundation, and is defeated when love begins to foster a lack of self-regard. At the close of the play Isabella can accept the duke's offer of marriage; she does so silently, because she has been spent in the struggle to accept her full self and its dangers.

These are subtle effects. They imply an ability to grasp general ideas, and to distrust them in judging human beings. They require an intuitive knowledge of the innermost resources of mind and body. They can be obscured by director or actor, and ignored by audience or reader. But I believe that they are truly and consistently written into Shakespeare's plays and that they contribute largely to their perennial power to hold 'our attention and illuminate our consciousness. We do ill service to our understanding to stress Shakespeare's presentation of various concepts, some commonplace and some obsolete. We must notice such significance, of course, but we must also try to appreciate his achievement in the less easily defined plane of his drama's action. Instead of presenting him as a Tudor conformist, let us see him as an Elizabethan empiricist – not as a sceptic or an ironist, but a thinking man who recognises that it is difficult to understand all the experiences that men enjoy and endure.

In some later plays Shakespeare seems to attempt a firmer delineation of the double dramatic perspective, as if he had gained conscious assurance in an effect that he had developed intuitively. When, at the end of *King Lear*, the hero is stretched on the rack of suffering, the audience is given only half-crazed words and actions by which to understand his state of being; critics have debated inconclusively whether he dies in joy or grief. Although the tragedy has many symbolic intimations of the redemptive power of love and the need for mutual truth and order, helpless, ignorant suffering is a major impression of the last scene. Of the survivors on stage, Albany speaks only in terms of a 'great decay' and the 'weight' of a 'sad time'. Kent recognises Lear's powers of endurance and, through his sense of involvement in some journey away from the others, he alone finds a task beyond 'general woe'. For viewing Lear's death the audience is given no explicit reminder of the concepts which helped to shape the tragedy and which seemed, at certain moments, to be capable of resolving pain and anxiety within a beneficent ordering of human affairs; a few men hold the stage at the close with no obvious relation to a symbolic idea. A comparison with the end of *Richard III* shows how far Shakespeare has travelled from his earlier diagrammatic groupings. An audience would have to be very self-convinced to avoid some measure of bewilderment and anxiety.

At the end of *The Tempest*, Prospero is reinstated as Duke of Milan, forgiving his enemies and attempting once again a life within an imperfect society. The charmed circle, the revealed lovers, the broken rod, the released Ariel, the procession which empties the stage are potent symbols figuring justice, mercy, regeneration, art, responsibility, affection. But Prospero then turns back, and faces the audience alone: he has more to say. Shakespeare clearly, and with assurance, reminds the audience that a human being does not fully complete a pattern. Having acted as Providence, Ruler, Sage and Artist, Prospero is now only any other man:

> Now I want
> Spirits to enforce, art to enchant,
> And my ending is despair.
> Unless I be relieved by prayer,
> Which pierces so that it assaults
> Mercy itself and frees all faults.
> As you from crimes would pardon'd be,
> Let your indulgence set me free.

The humanity of Prospero is finally affirmed in bare, conceptual terms.

Shakespeare's usual method was more intuitive and less specific in its demands upon the audience, but Prospero speaks for all: whatever symbolic force a character may have momentarily he can seldom be wholly known in symbolic terms. Shakespeare wrote to satisfy his conscious and unconscious mind; his dramatic form was not solely dependent on defined ideologies; his explicit meanings co-exist with those for which he himself had not discovered suitable words.

Notes

1   I have traced this technique in 'Mr Pinter's Shakespeare', *Critical Quarterly* vol. 5, No. 3 (1963), pp. 251–65.
2   Cf. R. W. Battenhouse, *'Measure for Measure* and the Christian doctrine of atonement', *PMLA*, 67 (1946) and Elizabeth M. Pope, 'The Renaissance Background of *Measure for Measure'*, *Shakespeare Survey*, 2 (1949).
3   Cf. N. Coghill, 'Comic form in *Measure for Measure'*, *Shakespeare Survey*, 8 (1955).

[1963]

A. D. NUTTALL

The argument about Shakespeare's characters

I

At one time, everybody used to talk about Shakespeare's characters as if they were real people. Today, simple folk, like Lord David Cecil and Professor Dover Wilson, still do; but the critically with-it do not, believing that this kind of talk makes no sense.

Such, in fiduciary terms, is the situation at the present time. And put so simply, this situation does look rather odd. When we say, 'as if they were real people', what is the precise force of 'as if' ? Does it imply that the people who talk in this way are the victims of some sort of delusion? Or does it mean that they are using language in a semi-figurative way to express something which may be perfectly sensible in itself? When the moderns claim that such talk fails to make sense, do they mean that such talk is based on a logical fallacy, a weirdly infantile misunderstanding of the fact and nature of fiction, or have they some more modest charge in mind? These questions are primitive enough, but they have never to my knowledge been satisfactorily asked or answered.[1]

The progress of Shakespearean criticism since the late seventeenth century can be seen as a rambling, gentlemanly conversation, into which (around the year 1933) there is a sudden and violent irruption. This irrupting voice tells the rest that almost all that has been said so far is without significance, and tells them so in a language quite unlike their own, using terms they are at a loss to answer.

The first voice to be heard in this conversation – Thomas Rymer's – is perhaps rather too shrill to be called gentlemanly. Yet Rymer, writing on *Othello* in 1692, uses a critical language recognisably akin to Bradley's, and crucially different from that of the irruptive L. C. Knights. Rymer's criticism of *Othello* is, of course, full of grievous faults, and, one might add, grievously has Rymer answered them. But the deficiencies of Rymer's sensibility are not in question. I am interested rather in his methodology. When Rymer extracted from *Othello* the ostentatiously flat-footed moral –

> First, This may be a caution to all Maidens of Quality how, without their Parents consent, they run away with Blackamoors.
> Secondly, This may be a warning to all good Wives, that they look well to their Linnen.
> Thirdly, This may be a lesson to Husbands, that before their Jealousie be Tragical the proofs may be Mathematical.[2]

– it seems that he was moved to regard Othello as a real Blackamoor and Desdemona as a real gentlewoman, and reacted to their plight almost as if they had been his personal acquaintances. He found the language of the play strained, bombastic and unnatural. The plot he considered to be wretchedly improbable and the morality disgusting. And he drew these strange conclusions because (we have been taught) he treated the persons and events of the play *as if they were real.*

From here on the story is a familiar one, and can be evoked by a few brief reminders. In 1765 Johnson published his edition of Shakespeare, which contained the famous note on *Henry V*, V.i.94, describing the departure of Pistol, the last of the 'comick personages' to be dismissed, and ending with the words, 'I believe every reader regrets their departure'. A sensitive nose could certainly smell out in this note the coming nineteenth century, with its talk of the friends we all make in the pages of Shakespeare. The scent is still stronger in an earlier note from the same play (IV.vii.80), where Johnson wrote, 'This is the last time Falstaff can make sport. The poet was loath to part with him, and has continued his memory as long as he could'. Then there is Maurice Morgann, who wrote in 1774 and published in 1777 his *Essay on the Dramatick Character of Sir John Falstaff*, in which he combed the text for legally acceptable evidence to show that Falstaff was not a constitutional coward. Finally, we have A. C. Bradley, Bradley the character-chaser, the motive-hunter. Where the modern critic is likely to ask 'What is this play really about?' Bradley asked 'What is this character really like?'

I I

But in 1933, all this desultory talk was halted by the publication of L. C. Knights's essay derisively entitled 'How many children had Lady Macbeth?' It included such inflammatory passages as this:

> The habit of regarding Shakespeare's persons as 'friends for life' or maybe, 'deceased acquaintances', is responsible for most of the vagaries that serve as Shakespeare criticism. It accounts for the artificial simplifications of the editors ('In a play one should speak like a man of business'). It accounts for the 'double time' theory for *Othello*. It accounts for Dr Bradley's notes.[3]

In these round terms Knights stated his case. I could only wish they had been a little less round and a little more detailed.

I suspect that, in most of us, the immediate urge to defend Johnson against Knights is stronger than the urge to defend Bradley. The case against the pre-romantic ought to be just as strong as the case against the romantic. Yet when the question is approached by way of the eighteenth century, a suspicion may well grow in the reader that there is something wrong with Knights's attack, that the whole debate may be complicated by the presence of unacknowledged historical factors. The investigation of these will not carry us through to the underlying logic of the conflict between Knights and the rest, but it may clear the way a little.

It is likely that many who blush at the 'biographical' extravagances of Bradley find Johnson's notes on the comedians singularly touching. Something which is cloying when we meet it in a late romantic proves invigorating when it occurs in a rugged eighteenth century commentary. It is helpful to consider these notes of Johnson's in relation to his critical use of the concept of 'nature'. By invoking nature, Johnson in the preface to his *Shakespeare* was able to grind under his heel the un-English doctrine of the Unities. Johnson's appreciation of Shakespeare's tragedies raises various tricky questions; but his love of the comedies is something perspicuously sane and delightful. It seems (witness his notorious comment on the 'blanket of the dark' passage) that when reading *Macbeth* Johnson was still hampered by neo-classical considerations of decorum, elevation and seriousness. But in the world of the comedies he was free. It is gratifying to find, in the age of well-turned epigram, a critic so receptive of the diffuse, humane wit of Shakespeare. Here, surely, the thing that helped him out of his own time and into Shakespeare's was the concept of nature. Shakespeare's comic characters may not be invariably decorous, but they are full of a vivid life; what more natural, then, than to regret their departure?

It is easy to see why the insistence on nature is more prepossessing in an eighteenth century context. The intrusion of warmth and humanity into a world of cold rules is very welcome. But – to trust for a moment to a wild condensation – the concept of nature forms a bridge between the critical theories of the eighteenth and the nineteenth centuries. In the hot-house atmosphere of romanticism an insistence on nature becomes otiose, even irritating. Now L. C. Knights in the thirties was clearly a post- and to some extent an anti-romantic. He, like everyone else, was in revolt against the over-heated Victorian age. This suggests that there is a *prima facie* case for attributing Knights's exasperation to a pre-rational historical reaction.

One can frame a similar historical argument with regard to Morgann's essay on Falstaff. Just as Johnson's attitude becomes more sympathetic if seen as a reaction against the formalism of his time, so Morgann's hyper-subtle account of Falstaff is more likeable when set in the context of eighteenth century dramatic practice. The Falstaffs Morgann saw on the stage were, he claimed, a coarsened travesty of the Falstaff any intelligent reader could discover if he read the text with an unprejudiced mind. This attitude, like Johnson's, looks forward to the nineteenth century. Thirty-five years later Charles Lamb was to write that he would a thousand times rather read a tragedy of Shakespeare's than see it acted,[4] and ninety-three years after Lamb Bradley asserted that *King Lear* was better read as a poem than seen as a play.[5] Once more we have a point of view which has in our own time become radically unfashionable. Once more all that is adventitious in our distaste can be cured if we look at the phenomenon through the eighteenth century end of the telescope. It is likely that the stage productions of the eighteenth and early nineteenth centuries were so bad that any man of sensibility could imagine a better *Lear* than Drury Lane could offer. All the rosy anecdotes of Garrick, Siddons and Kean will never establish the contrary. A whole galaxy of 'stars' cannot cure an over-all grossness of conception. If anything it will have an opposite effect, as anyone who has been moved by an innocent school production and irritated by Stratford will know very well. The Falstaff Morgann saw in the theatre was a simple buffoon, a gross figure of fun, afraid of everyone and everything, yet at the same time an idiotic boaster. In his text Morgann found something very different – a Falstaff who was not only 'a cause that there is wit in others' but also 'witty in himself', a Falstaff who was no fool but rather an overflowing fountain of incongruous intelligence, a figure miraculously combining the Shakespearean clod with the Shakespearean clown – and the whole invested with an incalculable humanity which is probably without parallel in the seventeenth century. It is not surprising that Morgann preferred close reading in his study to yawning in the stalls. Yet by the time of L. C. Knights the thing had swung the other way; the theatre had grown strong while the critics had grown tedious. So once again we may suspect that fashion played a part in the conception of his essay.

But historical arguments like these have a purely hortatory effect. They do not invalidate Knights's essay; they merely arouse our suspicions and invite us to probe more deeply. I may be able to prove you are a Socialist only because your father was a miner, but in doing so I have not refuted Socialism.

III

To get a closer look at our subject, let us take Morgann's statement of principle as cited by Knights together with Knights's own comment on it. Here is Morgann:

> The reader must be sensible of something in the composition of *Shakespeare's* characters, which renders them essentially different from those drawn by other writers. The characters of every Drama must indeed be grouped; but in the groups of other poets the parts which are not seen do not in fact exist. But there is a certain roundness and integrity in the forms of *Shakespeare*, which

21

give them an independence as well as a relation, insomuch that we often meet with passages which, tho' perfectly felt, cannot be sufficiently explained in words, without unfolding the whole character of the speaker . . . The reader will not now be surprised if I affirm that those characters in *Shakespeare*, which are seen only in part, are yet capable of being unfolded and understood in the whole; every part being in fact relative, and inferring all the rest. It is true that the point of action or sentiment, which we are most concerned in, is always held out for our especial notice. But who does not perceive that there is a peculiarity about it, which conveys a relish of the whole? And very frequently, when no particular point presses, he boldly makes a character act and speak from those parts of the composition which are *inferred* only, and not distinctly shown. This produces a wonderful effect; it seems to carry us beyond the poet to nature itself, and gives an integrity and truth to facts and character, which they could not otherwise·obtain: and this is in reality that art in *Shakespeare* which, being withdrawn from our notice, we more emphatically call *nature*. A felt propriety and truth from causes unseen, I take to be the highest point of Poetic composition. If the characters of *Shakespeare* are thus *whole*, and as it were original, whilst those of almost all other writers are mere imitation, it may be fit to consider them rather as Historic than Dramatic beings; and when occasion requires, to account for their conduct from the *whole* of character, from general principles, from latent motives, and from policies not avowed.[6]

It is odd that E. M. Forster should receive so much acclaim for his distinction between 'round' and 'flat' characters, while Morgann receives so little for the distinction he makes here. I suppose one reason for this is that Foster offers us a snappy and useful formula, while Morgann offers us none. Nevertheless, Morgann is making a shrewd point, basically a logical point, about the way a sort of incalculability, a special licence to the audience to make inferences, is *built into* certain dramatic characters. Here is Knights's comment:

> It is strange how narrowly Morgann misses the mark. He recognizes what can be called the full-bodied quality of Shakespeare's work – it came to him as a feeling of 'roundness and integrity'. But instead of realizing that this quality sprang from Shakespeare's use of words, words which have 'a network of tentacular roots, reaching down to the deepest terrors and desires', he referred it to the characters' 'independence' of the work in which they appeared, and directed his exploration to 'latent motives and policies not avowed'.[7]

It is strange how grossly Knights coarsens his material. I cannot feel that his perception of the fact that Shakespeare is a 'full-bodied' sort of writer improves on the subtle point Morgann is making. In so far as Knights's essay is to be considered as revolutionary, I think it must be taken as making a logical criticism, as attacking not merely poor critical execution, but vicious critical premises. Knights must mean that such criticism as Morgann's confounds fiction and reality; that it is not just tedious but also meaningless to ask whether Falstaff is really a coward or not, since Falstaff is not 'really' anything at all – he is a work of fiction. But Morgann too is making a logical point; and the strange thing is that he anticipates the criticism of Knights. Knights is more than half answered by the passage he cites.

For what exactly is claimed in this charge of Knights? – the charge that Bradley and the rest confound fiction and reality, the charge that it is absurd to ask whether Falstaff is *really* a coward? Is he (for example) claiming that Morgann, Bradley and the rest actually *mistook* Falstaff, Macbeth and the rest for real people? Obviously not. Such a state of mind would, I suppose, be legally certifiable as insane. It is true that Balzac once sent for Dr Bianchon, one of his own characters. But then Balzac was on his death-bed at the time. It is, in any case, not difficult to distinguish the delusions of a Balzac from the critical malpractice of a Bradley. When Bradley says that it is worth inquiring into the motives of Macbeth, there is certainly no question of his thinking of Macbeth as a real person. He is without doubt talking about the character in the play. You will not find Bradley burying his head in works of Scottish history which Shakespeare can never have read. Whatever the 'independence' of the dramatic character means, it cannot mean that.

But if Bradley was not actually deluded, what are we to say? Does his guilt merely consist in his using the *language* of delusion? Certainly we cannot pretend that Bradley invariably gives a signal of his awareness of fiction. There are indeed occasions when Bradley, instead of saying, e.g. 'The character Macbeth is represented as being actuated by ambition', will say 'Macbeth is ambitious'.

Well, of course *this* charge is quite absurd. If it can be deflated to so small a compass, it is no longer a criticism of the logic of Bradley's position, but rather an extremely inept piece of semantic pedantry. 'Inept', because of course the practice of simply naming the persons of a play without always designating them as 'character' has long been authorised by usage. It has become part of the shorthand of criticism to omit the designation of logical status once the over-all logical context is clear.

It is plain that the whole of Knights's argument is not conducted on this distressingly low level. Yet I suspect that there are times when he descends to it. For example, his mockery[8] of Bradley's platitudinous but unexceptionable 'Macbeth was exceedingly ambitious' is hard to account for on any other ground.

Knights's real objection is to the practice of drawing inferences from the seen to the unseen with respect to persons of the play. This argument is a little more respectable (but only a little). I will state it as fairly as I can. One of the differences between a fictitious and a real person is that you cannot make inferences about the first in the same way as you can about the second. But this (says Knights) is just what Bradley tries to do. Misled by the purely semantic licence described above, he insisted on making inferences outside the drama with respect to the characters. He would try to find out where Hamlet was at the time of his father's death. He may not go round to the Public Record Office to look up Mistress Quickly, but he is removed from this folly only by degree, not in kind. The semantic licence simply to name the characters has induced in him a sort of *partial* delusion. Likewise with Morgann. Morgann may not go to the War Office to enquire about Falstaff, but he does look into his war-record using any hint he can find in the play. He does ask what Falstaff was doing off stage, before the story we are *shown* begins. And this, Knights would claim, is absurd. For Falstaff before the action opens does not exist. A real person, we non-Berkleians know very well, is liable to be doing things when we are not watching him. But with dramatic characters this simply is not the case. They are the true Berkleian objects. Their *esse* is *percipi*. Their existence really does depend wholly upon their being perceived. It is illogical to ask whether Falstaff is *really* a coward since Falstaff is not *really* anything at all. Illusion is what he is made of.[9]

Now all this sounds much better. But here we must get down to business. For it is quite fallacious. Dramatic characters are not, as a matter of fact, constructed in a Berkleian *esse est percipi* way at all. It is just not accurate to say that their fictional existence begins and ends with what we actually see. The fact that dramatic compositions are representative implies that there is a difference between the representing token and what is represented. This is one of the main reasons why watching a play is different from watching a juggling act. Jugglers (as a rule) are not acting anything. They are just juggling. They come on the stage and throw Indian clubs around in a dexterous manner. But when a young man in a grey wig and beard shuffles on to the stage at the beginning of a play, it would be an insufficient description of his action to say 'He comes on to the stage wearing interesting whiskers, walking very slowly'. One is forced, in fact, to make inferences. One has to realise that while this may *be* a young man, he represents something else – namely an old, old man who has wandered long and far. 'He must have come a long way', the audience says to itself, 'he looks so tired' – and already it is making inferences about what happened before the play began. And of course this sort of inferring goes on all the time in drama. Furthermore, the moment audiences started refusing to do this, every drama ever written would grind to a halt. My great-uncle Alfred is just such an unconscious recusant. When he goes to the cinema he simply cannot be made to understand that time is sometimes deemed to have elapsed between successive sequences. If one ends with James Bond saying 'I'll see you in Venice on Tuesday' and the next begins with Bond in a gondola, my great-uncle will say 'He got there quick, didn't he?' There is a profound irony here. For my great-uncle is in a way being true to Knightsian principles. He is refusing to make any inference from the seen to the unseen. He refuses to think to himself, 'Bond must have boarded a plane in Pasadena and arrived on the Tuesday morning'. But it could easily be argued that here it is the Knightsian who is confounding fiction and reality. As Saint Augustine once said, how would a picture be a true picture, unless it were a false horse?[10] A proper awareness of the real status of dramatic elements *presupposes* a readiness to make inferences about off-stage events.

So the Knightsian argument in its radical form – against dramatic inference – collapses. There was also, dovetailed into it, the point as to whether it makes sense to ask if Falstaff was *really* a coward. This is really the old question of delusion all over again. For *of course* it would be absurd to enquire into what happened to Falstaff on the third of October 1402; but then this is not what Morgann did. He never asked, 'What was Falstaff like, apart from the play?' (an historical question). He asked, 'What is Falstaff really like in this play?' (as opposed to the Falstaff of popular misconception). We may allow that Morgann and Bradley were excessively meticulous in the attention they paid to detail, and sometimes allowed a hint to assume a disproportionate importance; but all these extravagances are faults in applying the premises. There is nothing vicious in the premises themselves – not so far, anyhow. It is strange that so simple an attack as Knights's should have attracted immediate support. So far from destroying Bradley's principles he rather betrayed the imperfections of his own.

IV

Yet here I must admit to a certain embarrassment in attacking Knights's essay. This centres on the fact that Knights's frequent silence on the rational basis of his opinion forces one to supply him with arguments, and so to lay oneself open to the charge of caricaturing his position in order to destroy it. It is true that there have already been several points in this article where, if I were asked 'Where does Knights say that?' I should be forced to reply, 'What else can he mean?' But my distress at this situation is in some measure dispelled on the rare occasions when I can watch Knights arguing for himself. Contrast the sophistication of Morgann's remarks on personification with Knights's remarks on abstraction. These follow a quotation from a rather staid specimen of eighteenth century criticism, Shaftesbury's *Advice to an Author* (1710). Shaftesbury, it appears, was bold enough to praise Shakespeare for 'the Justness of his *Moral*, the Aptness of many of his *Descriptions*, and the plain and natural Turn of several of his *Characters*'. Harmless enough, you will say? But hear Knights: 'We see the

25

beginning of that process of splitting up the indivisible unity of a Shakespeare play into various elements abstracted from the whole'.[11] Really, this is the beginning of the new priestcraft. 'Indivisible Unity' has the authentic theological ring about it.

The unity of a play (by Shakespeare or by anyone else) is divisible in all sorts of ways. One can certainly abstract the character of Richard II from his play and talk meaningfully about it if one chooses. Of course what Knights is really getting at is that this sort of talk leads to the *physical* division of Shakespeare's plays – the editing of Shakespearean anthologies. And to anthologies Knights is puritanically opposed. My own opinion is that anthologies can give endless delight, even if drawn from Shakespeare's dramatic works, but it is undoubtedly true that they are a poor substitute for the total *oeuvre*. Obviously, if Knights wishes to say that he thinks anthologies are a bad thing, he is free to do so. But the trouble is that he is not content just to do that. He must needs talk of 'indivisibility' and wrap the whole thing up in a pseudo-philosophical cocoon, so as to imply that anthologies are not only undesirable but logically impossible on top. Indeed, there can be little doubt that he is trying to smuggle in a conceptual point here, since part of his argument turns on the (erroneous) thesis that one cannot talk meaningfully about characters as such.

I imagine that the logical conclusion of Knights's curious antipathy towards abstraction would be that the only proper way to talk about a play would be to read the whole thing aloud. There is, of course, a real attraction in this idea, which lies I fancy in the fact that it is the only form of verbal representation of the play which could claim to come anywhere near exhaustiveness. But notice that, in attaining that end, it has forfeited any claim to be criticism. The only sensible consequence I can extract from this is that it is absurd to think you are talking about the whole play when you are talking about one character only. Which nobody does any way.

In fact, however, Knights does not follow his argument to its natural conclusion. Instead, he makes new abstractions of his own – 'image-patterns' and the like. These are in fact rather interesting and it is a pity that the consistency of his argument should properly entail their exclusion. I for my part would welcome them, but the suggestion that they, no less than character-studies, divide the Unity is hard to resist.

When Shylock says, 'I cannot find it: 'tis not in the bond' (*The Merchant of Venice*, IV.i.261), one can make two sorts of comment. One can observe that the word 'bond' has appeared repeatedly, like the tolling of a bell, and that this rhythmical reference has begun perhaps to give it a symbolic value, recalling the Old Law of the Old Testament. Alternatively, one can say that Shylock's insistence on the bond shows his nature, at once passionate and conscientiously legalistic. He sees in rules a supernatural authority (cf. 'I have an oath in heaven') and perhaps his vindictive hatred of Antonio is not uncompounded with love for his daughter. Both approaches are entirely meaningful. Both contain more or less speculative elements which admit of argument. *Both* are right on the map of common, reasonable, critical discourse. Does Richard III's opening speech about the sun of York *only* contribute to the image-pattern of planetary bodies in that play? Or does it also contribute certain information about his scheming nature? I would apologise for the childishness of these questions, but the truth is that criticism is suffering from a fit of temporary myopia, and facts as big as houses must be laboriously pointed out.

V

So far I have confined myself to the most fundamental aspects of artistic representation in their relation to Knights's critique. However, in Morgann's statement of principle, quoted above, a further, very relevant point is made. But this time it is a point, not about drama in general, but about Shakespeare in particular. Morgann observed that 'there is a certain roundness and integrity in the forms of *Shakespeare*, which give them an independence as well as a relation', and a little later that Shakespeare 'boldly makes a character act and speak from those parts of the composition which are *inferred* only, and not distinctly shown. This . . . seems to carry us beyond the poet to nature itself, and gives an integrity and truth to facts and character, which they could not otherwise obtain'. Morgann is attempting something very difficult here, and I think he has got just about halfway. He is aware in Shakespeare of a special dimension of inferable identity, an independent integrity *over and above* the usual dramatic allowance. Somehow or other, Shakespeare's Hamlet and his Falstaff are built to provoke questions. Subsequent romantic critics grasped his meaning intuitively. Then came the Knightsian reaction which ruled all such speculation out of court. However, various attacks on the problem were made – a brilliant one in John Bayley's *The Characters of Love* (1960). Bayley freely confessed that he for one would *like* to know how many children Lady Macbeth, in fact, had. He tried to get at the Morgann feeling of 'independence' by framing a distinction between 'open' and 'closed' characters. This contrast is similar to the 'round'/'flat' antithesis, but is distinguishable from it. To Bayley, the world of the great romantic writers (among whom he includes Milton) is a closed world, bounded by the author's own intuitions and intelligence. On the other hand, the world of the great non-romantics, of Tolstoy and Shakespeare, is open, always incalculable, always to be explored, always resistant to a final

27

classification. Proust, to Bayley, is a closed author. For all his subtlety, for all his attempted exhaustiveness, it is always the voice of Proust, the individual, that we are listening to. In reading *Paradise Lost* we are imprisoned by the personality and opinions of the author. Yet who knows anything at all about the personality and opinions of Shakespeare (beyond his liking for salad and hatred of dogs)? If we look at literature in this way it seems natural to say that *Paradise Lost* shows us the mind of Milton only, while Shakespeare's plays show us the whole world, in all its indefinite richness. Accordingly, the characters in an open work of art are different from those in a closed one. The author does not present them to the reader as if he understood them through and through. We have the feeling Morgann tried to describe, that they are ice-bergs, nine-tenths below the surface. They retain an inviolable area of incalculability. The case for or against them is never closed. The radical change of sympathy which attends the progress of Shylock would dislocate a 'closed' work of art. To Bayley, the relationship between Shakespeare and his characters is analogous to the relationship between true lovers. He does not attempt to tell us the 'whole truth' about them. In respecting their 'otherness' he endows them with personality.

This idea deserves a hard-headed interrogation. We might ask, 'How can you talk about undiscovered areas in Falstaff? Every dramatic character is purely formulaic, exists in so far as he is shaped'. The answer to this is that there are various sorts of shaping. One can describe, giving the impression that everything relevant has been said, or else one can describe giving the impression that much that is relevant has *not* been said. I do not allege that there *is* an undiscovered stratum in Falstaff's personality. Certainly I have no real hope of excavating it. I only say that Falstaff is described in such a way that we always feel there is more to be said. This is perfectly possible. By a curious irony this incompleteness, this want of finality in formulation achieves a greater naturalism than the most meticulous description. It is rather like the way in which a rough impressionist painting can bring one closer to the actual experience of looking at things on a sunny day than the most laboriously exact Flemish picture. The truth is that one of the characteristics of real people as opposed to the common run of fictitious personages is that there is much more about them which we do not know. But by this distinction, Shakespeare's characters fall into the category of real life. This is the truth behind all the figurative talk about Shakespeare giving us Nature herself, about the integrity and independence of his characters.

One wishes to say that while Lawrence's characters might surprise us, they never surprise Lawrence; but that Shakespeare is constantly surprised by his own creations. The trouble with this formula is that it seems to reduce itself to an unverifiable statement about the psychology of Shakespeare's creative processes. Yet I would guess that while Jonson would be dogmatic in a conversation about, say, Volpone, Shakespeare would be alert and receptive in a discussion of, say, the morals of Henry V. At all events, the effect of such indefiniteness in the work of art is to alert our speculation. It gives an enormous, one might almost say a paralysing licence to inference. And the cold hint of that word 'paralysing' brings me to my final point.

VI

For this is where I dissociate myself from the Morgann-Bradley-Bayley tradition. Certainly it has always been the habit of ordinary people (and this should have worried Knights), on leaving a theatre, or finishing a book, to speculate about the future of the characters. 'Do you think she'll get on with that old husband?' 'Do you think Mr Micawber really will reform when he goes abroad?' Actors exhibit the same Bradleian symptoms in a more developed form. For example, John Gielgud interviewed by Harold Hobson in *The Sunday Times* for 24 September 1961 gave the following account:

> The dons were astonished at the questions the actors asked them. They wanted to tell us about the beat of the verse, but we thought we could find that out for ourselves. What we wanted was to understand the characters' motives and progressions, and have effective business from us. The 'Othello', for example, that I'm going to play next month. Was Desdemona still a virgin when she arrived in Cyprus? I wrote to Rylands about this the other day. He replied that Shakespeare didn't bother much about that sort of thing. Yet it is very important to me – the actor who is going to play Othello.

Professor Nevill Coghill tells a very similar story about Olivier. In view of the way in which plays are constructed, such speculations can only be called an appropriate response. Now Bayley when he stressed the especial openness of Shakespeare's characters believed that this made them especially open to inference and speculative enquiry. He says at one point that when we look at a character in this light of indefiniteness it is hard to think of a question which would be irrelevant. And I reply, 'Certainly; *and it is hard to think of an answer that would be relevant*'. It is curious that both Morgann and Bayley seem to have thought that the openness of Shakespearean writing justifies the critical procedure of following up minute questions. In fact, though indefinite characterisation certainly provokes a multitude of questions, it simultaneously implies that those questions have no answers. If there were answers, the character would cease to be open and would become just an extremely complex closed character, requiring an unusually laborious reading. Thus the critical status of such explorations is left obscure. They seem in a way to be more like audience-response than objective description or judgement.

A. D. Nuttall

Of course there is in most Shakespearean plays a shading-off into unknowability whereby hints are given and pointers laid. I am of the opinion that these hints and pointers should be noticed. For example, I think it is worth scanning *Hamlet* to settle whether the Prince is in earnest in the horrific reason he gives for sparing Claudius. But it is the whole point of the special theory of openness that there is a point at which the hints shade off into nothing and yet there seems to be much more of the character to guess at. Here of course anyone's guess is as good as anyone else's. We have strayed into the region of the utterly unverifiable and it is quite true that you will occasionally come upon Bradley in this place. Such questions are an entirely appropriate reaction. The factual value of the specific solutions would appear to be nil.

I can see a sort of tangential value for such 'creative' criticism. If forcefully done it can awaken the reader's responses. Also, it can bring out vividly the way in which the original is mysterious. There is no more eloquent testimony to the mysterious humanity of Hamlet than the farrago of theory with which critics have tried to fill up the vacuum in our knowledge. A party of Knightsians could never have done it. In fact they could not have talked about Hamlet at all, having once cunningly perceived that he is an abstraction from his dramatic poem. In the world of art-criticism I suppose Walter Pater's rhapsody on the *Mona Lisa*,[12] or John Addington Symonds's prose-poem on Michelangelo's statute of Lorenzo de' Medici[13] is parallel. It took a critic as intelligent as Sir Kenneth Clark to perceive the appropriateness of Pater's observations.[14] They are more in tune with the humane genius of the Renaissance than the purely phenomenal approach of a Herbert Read. Symonds's very particular account of the worries of Lorenzo de' Medici has, I suppose, a very low cash value. Yet anyone who has read Michelangelo's seventeenth sonnet[15] will know that there is a sense in which Symonds can be said to be wandering in the right area.

So let us not be scared by L. C. Knights. We met when we first read Shakespeare a wonderful company of heroes and ladies, fools and wisemen, poet-kings, old, mad despots with flowers in their hair, melancholy humorists, men of action, distracted maids and acid commentators. They will stay with us through life. We shall find ourselves wondering about them even (be it said) when we have forgotten the plots in which they appear. There is much more to the plays of Shakespeare than the characters which appear in them. But then there are certainly characters in the plays of Shakespeare. I wonder, for example, whether Othello really did sleep with Emilia. I suppose not, but . . .

Notes

1   H. B. Charlton, in his *Shakespearean Tragedy* (1948), went so far as to confess himself bewildered by the anti-Bradleian reaction. Barbara Everett, in her 'Review: the figure in Professor Knights's carpet', *The Critical Quarterly*, 2 (1960), pp. 171–6, usefully deflated some Knightsian jargon, but did not, in my opinion, expose the true source of the disorder. I find myself puzzled by Lily B. Campbell's comment in Appendix B of her *Shakespeare's Tragic Heroes* (1962), for while on the one hand she seems to hold to the crude Knightsian distinction between reality and art (in reality you infer, in art you don't), on the other hand she seems to come very near the heart of the problem in her analogy from etching.

2   Thomas Rymer, *The Tragedies of the Last Age* ('A Short View of Tragedy'), 1692, p. 89.

3   L. C. Knights, 'How many children had Lady Macbeth?' printed in his *Explorations* (1958), p. 16.

4   Charles Lamb, 'On the tragedies of Shakespeare considered with reference to their fitness for stage representation', in *The Works of Charles and Mary Lamb*, ed. E. V. Lucas (1903), pp. 97–111.

5   A. C. Bradley, *Shakespearean Tragedy* (1905), p. 248.

6   In *Eighteenth Century Essays on Shakespeare*, ed. D. Nichol Smith (1903), pp. 246–7.

7   Knights, *op. cit.*, p. 12.

8   Knights, *op. cit.*, p. 3.

9   Cf. R. Wellek and A. Warren, *Theory of Literature* (1949), p. 15 – '[A character] has no past, no future, and sometimes no-continuity of life.'

10 Augustine, *Soliloquies* II.x, in *Patrologia Latina*, ed. J.-P. Migne (1845), Thomus XXXII column 893. The Latin text reads, ' . . . unde vera pictura esset, si falsus equus non esset?'

11 Knights, *op. cit.*, p. 10.

12 Walter Pater, *The Renaissance*, with an introduction and notes by Sir Kenneth Clark (1961), pp. 122–3.

13 J. A. Symonds, *The Life of Michelangelo Buonarotti* (1893), vol. II, p. 32.

14 Sir Kenneth Clark, *Landscape into Art* (1949), p. 46.

15 *The Sonnets of Michelangelo*, text and translation by J. A. Symonds (1950), p. 51.

[1965]

Postscript

Since this essay was first published it has been very reasonably pointed out (by S. Viswanathan and others) that I really ought to have taken notice of the fact that L. C. Knights himself was critical, later, of the position he had taken up in 'How many children had Lady Macbeth?'. See especially his 'The question of character in Shakespeare', first published in J. Garrett, ed., *More Talking of Shakespeare* (1959), reprinted in *Further Explorations* (1965).

JOHN EDMUNDS

Shakespeare breaks the illusion

The first time I ever directed Shakespeare was as a student in Paris, thirty long years ago. It was that brightest of jewels in the canon, *Twelfth Night,* and the posters had to be printed about three times because the French type-setters seemed unable to believe that a word could possibly have four con-sonants in succession: we had 'twefth', 'twelth' and 'twelf' before they got it right.

There's nothing quite like directing a play to make you scrutinise the text. And when we were rehearsing Act III Scene iv we came across a line of Fabian's which we decided must be among the cheekiest Shakespeare ever wrote. After Malvolio has been successfully gulled and from his false pinna-cle of new-found greatness has disdainfully rebuked Sir Toby and his fellow japesters, he sails offstage, and in the midst of his triumphant mirth Fabian comes out with:

> If this were played upon a stage now, I could condemn it as an improbable fiction.

What a nerve! This *is* being played upon a stage. To remind us at the very height of an elaborately contrived situation, when our belief in it is entire, when we are lost in the world of Illyria, to remind us that we are not watch-ing real life but something played upon a stage! Why break the illusion? Does Shakespeare *want* us to condemn the gulling of Malvolio as an 'impro-bable fiction', to say 'This is altogether too far-fetched', and reject it? That doesn't happen, and it's not the dramatist's purpose. But the line of Fabian's in no way develops the action, and yet was clearly inserted with some delib-eration. So what does it do? I would not suggest that Shakespeare gave it an *immense* amount of thought, or that the line has a very telling effect in per-formance, but reinforced by similar passages it may represent a clue to mat-ters of some weight.

What Fabian says is the kind of thing we all say from time to time: 'Truth is stranger than fiction', we pronounce when something extraordinary hap-pens. Or: 'If you put this coincidence into a play or a story, you'd never get away with it.' Now here is a character actually in a play saying just that about a highly contrived comic situation. This has two effects; the question is: are they consistent and compatible? The first effect is to make the action more like real life, because Fabian's comment is exactly what we should say in real life about a succession of events neat enough to serve as a stage plot. The second effect (and it strikes us, if indeed it strikes us at all, a moment later) is to remind us that the device *is* in a play and so is the character uttering the comment. And the sudden realisation of this paradox, if the line is played for it, can produce a laugh. So the comment *both* makes the play more like real life and reminds us that it is fiction. For Shakespeare, as I hope to show, there is no contradiction in this dual purpose. What Fabian is doing is momentarily stepping back from the action in which he is involved, and looking at it objectively *as an audience or critic* and commenting on its improbability. And we, as the audience for whom Fabian is playing his part, observe Fabian observing the situation. For a moment there is a play within the play, and Fabian is its audience. The line is an encapsulation of a device much loved by Shakespeare – as we shall see.

There are too many instances of Shakespeare's breaking the theatrical illusion for us to discount them as fortuitous. When Caesar has been stabbed before the Capitol, Cassius remarks:

> How many ages hence
> Shall this our lofty scene be acted o'er,
> In states unborn and accents yet unknown!

This does not simply mean: How often will potential tyrants be assassinated. Brutus takes up the theme:

> How many times shall Caesar bleed in sport,
> That now on Pompey's basis lies along
> No worthier than the dust!

When these lines are spoken we are as an audience immersed in an illusion – the willing suspension of disbelief indispensable to the dramatic experience – the illusion that we are back in 44 B.C. before the Roman Capitol witnessing the death of Caesar. These words serve to jerk us out of that illusion: suddenly (and, I think, *excitingly*) we realise that one of the 'states unborn' where Cassius says this 'lofty scene' will be 'acted o'er' is Britain and that this representation of Cassius to whom we are listening is speaking *now* in one of the 'accents yet unborn' that he is talking about. Past and present become thrillingly fused: we are momentarily whisked outside time; *for a short spell* we experience timelessness or eternity (The paradoxes are becoming more complex . . . and no other art form can make us feel paradox so forcefully.) The comments of Brutus and Cassius remind us that this Caesar in whom we have believed is bleeding only 'in sport'.

We are now touching on one of the most vital and valuable functions of drama for the community. Like Fabian, Brutus and Cassius suddenly see themselves objectively, as actors in a play which will be performed many times in years to come with many different actors assuming the parts they are now performing for the first time. But their realisation of this makes us realise that it is not the first time, that these historical personages who are seeing themselves as actors *are* actors and not the historical personages we

33

have been taking them for. (Of course, the players of Brutus and Cassius know that they are not Brutus and Cassius, though they pretend they do not know; and we in the audience know that they are only pretending not to know it, and we enter into that pretence – but let's not go into the levels of illusion too deeply. Just yet.)

The awareness of people that they are acting in daily life is fundamental to Shakespeare's purpose, but in this instance we can go further. The assassination of Julius Caesar is a mythical act, in that it forms a focal point of our culture. Awareness that they are creating a myth is built into the lines given to Brutus and Cassius. Whether or not in fact the conspirators would have been aware of the significance for Western culture of their deed is immaterial to Shakespeare's intention: what is vital to it is that the audience should be aware of the significance of the assassination, and not simply intellectually, but that they should be made to *feel* it with a sudden *frisson*. What the moment does is to induce in us, by means possible only in the theatre, a creative impulse of *recognition* (a kind of *anagnorisis*): we are struck by the apprehension that certain acts exist eternally, outside time, and momentarily we are placed in that other dimension. Tyrants or potential tyrants are repeatedly being assassinated in our world: the act is deep in the collective psyche; in the Platonic sense it is ever-present and ubiquitous. One of the functions of the drama is to actualise such truths as ritual. The lines of Brutus and Cassius are spoken while the conspirators are performing the ritual washing of their hands in Caesar's blood: their effect is to extend the significance of that sacramental act and suddenly to embrace audience as well as actors in the richer meaning.

Let us go a little further. If the killing of Caesar is an act of myth for us, this is partly because Shakespeare's play has made it so. I am not suggesting that the assassination would have been forgotten if Shakespeare had not immortalised it. No: but there are a great many people whose historical perceptions are shaped by the drama that Shakespeare made out of past events. Whatever the truth may be about Richard III, it is overshadowed in the popular consciousness by Shakespeare's attractive monster. *The artist not only provides the form of ritual, but also shapes the myth.*

Two other characters who reveal an awareness of their own mythical significance are Troilus and Cressida, who protest their love for each other by foreseeing that posterity will look upon them as paradigms of pure and constant love. Troilus' words – 'True swains in love shall in the world to come / Approve their truth by Troilus' – serve to make us see the immediate stage action in a larger context. Cressida's words a moment later (since we must know that she will betray her lover) add a powerful irony to the distancing effect:

> If I be false . . .
> Yea, let them say, to stick the heart of falsehood,
> 'As false as Cressid'.

The real Troilus and Cressida would not, one presumes, have been endowed with such prescience. Shakespeare gives them speeches that fulfil at least three functions at once: they further the surface action, or plot; they draw our attention to the mythical significance of the subject-matter; and they imbue the situation with bitter irony. As always, the illusion is broken in order to induce a more exciting and more penetrating experience in the audience.

Another breaker of theatrical illusion is Cleopatra. She describes the triumph that Octavius will be awarded in Rome if she permits herself to be captured alive:

> the quick comedians
> Extemporally will stage us, and present
> Our Alexandrian revels. Antony
> Shall be brought drunken forth, and I shall see
> Some squeaking Cleopatra boy my greatness
> I'the posture of a whore.

'I shall see some squeaking Cleopatra boy my greatness.' Shakespeare gives a boy-actor, impersonating Cleopatra, a line in which she draws attention to the fact that she is actually being impersonated by a boy. A cheap joke would clearly be out of place, so it's a bold and daring stroke. It isn't necessary to the action. Why does Shakespeare do it?

As with Brutus and Cassius, we see a historical personage aware of her significance as a mythical figure, so that the play has similar ritualistic overtones; but this time we see the character at a moment of critical choice: the moment when the shape of the myth is decided. Again, it is partly the artist who is creating the myth since these thoughts of Cleopatra are his imaginative reconstruction, but the interesting thing about this example of breaking the illusion is that the *moment of choice* is made timeless: included in the ritual which *is* the play *Antony and Cleopatra* is this sharing with the audience of an awareness of rôle-playing and of deliberate shaping of the rôle by the character. Cleopatra has two alternatives: she can be captured alive, leaving behind her the image of a cowardly whore; or she can kill herself and become a heroine for all eternity. The re-enactment of this moment of choice is the perpetuating of an existential crossroads: by what she does now Cleopatra creates her character to be fixed for ever as surely as the Six Characters of Pirandello, as surely as the pursuing lover on Keats's Grecian Urn: 'For ever wilt thou love and she be fair.' Or as Shakespeare puts it in his sonnet: 'So long as men can breathe or eyes can see' – so long will Cleopatra knowingly create her own heroic myth, and, sharing in that creative act, we may learn that we too can shape our destinies, determine the role that we play. Again, the theatrical illusion is broken to heighten our involvement, to lead us into closer empathy with Cleopatra as she moves toward her death, so that we respond to her on many levels: as mythical heroic queen, as boy-actor performing like a priest at the eucharist a ritual significant in our culture, as an individual like ourselves creating herself by her acts. Breaking the illusion is a technique that for a moment alienates only in order to enrich the dramatic experience.

As well as shaping history or legend into myth, Shakespeare is quite capable of making his own mythical characters. One of the greatest of these is surely Shylock. While directing students of the Drama Department for a production of *The Merchant of Venice* at Theatr y Werin, I was pulled up short in a rehearsal of the Trial Scene by what at the time seemed an illusion-shattering exchange. Just when Antonio has completed his courageous last words before baring his breast, as seems inevitable, to Shylock's knife, Bassanio is moved to say that he would sacrifice his bride to save his friend's life. At which his wife, present unbeknown to him and disguised as the lawyer, comments: 'Your wife would give you little thanks for that, / If she were by to hear you make the offer.' As if that were not enough, the interchange is repeated by Gratiano and *his* newly-acquired wife Nerissa, disguised as the lawyer's clerk. We stopped rehearsing to ask ourselves just what Shakespeare was up to. As yet there is no hint of Antonio's reprieve. An audience new to the play – and we expected to have many who would not be familiar with the plot, especially among the schoolchildren – the audience had been carefully led to believe in what is admittedly a most unlikely situation: that a Christian was about to have a pound of his flesh cut off by a Jew in open court. The play is so cleverly written that we do believe it. And at the very climax of our expectation of this horrendous act, the tension is snapped by a cheap joke. Or so it seems: certainly there is no way of stopping the audience from laughing. The moment passes, and the tension is restored as the knife is raised again – this time to be arrested by Portia's reprieve. Now: when the knife is raised the second time, is the audience in exactly the same frame of mind as it was before? Were the laughs just a matter of 'reculer pour mieux sauter' – just to heighten the ultimate tension by allowing the audience a moment's relaxation in legitimate laughter? We decided that there was more to it when we looked closely at the nature of the jokes. As a result of those apparently frivolous interchanges it seemed to us that something very significant had happened which should alter the nature of the audience response.

The audience had been reminded of several things: that the representatives of the law, the learned young counsel and his clerk, were false: they were not lawyers but dressed up in borrowed costume; they were not even male, but women with assumed names and manners. 'Robes and furred gowns hide all' – except from the audience who now, alienated by the comic moment, must be objectively aware that this trial is a mockery. In Shakespeare's day they would have looked at the action even more coolly than now, for in being reminded that Portia and Nerissa were women playing male lawyers, they would also become conscious that those women were being impersonated by boy-actors, and furthermore that Shylock and Antonio were only actors; indeed they see suddenly that the whole charade is a play. But alienation brings deeper recognition. Now the action is felt to be not just a particular struggle between two individuals, a Christian and a Jew, but as a symbolic contest between a community and an outsider in its midst, a tribe against a foreigner, a herd against an intruder. This is now a tribal confrontation in which the law is a mere pawn to be used in the implementation of a necessity deep in the collective unconscious, a matter of sacrifice and survival. So once again the illusion is broken in the interest of universalising the particular, turning an individual case into the material of myth, and reinforcing the participation of the audience by opening up a deeper level of response. And it is precisely by sounding such deep resonances that Shakespeare turns somewhat improbable stories into great and enduring art: so it is interesting to examine the dramatic techniques he employs to manipulate the response of his audience.

All the examples I have cited involve characters' changing their rôle from actor to observer, or observing themselves playing a rôle in a situation the audience has been lulled into accepting as real, thus obliquely drawing their attention to their own rôle for the nonce as observers, and so to rôle-playing in real life. The metaphor of the theatre is an obvious one for an actor-dramatist, but Shakespeare's constant recourse to it is not superficial, as has been frequently pointed out. Just as his characters sometimes reveal an understanding of their own significance which amounts to a flash of almost god-like objectivity, so Shakespeare seems to be inducing in us a new insight into our own situation. If these moments *work* in the theatre, they can be profoundly exciting, although at the time we cannot be expected to understand why.

Shakespeare was fascinated by kingship. Of course: in life the king is the leading actor, the man with the most heavily stylised and responsible rôle, the man with the most special words to say, the grandest costume, and the most attentive audience. His part is difficult, dangerous, and he's always on stage even in his bed-chamber. We all play our alloted parts, but kings and queens far more conspicuously than the rest of us. Of all Shakespeare's kings the one who is most aware of rôle playing is Richard II. And the play is about his having his rôle taken away from him in mid-performance. No leading actor likes to be told that his interpretation is so execrable that another actor is to play his part for the last one-and-a-half acts. It happens to Richard. The experience is deeply traumatic, and it is partly the trauma of his being forced to create a new rôle for himself that the play explores.

The moment of transition for Richard, the moment of adjustment to his new situation, is marked by a visual image and a gesture so memorable, so bold, and so complex in its implications that it leaves one gasping. The tormented leading actor (in the play as in the historical situation), deprived of his part (in the historical situation but not in the play), sends, as it were, to his dressing-room for a mirror to learn from his appearance how he should now perform. Again, Jean-Paul Sartre is anticipated, and the notion that we learn who we are from the image we see of ourselves in the eyes of others: that is, we behave in response to the way other people behave towards us. We need an image of ourselves in order to know our identity. In the Hell of Sartre's *Huis Clos* (variously translated as *In Camera, No Exit, Vicious Circle*) there are no mirrors, and the characters' torment is the frustration of not finding a bearable image of themselves in the eyes of one another. Richard, so far, has been confirmed in his rôle by the lustre reflected in every eye around him. That deference has gone. What will the mirror tell him about his new self?

Already he has expressed the wish to become nothing, to let the performer vanish with the rôle: 'O! that I were a mockery king of snow . . . To melt myself away in waterdrops.' Now, to destroy the face that looks just as it did when he played the king, he shatters the mirror. The act is pseudo-suicide: if he cannot be king he will not exist. But Bolingbroke reminds him that, though the rôle has been transferred, the actor remains. 'The shadow of your sorrow hath destroyed / The shadow of your face.' The show, the props, the gestures, the signs of inner suffering – in a word, the playing, the theatricality, the performance – is not all. On the stage, in life, 'these external manners' are but reflections of an unseen reality. The nature of this 'reality' is the problem that obsesses Richard for the remainder of his short life, and although his struggle to come to terms with the loss of 'himself' gains our respect, there are signs that, had he not been killed, his dilemma would lead him into madness rather than a solution.

But Bolingbroke's words seem to cause him to reject all further thought of suicide. Asking for leave to go from 'their sights', he leaves the stage both literally and metaphorically, and retires to commune with himself alone.

The equation with rôle-transference is maintained in York's description of Bolingbroke's triumphant entry into London as the new leading man, followed by the demoted Richard:

> As in a theatre the eyes of men,
> After a well-graced actor leaves the stage,
> Are idly bent on him that enters next,
> Thinking his prattle to be tedious;
> Even so, or with much more contempt, men's eyes
> Did scowl on gentle Richard.

Alone in his prison, battling with himself in search of his new rôle, Richard sustains the metaphor, finding in himself the potential of many different characters: 'Thus play I in one person many people, / And none contented.' Yet a new identity he must find as long as he is still living:

> But, whate'er I be,
> Nor I, nor any man that but man is,
> With nothing shall be pleased, till he be eas'd
> With being nothing.

On the stage of life we need, fundamentally, to know who we are. But do we ever? This is the question the Father asks of the Producer in Pirandello's *Six Characters in Search of an Author*. 'Man', he says, 'can quite well be nobody.' Which is exactly the sad state that Richard feels himself to be in. The Father goes on to demonstrate to the Producer that every man's identity is in such a state of flux that he cannot know who he is: in fact, that every man is always, did he but realise it, in the horrifying condition of limbo in which we find Richard in his prison. The whole point of the Father's argument is to show the superiority of fictional characters like himself to real people. A *character*, he says, knows who he is: '[Our reality] doesn't change! Do you see? That's the difference! Ours doesn't change, it can't change, it can never be different, never, because it is already determined, like this, for ever, that's what's so terrible! We are an eternal reality.' Human beings are always in flux; fictional characters are eternally fixed. But Richard is a historical personage who has become a character; and a character who is only too keenly aware that he is subject to precisely that flux, that breaking of illusion which the Father ascribes to real people but not to fictional characters! (Of course, Pirandello's Producer is a fictional character too, but let's not clog the argument!)
Richard, like Pirandello's Six Characters, is frustrated by lack of a script – but it's worse for him because he had one – a magnificent one – and it's been torn away from him halfway through his performance, halfway through his expectation of life.

What I'm saying of course is that Shakespeare anticipated not only Brecht and Sartre but Pirandello too (as well as Artaud and any other theoretician of the drama you care to name). Shakespeare's treatment of the theme is much cleverer than Pirandello's because he fuses the Producer and the Father into one character: Richard is the eternal fixed immutable archetype of a man in a state of flux. Well, paradox is the usual basis of creative leaps in art. Once again the artist has imposed a shape on the shifting chaos of life and created a permanent structure more enduring than the statue of Ozymandias and imbued with the rich ironies crystallised by Shelley: 'Look on my works, ye Mighty, and despair': despair, indeed, of ever getting to the bottom of them.

We have seen Shakespeare break the illusion as a technique used variously to underline the qualities of drama as myth, ritual and rôle-playing. It can also help us share in his own deep optimism. His shaping mirror is ultimately bright and consolatory, suggesting that there is a glowing substance behind the gloomy shadows we perceive. In *The Winter's Tale,* at several particularly incredible moments, Shakespeare inserts lines clearly intended to draw attention to, rather than conceal, the improbability of the action; 'This news which is called true', says the Second Gentleman reporting that Perdita is found, 'is so like an old tale that the verity of it is in strong suspicion.' When asked what happened to Antigonus, the Third Gentleman relates what we have seen and stresses its unlikelihood; 'like an old tale still, which will have matter to rehearse though credit be asleep and not an ear open: He was torn to pieces with a bear'. A likely tale! But we have seen the bear. This shaping art is conscious of its unreality, and again the daring breaking of illusion serves to strengthen our apprehension of deeper purposes we cannot fathom, of a benevolent substance behind the visible shadow of events.

At the climax of the action (the miraculous restoration of Hermione to Leontes) the device is used with even more telling effect: 'That she is living', says Paulina, 'were it but told you, should be hooted at like an old tale'. We are made aware that we are watching an old tale that is even so entitled; and in this tale she is indeed living. The mirror of Shakespeare's stage gives us a glimpse of a substance kinder than the shadow we normally see – and infinitely more encouraging. There is no sin that may not be forgiven, no loss that cannot be restored. There is no artist more capable of filling us with hope. How is it done?

The restoration of Hermione, the apparent bringing to life of the statue, is a play within a play. Paulina is the author and producer; Hermione the sole performer; Leontes is the audience. Because we are not in the know – and this is important: dramatic irony would not serve Shakespeare's purpose here – we share the miracle with Leontes, his belief creating ours in the power of contrition to heal and make whole. The self-conscious breaking of illusion in Paulina's words has relaxed our critical barriers, so that we are induced to accept the impossible, to be led with Leontes into the apprehension of a spiritual world superior to our everyday awareness and expectations: 'There are more things in Heaven and earth, Horatio, than are dreamt of in your *philosophy*.' Philosophy cannot take us into the realms of the sublime. But Drama can. And part of Shakespeare's technique for affording us this treasured experience is to break the regular stage illusion, break down our rational defences so that we may become receptive to a different level of truth.

Shakespeare gives us an explanation of his method of working in *A Midsummer Night's Dream*. There we may discover his attitude towards theatrical illusion, what induces it and what destroys it, and a statement of the kind of belief that the poet can create in his audience. In a successful dramatic experience the imaginative resources of the poet, the actor and the audience will be fused in unison. Like all dramatists writing before the establishment of the tedious conventions of Realism, Shakespeare always expected to work on his audience's 'imaginary forces' to 'piece out' what he was pleased to call the 'imperfections' of his staging. But his contempt for realism has nothing to do with theatrical illusion: no play can work unless the audience believes in it, however scanty the scenery, costumes and props; it is the belief of the actors in their characters, situations and relationships that creates belief in the audience. In about five minutes of Act III, Scene i, of the *Dream* Shakespeare encapsulates centuries of scholarly argument concerning the nature of stage illusion.

Bottom and his fellow actors are worried about certain elements in the script of *Pyramus and Thisbe*. The three solutions proposed by members of the company imply three different approaches to this matter of illusion.

First, Bottom takes it for granted that the court audience will believe in the action so completely that the ladies will be frightened by the violence in the play, that is by the suicide of Pyramus and the appearance of a lion. His solution is to allay their fears by assuring them that they are not witnessing reality but only make-believe: the Court ladies will be told that the actors are only pretending.

Since this is clearly intended to be comic, we may assume that Shakespeare's audience were sufficiently sophisticated not to believe that what they saw on stage was real life, that they knew that only clodpoles like the mechanicals themselves would imagine anyone could be so utterly deceived. But of course there are recorded instances of simple folk believing absolutely in the reality of stage performance. There's a famous story about a nineteenth-century production of *Othello* being interrupted by a woman shouting from the gallery: 'Can't you see she's innocent, you great black fool!' Theatrical illusion is a more subtle matter, we all know, and yet the complex edifice of neo-classical rules with their insistence on the unities of time and place were founded on the assumption that an audience could not be expected to believe that the stage was first one place and then another, or that an extensive period of time elapsed during the performance of only three hours. This misconception, which bedevilled dramatists particularly in seventeenth-century France, was not properly exposed as nonsense until Addison and Johnson stamped on it with scorn. But Shakespeare in his wisdom never subscribed to such silliness, and pokes fun at it here through Bottom and his fellows. The audience does not believe in a literal sense in the action on the stage.

But what are we to make of the second suggestion contained in the scene? The play of Pyramus and Thisbe calls for moonlight. Bottom's solution is that they should open the casement windows in the palace where they will be performing, and use the real moonlight that will stream in. This notion absolutely anticipates nineteenth-century naturalism. Antoine in Paris created a sensation by using real meat in a setting representing a butcher's shop; in Chekhov's *The Seagull* Constantine comes closer by timing the presentation of his play to coincide with the rising of the moon: his setting was a real lake and a real moon. Not that such realism was original: if we go back to the decadent days of the Roman Empire, there are tales of criminals condemned to death being executed on stage as part of a performance. Less horrifically, a few summers ago Albee's *The Zoo Story,* which is set by a park bench near a zoo, was performed in Regent's Park open-air theatre which is close to London Zoo. What could be better, one supposes. But the result of such realism was somehow to make the play seem false. Props and settings that are too real don't, in fact, reinforce the illusion: they break it. In Theatr y Werin, in a Drama Department production of Coward's *Hay Fever,* stage-management used real boil-in-the-bag haddock for the breakfast scene in the last act of the play. The authentic aroma filled the auditorium. The result was that the audience were so intrigued they kept nudging each other and stopped listening to the dialogue. Reality swamped the desired illusion. Antoine found the same effect produced by his real meat, to his chagrin. But Shakespeare, to judge by the comic tone of Bottom's proposition, scorned the naturalistic movement three hundred years before it was thought of. He knew that the real thing is less theatrically effective than the imitation, or suggestion. In the event, the mechanicals don't adopt the idea (perhaps because real moonlight would have been difficult to come by in the Globe Theatre in the afternoon) but instead they take up Quince's notion, which is Shakespeare's comment on our third dramatic theory.

The moonlight is to be represented by an actor with a bush of thorns and a lantern. Similarly, the Wall will be portrayed by an actor with loam or rough-cast about him. Most of the Court audience find this wildly funny, but Theseus's rebuke suggests that Shakespeare meant us to find it endearing. The mechanicals are like children, and this solution to the problems of staging their play is exactly what children do instinctively, what we encourage them to do in modern drama classes: 'Be the train', we say; 'Be the sea', 'Be a great white bird' – or whatever. These simple workmen become moonlight, a wall, a lion. Whereas realism is childish, this approach is childlike; it is Brechtian: it expects the audience to build on the suggestion, using its own imagination. Theseus is sympathetic: 'The best in this kind are but shadows', he says, 'and the worst are no worse *if imagination amend them'*.

We are not far from the Chorus in *Henry V* in Theseus's apology for the mechanicals' representation. The best acting requires the willing co-operation of the spectators' imagination; the worst acting needs more help from the audience.

The Tragedy of Pyramus and Thisbe is an old style of theatre and acting, badly written and executed, introduced into Shakespeare's up-to-date form of drama. Like the Mystery Plays, *Pyramus and Thisbe* is performed by artisans, the main play by professionals – better done but not so different. The lovers lose out in the amateur play, in the *Dream* they are happily paired off: well, one's a tragedy, the other a comedy: that's what you would expect. Both plots depend on incredible contrivances: chance and magic potions. In neither are the characters in control of their destinies. Demetrius loves Hermia, and to suit the plot his rôle is arbitrarily changed: he's given the rôle of *Helena*'s lover. Hermia's father, despite Theseus's insistence in Act One on his powerlessness to over-rule the law, in the end has to put up with the unwanted Lysander as his son-in-law: the situation set up in Act One – Helena must marry Demetrius or die or go into a nunnery – is knocked down in Act Four with one arbitrary line from the Duke: 'Egeus, I will overbear your will.' If he'd done that in the first place, there'd have been no play. There's not much more rhyme or reason on the face of it in the main play than in Bottom's when all's said and done. We can't believe in it literally however good the acting or even when performed as it often is in real woods and by real moonlight.

The difference in quality between the two works – the reason why one succeeds and the other fails – has nothing to do with stage conventions: the most improbable plots and the most artificial styles of writing and acting (or singing, as in grand opera) can happily suspend disbelief. Through Theseus and Hippolyta, Shakespeare explains why the one play is a work of art and the other not. In reply to Theseus' attempt to defend the workmen's efforts, Hippolyta retorts: 'It must be your imagination then and not theirs.' In other words, 'Yes, all poets and actors are entitled to expect the audience to work with them at creating the dramatic experience, but the stimulus must come first from them: where there's a lack of imaginative power in the writing and the interpretation you can't expect the latent 'imaginary forces' of the audience to be released. Before the tragedy of Pyramus and Thisbe begins, Theseus explains the true poet's way of working: the imagination can create what it desires. 'If it would apprehend some joy, / It comprehends some bringer of that joy.' This is a most significant and bold statement concerning the function and power of art. Shakespeare uses the word *apprehension* in a famous passage in *Hamlet* where the prince is discussing the attributes of Man: 'In apprehension how like a god.' That is, man has a god-like ability to *conceive*, first in the mind as God conceived the world, and also in the further sense embraced by the word, to *grasp* by making real what had' been imagined – as God then made the world He had conceived. Hamlet is saying Man too can conceive things that do not exist and make them actual. How? In his working as an artist. The thought is expanded by Theseus: 'If it would apprehend [that is, conceive and grasp] some joy, it comprehends some bringer of that joy.'

When the imagination of the poet conceives some joy, it is capable of creating the means of making that joy actual. Shakespeare the poet conceived the joy of the restoration of Hermione. He was able to go further and to *comprehend* some bringer of that joy. *Comprehend* means to apprehend with the senses, with sight, touch and hearing. The theatre is the art of the senses, the means by which Shakespeare could most effectively make actual the joy conceived by his imagination. And this power of his art is most movingly exercised in the late plays *The Winter's Tale* and *Pericles*, where he awakens the imagination of a co-operative audience to share in a pure joy such as we cannot experience on earth but believe that Heaven is for. We don't believe literally that Hermione lives and is found again, nor in the magical events of the midsummer night, but, in Hippolyta's words:

> All the story of the night told over,
> And all their minds transfigured so together,
> More witnesseth than fancy's images,
> And grows to something of great constancy
> But, howsoever, strange and admirable.

This 'something of great constancy . . . strange and admirable' – to be wondered at – is the deeper truth which, by means of the theatre, Shakespeare makes actual.

In *Hamlet*, as in the *Dream*, an old-fashioned kind of play is presented to the Court but this time with professional competence. The play he asks the players to perform Hamlet calls *The Mousetrap*, and, like Bottom's play, it is a distorted reflection of the action of the main play, as any theatrical presentation is a distorted or at least artistically shaped reflection of what we are pleased to call real life. The situation of *The Mousetrap* or *The Murder of Gonzago*'s performance has a dazzling multi-faceted complexity. What exactly is happening? Some of the actors in Shakespeare's company are pretending to be actors of an earlier generation performing a play in an outmoded but still powerful style. Watching them are the rest of the Company, pretending to be members of the Danish Court in the main play, except that two of them, those assuming the rôles of Hamlet and Horatio, are more interested in watching Claudius for signs of recognition and guilt. Beyond that, watching everything on stage and Hamlet in particular, are we, the audience. A watches B, watching C, watching D. A series of shows, each an illusion for its observers, each illusion broken for the observers of those observers. D, the *Mousetrap* players, know they are being watched by C, Claudius, and B, Hamlet: their stylised speech and actions betray a constant awareness of spectators. Ophelia asks Hamlet about the Prologue: 'Will he tell us what this show meant?' And Hamlet replies: 'Ay, or any show that you'll show him: be not you ashamed to show, he'll not shame to tell you what it means.' To Ophelia this is 'nought'. Not surprisingly: it is spoken for our benefit in the audience. (I do not believe that Claudius is intended to hear the remark.) The style of the main play is positively naturalistic compared to *The Mousetrap*. But it is also aware of our listening presence. What is Hamlet telling us through Ophelia? The particular reference is not to Ophelia but to Claudius: Claudius's actions will be shown for what they truly are by the players. And as a general statement, the craft of the actor will interpret the outward signs of our inner life: it is the function of drama to interpret, not merely reflect, reality. Just as *The Mousetrap* is interpreting the situation in the Danish court, revealing it, making overt what is concealed, so the main play of *Hamlet* is interpreting the inner, concealed life of the observing audience whose reality it reflects, showing, in Hamlet's own words, 'the very age and body of the time its form and pressure'.

The players in *The Mousetrap* perform showing awareness of the Court audience but pretend they are unaware that they are also being watched by us, although as actors in Shakespeare's company they know it very well. The Court audience watches *The Mousetrap* in order to show us they are watching it, implicitly revealing an awareness of our presence. But, as Shakespeare's actors, they know that the real drama is not that which seems. The spotlight is really on Claudius, whose behaviour is to be interpreted by the actor Hamlet, whose reactions in turn we see as the reflection and interpretation of ourselves, since it is with him that we have been principally induced to identify.

Watchers and watched. Interpreters and those interpreted. Conscious and unconscious pretenders and rôle-players. All that is being presented on that wooden O is for our benefit. Unless we were watching there would be no show, no rôle-playing, no inter-relationship, no tension; the complex delicate structure would collapse and disappear. So we are an integral part, indeed the motivating factor, in the ritual. We too have our rôle, our interpretation to fulfil.

Extend the theme: The man playing Hamlet is watching the man playing his uncle who is watching the men playing the characters in *The Mousetrap*, who know they are being watched but pretend they do not know. Yet if they did not know they would not perform.

The man playing Hamlet knows that we are watching him but behaves as if he did not. Yet if we were not watching he would not play because he plays to show us something.

The question must arise: Is anyone watching us watching Hamlet watching Claudius watching the play? If no one were watching, would we play our parts? Could there be a play for us to be in? Are we aware of being watched? Do we pretend that we are not playing for someone's benefit? To whom could we make such a pretence? To ourselves? To one another? To the watcher? It is of course the old philosophical question. Can we exist if we are not perceived?

If the world is a great theatre, as both Shakespeare and Calderón saw it, there has to be an audience. What is the nature of that audience? Again, both Shakespeare and Calderón came to the same independent conclusion: the audience is a dreamer, and we are in his dream. To Calderón's Sigismund, and so to Calderon's audience, life seemed to be a dream: while we are experiencing a dream there is no difference from what we call reality, except that sometimes we are aware that we are dreaming. But that sensation of dreaming can also occur in so-called reality. It is left to Prospero to sum it up when he equates the masque, or theatrical show, which he has just abruptly broken off, with the real world: like the airy spirits, we are all figments of an imagination, a great creative consciousness. As he, the poet-magician, created the performers of the masque, so he and the creatures of the play *The Tempest* are figments of Shakespeare's imagination, and so Shakespeare himself and his audience are all figments of a greater brooding imagination.

> We are such stuff
> As dreams are made on, and our little life
> Is rounded with a sleep.

That is (I would interpret), our little life is a brief dream within an infinite sleep. To have sleep you must posit a sleeper. But of whose dream does that sleeper form a part?

Shakespeare breaks the illusion to reveal a truth which in turn is found to be a more subtle illusion.

The illusion that the play is reality is broken to take us into the sphere of myth.

The illusion that the character is a person is broken to make us feel that we too are rôle-players.

The illusion that we in the audience are unseen observers is broken to make us aware of being ourselves observed.

The illusion that the theatre is a world is broken to show us that all the world's a stage.

The illusion that the stage-mirror's reflection is the substance is broken to teach us that Nature herself is only a shadow.

As we draw nearer to the apparent substance we perceive it to be the shadow of a further substance. Just as, when we climb a mountain, the peak at which we aim is discovered to conceal a further peak which in turn gives away to yet another. What may or may not be beyond the veils of seeming Shakespeare cannot tell us: that is not his function. But he does share with us his instinctive faith in a beneficent power and the beauty of truth as far as he can discern it. Perhaps that is all we know on earth – and all we need to know.

[1981]

MARTIN BANHAM

BBC Television's dull Shakespeares

This review, to be about as unoriginal as its subject matter, is written more in sorrow than anger – though some anger at the disservice the BBC's worthily intended production of the Shakespeare canon is in fact doing must occasionally surface. It is a measure of my response that words such as 'dull' and 'worthy' are the ones that come to mind when trying to assess the series so far. We are offered fine actors working seriously, with no doubt equally fine directors, and with financial resources to match, plus the great enterprise of the presentation of thirty-seven of Shakespeare's plays, but all this leads us, in the end, only to something *dull*. Sadly we have to look on this venture, on the evidence to date, as the lost opportunity.

The evidence that I will offer centres around the productions in December 1979 of the two parts of *Henry IV* and of *Henry V*.* Here are three plays full of intrigue, power politics, broad and sharp comedy, excitement of the battlefield, poignant and sentimental relationships, and offering an opportunity to travel in history and scene in the company of some of Shakespeare's most famous characters. If, with such opportunities, we are eventually left disappointed and frustrated, where can the fault lie? Is it inherent in the medium? Is it that television cannot capture those qualities that make Shakespeare, at his best, such a marvellous experience in the theatre and an equally satisfying one in the imagination of the reader's mind? When thinking of *Henry V* many of us think first of the play as a film – Laurence Olivier's famous version, and our memories of that (in contrast to the compressed scale of the television production) include the thrill of the splendidly recreated Globe Theatre for the opening sequences (architectural pedants apart!) and the essentially filmic reconstruction of the battle scenes. It may not have been pure, but it was fun! We *did* come out of the cinema playing at being our own Henrys, stimulated and delighted by the experience. We had been entranced and captured by the power of the language and the presence of the actor. We had laughed, and done so in the company of others. And this point seems to me to be important. In the theatre the experience of the play is a shared one – shared not only between the individual in the audience and the actors but by members of the audience among themselves. Theatre is a public medium, television, from a viewer's (that very word!) angle, a private

*_Henry IV, part 1_, 7.15 p.m., Sunday 9 December 1979, BBC2.
Henry IV, part 2, 7.15 p.m., Sunday 16 December 1979, BBC2.
Henry V, 7.15 p.m., Sunday 23 December 1979, BBC2.

one. Plays, it must be argued, and notably Shakespeare's, are written consciously for audience response and participation. The audience is invited, in creating the scene, to use the resources of its own imagination, and, in listening to the characters on stage, to offer them the feed-back and focus that is at the heart of the shared experience. Does television fall between two stools, being able to offer neither the visual scope and communal audience experience of film and the cinema, nor the total qualities of the act of theatre? To develop this point a little let us look at three particular problems that television seems to produce, those of settings, speech and visual selection.

It is a cliché, but a perfectly respectable one, to assert that, in a Shakespearian play, the best scenery is created in the mind of the audience, and that to dress the set in a realistic way may only serve to confuse the audience and edit the individual's response. We all know of the great Victorian stage productions of Shakespeare that allowed the spectacle to dominate and decimated the text to accommodate it, and though we might have enjoyed the effect we cannot pretend that such productions served the plays or the playwright particularly well. If we allow that the film is likely to resort to some of the same literal reproductions of the scene, then we accept that as part of the nature of the beast, and sit back and enjoy it in its own terms. But television, certainly as evidenced by the Shakespeare series to date, too often aims between the spectacle of film and the simplicity and directness of theatre, giving settings that may in themselves be attractive, but which too often lack coherence and overall shape. They fail to contribute to the experience: prettiness is not enough. The second problem is that of speech. The range and dimension of language in any Shakespeare play is considerable. We share the secret thoughts and the public squabbles, we participate in ritual and in rhetoric. The scale is always changing. Of course we find this particularly in the *Henry* plays, and part of our pleasurable anticipation of them is for the language that they offer. But the key words *are* range, scale, dimension, and it is arguable that television proves itself unable to cope with the full demands of Shakespeare's language. The quieter, private moments may succeed (thus Anthony Quayle's Falstaff could address us conspiratorially throught the intimate window of the television screen) but the more robust, declamatory speeches often come perilously close to bluster – or, even worse, to petulance. Witness David Gwillim's uncomfortable handling of the famous 'Once more unto the breach, dear friends' speech in *Henry V*. Deprived of the physical space in which to deliver this fine piece, he was diminished in scale and impact. A considerable part of this was also due to the fact that he didn't really have anyone to talk *to*. A few actors on a small set on a small screen do not a Harry make! Here, above all, the play (and the actor) needed *audience.* The third related point is that of visual selection, and here I am concerned about the interference of the director in terms of what the viewer may see. Again it may be argued that Shakespeare, in writing and constructing his plays, always had in mind the fact that the audience could see all that was happening on stage at any given moment. The action off the ball may be as significant as that on it. We, the audience, make our own selection and that contributes essentially to our feeling for and sense of the complete drama in which we are participating. When a television (or, to be fair, a film) director cuts to a particular character, or comes into a close-up, or otherwise shapes our image of the action, he is intruding his own interpretation of what is significant between the action and the spectator. In so doing not only does he interfere with our imaginative liberties, he also runs the risk of destroying the sensitive integral framework of the play itself. One result of this, and of associated actions, has been to give these Shakespearean productions on television a linear feeling – a sense of being formed not with the circular, ultimately rounded and complete style of the 'wooden O' (which is not merely a description of a theatre but of the whole embracing experience of the drama) but with an episodic, strung-out, single line of action. The television audience, not being allowed to stand at once within and beside the action, is pointed in various directions not by its own will and decision, and not by the logic of the play in its entirety, but by technical decisions in order to accommodate the workings of the medium. So, to return to an earlier question, are we in the wrong medium for Shakespeare?

Quite obviously the BBC (and Time Life Films, their co-producers, and no doubt the source of the 'measure of financial support' that BBC's advertising for the series refers to) don't think so. But it is worthwhile spending some time looking at the basis for the overall production style as it is revealed in the publicity handout accompanying the launching of the series. This rightly draws attention to the acting talent that has been employed by the series and to the generally high standards that may be expected from BBC television's scenic and costume designers. It reminds us, and fairly too, that 'Since its foundation, the BBC has led the world in the production of classic drama . . .' (hence 'more in sorrow' *etcetera*). But it then goes on to make other claims which, if they have informed the general production style as they certainly appear to have done, could unkindly be referred to as wrong-headed, or more generously as debatable. Here is a sample:

> . . . it has been possible to record entire productions on location . . . The settings are those the layman would expect to see when he hears the name of Julius Caesar or Richard II. The Forum belongs to ancient Rome. Italy of the high Renaissance, setting of many of the dramas, is brought to life in squares and palaces that might well have been created by the artists of their time. *As You Like It* has been recorded in a real forest. The Tudor pageantry of *Henry VIII* has been re-created in all its splendour at Leeds Castle.

Shakespeare wrote to please an audience that was neither particularly sophisticated nor literary. He wrote for people, not coteries. It is our intention to bring his plays on the same plain terms to a mass audience . . . we think he would have been delighted by the resources on which we have been able to draw.

There has been no attempt at stylisation; there are no gimmicks; no embellishments to confuse the student.

Now let it be said that I have quoted these extracts slightly out of context, but not in any way to alter their meaning. The first section deals with the settings, and emphasises the fact that the producers saw the re-creation of authentic settings as an advantage, indeed a virtue. Or did they see it as the only possible way for television to work and therefore set out to make it a virtue? Is it really supposed to be authenticising the play to have *As You Like It* in a real forest? To reiterate: prettiness is not enough. Another, and interesting side issue becomes pertinent here. Much of the internal rhythm of a scene in Shakespeare, as with the Elizabethan drama in general, may be seen to be related to the physical dimensions of the stages of the period, as we understand them to have been. In other words, a scene and a sequence of scenes is constructed in a way that is aware of the pacing and shaping implicit in the dimension of the acting area. Thus quick shifts of action may be especially sensitively contrived, the comings and goings may have been written to cover particular distances or to allow for moments of comedy or tension that are effected by subtle use of the specific playing area. This particular round peg will not fit comfortably into a square hole. In other words, change the staging conventions and you may destroy the integral rhythms of speech and action, and this brings us back again to observing the deadeningly linear experience of television. The further comment, in the quotation, about what the layman would expect to see, really does have to be begging the question. The opportunity in this television series was to astonish and delight 'the layman', not to confirm his prejudices that Shakespeare is wordy and dull or to seduce him with a scenic tour of Europe.

The second quotation challenges us with a question that is often raised – basically a sophistication of the 'if Shakespeare had had TV he would have used it' argument. This may well be true, but again it seems to miss the point, which is that he didn't and that he wrote within the terms of his own world and his own stage, and that an acknowledgment and understanding of that is an essential *starting point* for any production of a Shakespeare play. The third quotation offers us 'the student' (who, like the 'layman' is not to be confused) who is to be given a gimmick-free production. The irony is that many of the most interesting, entertaining, thoughtful and revealing Shakespearean productions of the last twenty-five years have been the 'gimmicky' ones – if one replaces the word with the alternative word 'adventurous'. The caution implicit in the third quotation is, perhaps, the downfall of the series – a lack of boldness, a lack of imagination, a cautious concern for the elusive idea of a straightforward definitive production. Good Shakespearean production has a base of scholarship and understanding and then a superstructure of ideas and ventures and risks. It is a living thing, full of embellishments, full of stylisation, full of intelligent constructive 'gimmicks'.

Perhaps at this point it would be helpful to look at a number of scenes from the three *Henry* plays, as produced on television, and to see how and where the problems that I have been discussing in more general terms arise in specific scenes. After that, and in conclusion, I shall try and offer a more positive comment with some ideas towards the successful presentation of Shakespeare on television.

Henry IV, part 1, Act 2, scene 2. The battle at Gad's Hill. This is a comic scene, the basic comic business being at the expense of Falstaff who, being the robber is himself 'robbed' by Prince Hal and Poins. Various points make the comedy, amongst them, of course, the figure of Falstaff himself (admirably played in the TV production by Anthony Quayle) and the amiable trickery of the Prince. It is a scene full of hiding and seeking, set in the half-light of early dawn. This last fact is important, and the time is established quite clearly in the preceding scenes. But of course on Shakespeare's stage this scene would generally have been played in full daylight, and the illusion of semi-darkness would have been created by the comic action. Without that visual trickery (to which the audience is a party) the scene loses something of its fun. More important though is the implicit buffoonery of the action, with fat and foolish men hiding behind little pieces of cover on the stage in order to ambush others, and then themselves being ambushed by 'thieves' whom the conventions of the comedy allow them to fail to recognise as their companions, and the audience to accept as disguised beyond recognition and covered by the mists of dawn. This is a big scene – and a lot is made of it a little later in the play. It should be riotous and ridiculous, and above all it should be clear. The essence of the humour is in the willing illusion that what everybody can clearly see is in fact invisible. In the television version this became a rather confused tumble, more of a giggle than a belly-laugh, and the realistic creation of the light of early morning and mists of dawn stole much of the wit from the scene. What should have been a memorable vehicle for the clowns, became a rather hurried scuffle. I think we have an instance here of a scene that unless treated in an entirely unrealistic way fits most awkwardly into the medium.

Henry V, Prologue. The prologue, through the character Chorus, gives a fascinating impression of the Shakespearean stage, certainly of the early theatres, with his famous reference to 'The flat unraised spirits that hath dared / On this unworthy scaffold to bring forth / So great an object. Can this cockpit hold / The vasty fields of France? Or may we cram / Within this wooden O the very casques / That did affright the air at Agincourt?' Even, a little later, the description 'the girdle of these walls' reinforces the sense of being within a theatre where the audiences are *gathered around* the story-teller and the players. It is this intimacy, this gathering around, that invests the play with its extraordinary charm, its sense of oneness and companion-ship, of partisanship and patriotism. Chorus's comments are not an excuse, they are a carefully devised creation of a sense of unity and community – quite literally a statement 'we are all in this *together*'. A challenge for any director and designer on a modern stage, which may not lend itself architec-turally to this closeness between players and audience, is to find a solution that will capture this precious moment. It seemed particularly perverse, therefore, of the television production to play this scene with Chorus walk-ing straight down towards the camera between two lines of gradually revealed characters. The sense of the round was totally contradicted and replaced by visual signals which, far from drawing us into the action, placed us at a distance from it. Chorus thenceforth became a mannered and (spare the thought) gimmicky character, popping up from unexpected places, rather than the companion to our view and experience of the action as he should be.

Henry V, Act 3, scene 1, and Henry IV, part 1, Act 5 (the battle scenes). I have referred earlier to the difficult circumstances in which David Gwillim was asked to deliver the 'Once more unto the breach' speech, but it is worth look-ing in a little more detail at the scene. Battle scenes *are* difficult to stage, and we are all aware of productions where a few actors chasing each other over vast stages with pikes or swords have not exactly persuaded us of the reality of the conflict. Here we are firmly up against the possibilities and limitations of the Elizabethan stage. The battle scenes are peopled by a few actors at least to some extent because it didn't take many actors to look a crowd on a small stage, and certainly because the sense of a running battle, one that was passing in front of one's eyes but actually taking place on a wider battlefield was more easily achieved within the confines of a small stage and theatre, making full use of available exits and levels, and never allowing realism to take away the ability of the imagination to 'Into a thousand parts divide one man'. The battle scenes lacked focus in the television productions, offering no clear sense of arena or direction, and compromising between the simplic-ity of the stage and the vast panoramas of the film with an indoor set dressed in unconvincing grass and shrub. And back at the breach itself, no one looked more lonely and embarrassed than poor King Henry urging on invisible troops to an indistinct objective via an improbable scaffold. Again we found ourselves in a kind of televisual limbo-land, halfway between the imagination and the reality.

Henry V, Act 3, scene 4. This is the scene where we are introduced to Katherine. It is an accurately placed scene, a moment of charm in the middle of turmoil, a hint of action to come, and a knowing moment for the audience to share in. In the BBC production the roles of Katherine and Alice were delightfully and wittily played by Jocelyne Boisseau and Anna Quayle, and the specific scene we are concerned with was a pleasure to watch and listen to in itself. But the problem was that it *was* in itself. It suddenly emerged on the screen, set in soft edges, like a dainty picture illustrating the text. In the sense that the director was presumably trying to capture the other world beyond the carnage and the politics the scene had its logic – but to divorce it from the action in quite such a way again runs the risk of upsetting the total rhythms of the action. It made the scene feel awkwardly placed, whereas in fact it is most subtly located.

So now to return to my responsibility not to be merely a destructive and grumpy critic but to offer some more constructive comments. They are in the form of three possible and not entirely exclusive approaches to both the style and the philosophy of Shakespeare on television, and they are offered in the belief that my earlier question about the incompatibility between Shakespearean production and television has to be resisted. It has to be asserted that there are ways of presenting Shakespeare on television, most particularly because this is a great, developing and influential medium which must be able to take the classic drama into its repertoire.

The first concerns audiences. I have suggested earlier in this review that the role of the audience in a Shakespeare production is an important one, and one understood and exploited by the playwright. So much of the power and impact of the action depends upon the presence of an audience. I have instanced Henry V's great rallying speeches, but equally one may think of his more introspective moments, when the audience is needed to give a full dimension to his words and thoughts. But a more urgent case has to be made out for the comic actors – in which our three history plays abound, and who, without the return of laughter and comment from the audience have nothing to play to but the empty air. No wonder that on television their comedy falls flat, or survives at the level of self-indulgent posturing. This is not the fault of actors of the quality of Bryan Pringle or Gordon Gostelow, but rather the consequence of the dilemma in which they find themselves. It is a situation that television would not expose its contemporary comics to. It is no accident, surely, that Morecambe and Wise, Mike Yarwood and company perform on television with audiences? It enables their acts to work, and it enhances the enjoyment for the viewing audience. The audience provides the essential ingredient which brings the entertainment to life. It may be quite inappropriate and unnecessary for there to be an audience for a play specifically written for television, but is there any reason to deny an audience to one written for its living presence? It may not even be necessary for an audience to be in vision, but the fact of its being there could revitalise the experience of televised Shakespeare. I can see this suggestion being greeted with horror by television drama producers (and perhaps some television actors) to whom the live audience is often a strange experience and for whom it would merely conjure images of the early days of television when cameras entered the theatre and pointed themselves straight at the stage. But that is surely not the limit of the imagination and skill of contemporary television drama production? And which is more important, contemporary wisdom as to what television drama is, or the lifeblood of our greatest playwright?

My second suggestion concerns ways of giving a real unity and uniqueness to the series. I return to that opening sequence of the Olivier *Henry V* with the camera flying over 'London' and settling on to the Globe stage. Given all the intriguing scholarship of this century which has gradually revealed for us the form and resources of the Elizabethan stage, what an opportunity there would have been for this series to have undertaken informed reconstruction of the various stages upon which Shakespeare's plays may have been performed, and to have brought them to life again in their finest setting. Here we might envisage a most fruitful blending of the simple imaginative arena of Shakespeare's own experience, and the ability of modern TV technology to bring this to the screen. A danger would certainly lie in mere historical pedantry, and museum Shakespeare is not what would be intended. But one thing is certain and that is that the present series will disappear rapidly from the mind, having nothing special to offer, whilst a lively reconstruction might have regenerated the thinking of our whole theatre towards Shakespearean production. It would only be pedantic in the hands of pedants, so let that not be used as an excuse!

Lastly I offer what I would regard as probably the most realistic approach, and this takes us back to that self-satisfied but erroneous belief that in 'no stylisation . . . no gimmicks . . . no embellishments of any sort' we have the recipe for excellence. What this series really demands is a number of individual productions that are strikingly original, daring, experimental – productions that exploit and explore the potential of television rather than sit sedately within the empty box. We should not be content with productions that simply confirm the layman's expectations, but productions which stimulate, enrage, excite and delight us – and which make us keep coming back for more. Jacqueline Pearson concluded her review of the first television Shakespeares (*Critical Quarterly*, vol. 21, No. 1, spring 1979) by saying that she remained 'cautiously pessimistic' about the future of the series. The most recent evidence suggests that, like me, she should throw away her caution. But, dear BBC, for Shakespeare's sake, there is time (and life?) to change.

[1980]

JOHN WAIN

The Shakespearean lie-detector: thoughts on *Much Ado about Nothing*

I

Much Ado about Nothing is a play that might well halt the critic of Shakespeare in his amble through the plays, in much the same way as *Hamlet* halts him: a strong, buoyant, uneven piece of work. It could not possibly be called a failure, and yet it could not be described as a total success either. I believe the play has interesting things to tell us about the nature of Shakespeare's impulses as an artist, and in particular about the state of his mind in the closing months of the sixteenth century.

This essay will be concerned mainly with two topics: the play's overwhelmingly prosaic nature, its almost complete lack of the poetry which permeates Shakespearean comedy in general; and its novelistic quality, that drive towards three-dimensional characterisation which forces us to stand back and allow the characters, at whatever risk, to come out of their dramatic framework; for both of which I hope to suggest plausible reasons.

II

To begin with the play's undeniable success. It has always been a great favourite on the stage. If the verses contributed by Leonard Digges to the 1640 edition of Shakespeare's Poems are to be accepted as evidence, and I see no reason why they should not, this play already stood out as one of the most popular in the theatre:

> let but Beatrice
> And Benedick be seen, lo in a trice
> The cockpit, galleries, boxes, all are full.

Yet Digges's manner of referring to the play by its sub-plot indicates, thus early, an imbalance that has continued to make itself felt. *Much Ado*, for all its glitter and pace, does not leave us, either as spectators or readers, with that complete satisfaction, that sense of participating in something perfectly achieved, that we associate with *As You Like It* or *Twelfth Night* – and, for that matter, with the earlier *A Midsummer Night's Dream*. In all those plays, Shakespeare has been able to create a unity of mood which encircles and contains the many abrupt changes of tone – changes which a comedy, far more than a tragedy, is apt to invite and to live by. The total effect is of a

57

glittering restlessness subjected to a harmony that governs and enriches. *Much Ado* lacks this harmony. It belongs, in that respect, with the notoriously fragmented *Merchant of Venice*.

Still, there is a fascination in the failures or near-misses of a great artist. If we are interested in those works in which he completely succeeds, we cannot help being interested in those in which the success is limited and flawed. And some failures are resplendent. The Romantic poets, we recall, honoured Milton for his failure to carry out in poetry the full range of his Puritan programme. Blake praised him for being 'of the devil's party without knowing it'. Odd, to praise a great poet for a failure of self-knowledge! Yet that is what we sometimes find ourselves doing with Shakespeare. Like Milton in *Paradise Lost* – or, more strictly speaking, like Milton in the Romantics' characteristic account of him – he failed to estimate in advance, when blue-printing a work, which parts of it he could warm and illumine with his imagination and which parts would remain obstinately cold and dark.

The parallel with Milton, however, I introduce only to indicate the drift of my argument. It certainly does not hold good in any but superficial respects. For Milton's art, like his biography, shows everywhere the marks of a grand stubbornness. He confronted literary problems as he confronted political ones, by large and extreme solutions, carried through with courage and inflexibility. Cut off the king's head; leave your wife and sue for divorce; plan an immense epic and drive it through like a super-highway. Even in the weakest and dullest parts of *Paradise Lost* – those passages towards the end where plainly the poem is being heaved along by heroic will-power rather than driven by the immense and flowing urgency that we feel in the opening Books – Milton is still in control, still, though with a painfully visible effort, mastering his materials. Shakespeare is the opposite. As an artist, he is more often commanded by his imagination than commanding it. He is instinctive, spontaneous, lacking in the effrontery which can simulate inspiration in those parts of a large construction where it fails to come naturally. Where Shakespeare fails, he makes no attempt to varnish the failure. He is always doing several things at once, and if he loses interest in one of them, he leaves it frankly as a mock-up. But always for a good reason. He worked at speed, had to make a rapid choice of materials, and when a situation, or a character, fails to come to life under his hand, the fault is rarely – I think, never – the poet's. Some surfaces will not take a mural; some clay resists life; some situations, which looked neat enough in the blue-print, disintegrate under the weight of actuality and energy that Shakespeare cannot help putting into them.

Shakespeare, to put it in a more pedestrian way, was not a good hack-writer. He lacked the unvarying professional skill that can arrange even the poorest material into a pleasing shape, keeping its weaknesses out of sight. When things began to go wrong, he had his own remedy, which was to send even more energy flowing through those parts of the work which he *did* find congenial. As a result, the typical Shakespearean failure is a play at once lop-sided and brilliant – so brilliant that the lop-sidedness does not keep it from being acted and read.

III

These general considerations should help us in making our estimate of *Much Ado*. The comic scenes are warm and genial as well as genuinely funny; the story of Beatrice and Benedick, couched in a dialogue that sparkles like a handful of diamonds, is also a gentle and sympathetic story of how two gifted people are led towards a happiness they were in danger of missing; dramaturgically the play is brilliant, working out with a deft intricacy its major theme. This theme, as usual in Shakespearean comedy, is self-recognition, the journey from confusion to clarity: knowledge of one's own truth, leading to the possibility of happy relationships, symbolised by the multiple wedding and the dance. But in *Much Ado* this habitual theme is given an original twist, which John Masefield aptly described as 'the power of report to alter human lives'. All the truths that are discovered, as well as all the lies and fake reports that are spread, are communicated by report. And this anchors the theme of self-recognition firmly to the related theme of social harmony. We form our opinions of ourselves and others always partly, and sometimes largely, on the basis of what other people say. No one quite trusts his own unaided perception of the world. 'What a beautiful child you have', says one woman to another. 'That's nothing', is the reply, 'you should see his picture'. When Claudio is denouncing Hero's supposed faithlessness at the altar, he says to her father,

> Leonato, stand I here?
> Is this the Prince? Is this the Prince's brother?
> Is this face Hero's? Are our eyes our own?

The play's answer to that last question is, of course, No. Our nature as human beings is such that we inevitably see as much through other people's eyes as through our own. When Claudio, in the first bitterness of his impression that Don Pedro has robbed him of Hero, says,

> Therefore all hearts in love use their own tongues;
> Let every eye negotiate for itself
> And trust no agent,

59

he is asking the impossible. He himself, on first seeing Hero after his return from the wars, has turned to Benedick and asked, with a kind of rapturous anxiety, 'Benedick, didst thou note the daughter of Signior Leonato? . . . Is she not a modest young lady?' And, longing to be serious in spite of Benedick's joking, pressed him, 'I pray thee tell me truly how thou likest her'.

In the same vein is Friar Francis's remark (IV.i) that Claudio's attitude to Hero will change when he hears the report that she is dead; report will do for him what his own unaided perceptions would not:

> When he shall hear she died upon his words,
> The idea of her life shall sweetly creep
> Into his study of imagination.

Thus the machinery of this play links up with the cheated-vision symbolism of *A Midsummer Night's Dream* and also with the clothes-symbolism of *Cymbeline*; it is an essential Shakespearean preoccupation.

Yet the major deficiency remains. Everything is seen in the dry light and the straight perspective of prose. Poetry – however we define the word – is missing. Except here and there in the turn of some phrase of Beatrice's, the play never approaches it.

Like virtually every play of Shakespeare's, *Much Ado* is written in a mixture of prose and verse, and one of the first things we notice when we look at it attentively is that the prose is everywhere more memorable and satisfying than the verse, which at its best is workmanlike and vivacious, but never more; and, at its all too frequent worst, weak, monotonous and verbose.

The nature of the malaise is clear enough. The verse is weak because the verse-plot is weak. It was Shakespeare's custom, in comedy, to use a verse-plot alongside a prose-plot. In *As You Like It* and *Twelfth Night*, the two are of equal ease and vivacity. As the prose is supple and vivacious, so the verse is springy and memorable; the change from one to another falls on the ear as a delightful variation. It also serves as an aid to the attention. All plays are to some extent written for the first-night audience, and even the Elizabethans, with their quick wits and boundless appetite for complicated intrigue, must have welcomed the decisive difference in idiom which signalled the switch from plot to plot and back again. But in those plays, as in *A Midsummer Night's Dream* whose moonlit atmosphere effortlessly embraces a prose-plot and a tight web of three verse-plots, Shakespeare's imagination was equally involved in all parts of the play. In *Much Ado*, it was not. The verse-plot fails to convince or interest us because it failed similarly with Shakespeare himself.

IV

This, I know, is the conventional view, and recent critics like Graham Storey and John Russell Brown have registered various disagreements with it. Their arguments are ingenious and interesting and I find myself giving assent to them – until the next time I turn back to the play. That spoils everything. The old objections reappear in full force. Shakespeare has fallen into his old trap of beginning to handle a story without realising that at bottom it simply does not interest him. When the realisation comes, it is too late; he is stuck with the intractable material, and, as usual, he gives up any attempt to make it live.

Why did the Hero-and-Claudio plot go so dead on its author? The answer is not easy to find. Because it is not, *per se*, an unconvincing story. Psychologically, it is real enough. The characters act throughout in consistency with their own natures. Hero, her father Leonato and his brother Antonio, are all perfectly credible. Don John, though he is only briefly sketched and fades out early from the action, is quite convincing in his laconic disagreeableness, a plain-spoken villain who openly wishes others harm. Conrade and Borachio, mere outlines, are at any rate free of inherent contradictions; so is Margaret. None of these characters presents any major difficulty. It begins to look as if the trouble lay somewhere in the presentation of Claudio.

This young man, according to the requirements of the story, has only to be presented as a blameless lover, wronged and misled through no fault of his own; convinced that his love is met with deception and ingratitude, he has no choice but to repudiate the match; later, when everything comes to light, the story requires him to show sincere penitence and willingness to make amends, finally breaking out into joy when his love is restored to him. On the face of it, there seems to be no particular difficulty. But Shakespeare goes about it, from the start, in a curiously left-handed fashion. First we have the business of the wooing by proxy. Claudio confesses to Don Pedro his love for Hero, and Don Pedro at once offers, without waiting to be asked, to take advantage of the forthcoming masked ball to engage the girl's attention, propose marriage while pretending to be Claudio, and then speak to her father on his behalf. It is not clear why he feels called upon to do this, any more than it is clear why Claudio, a Florentine, should address Don Pedro, a Spaniard, as 'my liege' and treat him as a feudal overlord. Doubtless we are supposed to assume that he is in Don Pedro's service. It is all part of the *donnée*. There cannot be much difference in age between them, and Don Pedro is represented throughout as a young gallant, of age to be a bridegroom himself.

John Wain

The scene is perfunctory, and carries little conviction; it seems to have been written with only half Shakespeare's attention. Why, otherwise, would he make Claudio bring up the topic with the unfortunate question, 'Hath Leonato any son, my lord?' as if his motives were mercenary. Don Pedro seems to fall in with this suggestion when he replies at once that 'she's his only heir'. This is unpromising, but worse is to come. Immediately after the conversation between them, we have a short scene (I.ii) whose sole purpose seems to be to provide the story with an extra complication – one which, in fact, is never taken up or put to any use. Antonio seeks out his brother Leonato; he has overheard a fragment of the dialogue between Claudio and Don Pedro, and evidently the wrong fragment, so that he believes the prince intends to woo Hero on his account. Leonato wisely says that he will believe this when he sees it; 'we will hold it as a dream till it appear itself'; but he does say that he will tell Hero the news, 'that she may be better prepared for an answer'. Apart from confusing the story, the episode serves only to provide an awkward small problem for the actress who plays Hero. When, in the masked-ball scene in II.i, she finds herself dancing with Don Pedro, and he begins at once to speak in amorous tones, is she supposed to know who he is? Since she has been told that Don Pedro intends to woo her, she can hardly fail to guess that he will seek her out; presumably she is ready to be approached by him; does she intend to consent? There is no coldness or refusal in her tone, no hint of disappointment at not being approached by Claudio; she is merely gay and deft in her answers. It is a small, obstinate problem that is in any case hardly worth solving; on the stage, most producers cut out the scene where Antonio makes his mistake, and this is certainly what I should do myself. But it is hardly a good beginning.

Claudio is then convinced, by the unsupported assertion of Don John, that the prince has double-crossed him, that he made his offer merely to get Claudio to hold back while he went after the girl himself. If Claudio were a generous character we should expect him to put up some resistance to the story; he might say something like, 'I have the prince's own word for it that he would act on my behalf; we have been comrades in arms, he wishes me well and I trust him; I know him better than to believe he would stoop to this'. In fact, he believes the story straight away, with a depressing, I-might-have-known-it alacrity.

> 'Tis certain so; the Prince woos for himself.
> Friendship is constant in all other things
> Save in the office and affairs of love;
> Therefore all hearts in love use their own tongues.
> Let every eye negotiate for itself,
> And trust no agent; for beauty is a witch

Against whose charms faith melteth into blood.
This is an accident of hourly proof,
Which I mistrusted not. Farewell, therefore, Hero.

Benedick, who has heard the rumour and sees no reason to disbelieve it, now enters and tells Claudio the unwelcome news again, in no very gentle manner; when Claudio goes off to nurse his grievance, Benedick looks after him with 'Alas, poor hurt fowl' Now will he creep into sedges'. This though unconcernedly genial, is a contempt-image: Claudio has no more spirit than a dabchick.

At the next general muster of the characters (II.i) Claudio appears with a sour expression that makes Beatrice describe him as 'civil [Seville] as an orange', an image that later recurs in his bitter speech of renunciation at the altar ('Give not this rotten orange to your friend'). When the misunderstanding is abruptly removed, and he is suddenly thrust into the knowledge that Hero is his after all, he is understandably speechless and has to be prompted by Beatrice, who, like Benedick, seems to have a slightly contemptuous attitude towards him.

Claudio is now launched on felicity, yet he has so far been given no memorable lines, has shown no gaiety or wit, and we know nothing about him except that he has a tendency to believe the worst about human nature. He has been brave in battle – offstage, before the story opens – but all we have seen is the poor hurt fowl creeping into sedges. Why Shakespeare treated him like this, when it was important to win the audience's sympathy for such a central character, I cannot say. But it is clear that, for whatever reason, Shakespeare found him unattractive. Already the altar scene, at which Claudio must behave with cold vindictiveness, is casting its shadow before.

The trick is played; the victims are planted, the charade is acted out, Don Pedro and Claudio believe that Hero is false and vicious. What, one wonders for the second time, would be the reaction of a generous young man, with decent feelings and a tender heart? There are several possibilities; he could seek out the man who had stepped into his place and challenge him to a duel; or he could take horse and gallop out of town within that hour, leaving the wedding-party to assemble without him and the girl to make her own explanations. What he actually does is to get as far as the altar and then launch into a high-pitched tirade in which he not only denounces Hero but sees to it that her father is made to suffer as much as possible.

In all this, there is no psychological improbability. Such a youth would in all likelihood behave just in this way, especially if he were a Renaissance nobleman, touchy about his honour. Claudio's basic insecurity, already well demonstrated in the play, would naturally come out in vindictiveness if he thought himself cheated. The story, *qua* story, is perfectly credible. The reason we do not believe it is simply that it is put into an artificial idiom. If Shakespeare had told this story in the same swift, concrete, realistic prose with which he presented the story of Beatrice and Benedick, it would be perfectly convincing. But he has, for some reason, written consistently poor verse for the characters to speak, mishandled the details (we will come to that in a moment), and in general made such a poor job of it that everyone feels a blessed sense of relief when Leonato, Friar Francis and Hero take their departure, and the stage is left to Beatrice and Benedick. How reviving it is, to the spirits and the attention to drop from the stilted heights of Friar Francis's verse, full of lines like 'For to strange sores strangely they strain the cure', to the directness and humanity of

- Lady Beatrice, have you wept all this while?
- Yea, and I will weep a while longer.

The tinsel and the crape hair are laid aside with the attitudinising and the clumping verse; we are back in the real world of feeling. Shakespeare obviously shares this relief. His writing, in this wonderful scene in which Benedick and Beatrice admit their love, has the power and speed of an uncoiling spring.

But to come back to Claudio. His vindictiveness towards Hero and her father is not in the least unconvincing; it springs from exactly that self-mistrust and poor-spiritedness which we, and some of the other characters in the play, have already noticed. The question is, why are they there? Why does Shakespeare give this kind of character to Claudio, when he could easily have made him more sympathetic?

The answer, as so often, lies in the exigencies of the plot. Claudio has to humiliate Hero publicly, has to strike an all but killing blow at her gentle nature, for the same reason that Leontes has to do these things to Hermione. In each case, the woman has to be so emotionally shattered that she swoons and is later given out as dead. So that Shakespeare had no alternative but to bring the whole party to the altar and let Claudio renounce his bride before the world. This, I believe, is the central spot of infection from which the poison pumped outwards. Having to make Claudio behave in this way, Shakespeare could feel no affection for him. And he had, as I remarked earlier, no gift for pretending. If he disliked a character, one of two things happened. Either, as in the case of Isabella in *Measure for Measure*, his pen simply ran away with him, providing more and more repulsive things for the character to say; or it refused to work at all. In *Much Ado* it was the second of these two fates that befell Shakespeare. As the play went on, he must have come to dread those scenes in which he would have to introduce Claudio. It

64

became harder and harder to think of anything to make him say. Perfectly good opportunities presented themselves and were refused; he just *could* not try hard. The Shakespearean lie-detector was at work.

Think, for instance, of the closing scenes of the play's last act. Claudio, however heartless he may have been, has here several golden opportunities to redeem himself. Shakespeare has only to show him as genuinely penitent, give him some convincing lines to say, and we shall begin to feel sorry for him, to look forward with pleasure to the time when his happiness is restored. In fact, nothing of the kind happens. In spite of the harm done to the play by Shakespeare's true opinion of Claudio, he cannot help showing that opinion. In the scene (V.i) where he and Don Pedro are confronted by Leonato and Antonio, he appears as having disengaged himself, emotionally, from the whole situation.

> *Don Pedro* Nay, do not quarrel with us, good old man.
> *Antonio* If he could right himself with quarrelling,
>   Some of us would lie low.
> *Claudio* Who wrongs him?

An unfortunate question from one in his position; and it would be difficult, to say the least, for an actor to speak it in a tone of kindly innocence. It comes out inevitably with a hard, sneering edge.

That scene develops interestingly, bearing out the view that the story in itself was not repugnant to Shakespeare; he found plenty of interest in it. Antonio, a very minor character whose general function in the play is simply to feed the plot, suddenly comes to life in this scene. Leonato, knowing that his daughter is not really dead yet unable to keep down his anger at the sight of the two smooth young gallants who have brought such sorrow on his grey hairs, begins to rail at Claudio and the prince, whereupon Antonio, catching his mood and feeling it more deeply – for we have no reason to suppose that he is in the secret – begins to rage and threaten, becoming more and more beside himself while his brother, alarmed at the passion his own words have set in motion, plucks at his sleeve with 'Brother – ' and 'But, brother Antony – '. 'Do not you meddle; let me deal in this', cries the enraged old gentleman. The whole tiny episode is splendidly alive and convincing. But that life does not reach as far as Claudio. He says nothing until the two old men withdraw and Benedick comes onstage. Then he at once begins his accustomed teasing. He has it firmly in his head that Benedick is there to provide sport, either by his own wit or by proving a target for the infinitely more clumsy jokes that occur to himself or Don Pedro. Lightly dismissing the grief and answer of the previous encounter with, 'We had lik'd to have had our two noses snapp'd off with two old men without teeth', he challenges Benedick to a wit-contest, and in spite of Benedick's fierce looks and reserved manner, goes clumping on with jokes about 'Benedick the married man' until he is brought up sharply by an unmistakable insult followed by a challenge. He can hardly ignore this, but his is a mind that works simply and cannot entertain more than one idea at a time. He can change, when something big enough happens to make him change, but he cannot be supple, cannot perceive shifts in mood. Even after Benedick has challenged him, he cannot get it clear that the time for teasing is over; he keeps it up, woodenly enough, right up to Benedick's exit. So unshakable is his conviction that Benedick *equals* mirth and sport.

Psychologically this is exactly right. Shakespeare saw clearly what kind of person Claudio would have to be, if he were to behave in the way called for by the plot. What depressed him, inhibiting his mind and causing him to write badly, was the iron necessity of making such a man – cold, proud, self-regarding, inflexible – the hero of the main story in the play.

We see this more and more clearly as the last act unfolds. In Scene iii, when Claudio, accompanied by the prince and 'three or four with tapers', comes to do penance at Hero's tomb, Shakespeare shies away from the task of putting words into his mouth. Instead, he makes the scene a short formal inset; Claudio recites a few stiff, awkward rhymes and then a song is sung. The song has merit; the scene, lit by tapers and with a dramatic solemnity, is effective on the stage; but Shakespeare has missed the chance of bringing Claudio nearer to a humanity that would help us to feel for him. It is too late for that; the case is hopeless.

The characters then go home (evidently they are no longer houseguests at Leonato's) and put on 'other weeds' for the marriage of Claudio and the supposed daughter of Antonio, which he has agreed to with the words,

> I do embrace your offer, and dispose
> For henceforth of poor Claudio.

Arriving there, they find Benedick waiting with Leonato. Incredible as it may seem, Claudio again begins his clumsy pleasantries about Benedick's marriage ('we'll tip thy horns with gold', etc. etc.). Neither the challenge, nor the sobering effect of the occasion, nor the fact that he is newly come from the tomb of Hero, can make him forget that Benedick's presence is the signal for an outbreak of joshing. Shakespeare knows that this is the kind of man he is, and with his curious compulsive honesty he cannot help sharing that knowledge with us, whatever it may do to the play.

The cost is certainly great. Antonio goes off to fetch the girls, and brings them in wearing masks. Here, obviously, is an excellent opportunity for Shakespeare to give Claudio some convincing lines. When he is at last confronted with the girl he is to marry instead of Hero, there is plenty that even the most ordinary writer could make him say. He can speak, briefly but movingly, about his love for the dead girl, and his remorse; he can declare his intention of doing everything in his power to bring happiness into the family that has been plunged into misery through his error; he can thank the good fortune that has made him happy, even in this misery, by uniting him to a girl closely related to his love and closely resembling her. Then the unmasking and the joy. It is not my intention to try to take the pen out of Shakespeare's hand and write the play myself; I give these simple indications merely as a way of showing that it is not in the least difficult to imagine an effective speech that Claudio might make at this point in the action – how he might, even now, show some saving humanity.

What Shakespeare actually does is to give him the one line, 'Which is the lady I must seize upon?' This, coming as it does at a crucial moment, has a strong claim to be considered the worst line in the whole of Shakespeare. It is the poet's final admission that Claudio has imposed his ungenerous personality on the story and ruined it beyond repair. After that, there is nothing for it but to get the unmasking scene over as quickly as possible and hurry on to the marriage of Beatrice and Benedick. Hero unmasks, and Claudio utters two words, 'Another Hero!' before the action sweeps on and everyone turns with relief to the sub-plot.

V

Before we can so turn, however, we must pause and consider the extent of the damage that was done to the Hero-and-Claudio plot by Shakespeare's distaste for it. Dr Johnson, in dismissing the plot of *Cymbeline*, spoke of 'faults too evident for detection, and too gross for aggravation'. This could certainly be applied to the Hero-and-Claudio story; one can more easily say what isn't wrong with it than what is. To begin with we might note that the whole contriving of the plot by Borachio is just about as maladroit as it could be. When he is outlining to Don John what he means to do, Borachio says,

> They will scarcely believe this without trial; offer them instances; which shall bear no less likelihood than to see me at her chamber-window; hear me call Margaret, Hero; hear Margaret term me Claudio; and bring them to see this the very night before the intended wedding.

There is here one of those contradictions 'too gross for detection'; how would it serve the deception to 'hear Margaret term me Claudio'? If Claudio is supposed to be listening, he would surely suspect that something very strange was happening if he heard someone else called by his name. To be fair, this particular bit of the scheme is never afterwards referred to, and it has been argued that 'Claudio' is a slip of the pen for 'Borachio'; many editors, from Theobald to Peter Alexander, boldly substitute the name 'Borachio', thus tidying up after a fit of Shakespearean absent-mindedness. But even if we accept this, we are still left with the problem of Margaret. Why should she consent to take part in the masquerade, to wear her mistress's clothes, and then remain silent when the storm breaks? What is she supposed to be doing? Why is she absent from the wedding, which as Hero's personal lady-in-waiting she might naturally be supposed to attend?

Margaret, obviously, is one of those characters on whom Shakespeare has simply given up. After the Watch has unmasked the plot, Leonato expresses his intention of seeking Margaret out and confronting her with Borachio. In the very next scene (V.ii) we see her, talking to Benedick, but the scene is entirely without function except in so far as Benedick asks her to go and fetch Beatrice and she agrees to do so; the rest is merely an interlude of rather arid sparring. Shakespeare was glad to bundle Margaret out of sight, just as he was wise to provide such good comic by-play in the scene of the overhearing of the plot by the Watch ('I know that Deformed'), to keep us from noticing the threadbare device that is being used. Conrade, evidently, is a character whose sole function in the play is to be present in the street in the middle of the night (why?) and have Borachio tell him what has happened. They do not meet by arrangement; Conrade, though he has earlier declared that he will back Don John in any wickedness, is not present when Borachio outlines his plot, and knows nothing about it until the pair happen to meet in the street. We do not, at any rate in the theatre, feel the weakness of this device, partly because the antics of the Watch are so amusing and partly because, in the rather laboured dialogue with which they work up to the disclosure, the pair introduce the important theme of appearance versus reality. 'Thou knowest that the fashion of a doublet, or a hat, or a cloak, is nothing to a man'. And this is part of the 'nothing' that causes all the play's much ado. It is excellent dramaturgy to have the audience reminded, at this point, of the play's serious backbone; it keeps our attention busy at an awkward moment. The same function is served by the brilliant stagecraft of the altar scene itself, which gives every character something to say and do, so that we are carried along on the dramatic current and do not pause for questioning. For that matter, it is likewise excellent dramatic sense to have the Watch overhear the plot *before* we come to the altar scene and not after; it prevents the altar scene from being flooded with that dark tragic colouring that would overbalance the lighter tones of the rest of the play. Shakespeare had learnt this lesson the hard way in *The Merchant of Venice*, and it is interesting to see him getting out of trouble by shaping the plot so artfully: since there is, of course, no inherent reason why

Borachio should not have met Conrade in the street on the night after the wedding débâcle rather than the night before.

VI

The Hero-and-Claudio plot, we have now established at perhaps tedious length, is a ruin. And what ruined it, in my opinion, was the pull towards psychological realism that seems to have been so strong in Shakespeare's mind at this time. Certainly this made the character of Claudio unworkable, and once that was hopeless it was all hopeless. Because the plot demanded that Claudio should behave ungenerously to a girl he was supposed to love, because Shakespeare could not stick to the chocolate-box conventions but had to go ahead and show Claudio as a real, and therefore necessarily unpleasant, youth, the contradictions grew and grew until they became unsurmountable.

It is this that must be my excuse for applying realistic criteria to the play, probing into questions of probability and motive, tut-tutting at the flimsiness of the main plot, and generally talking about the play as if it were a novel. In the last thirty years we have had many sharp warnings against this. It has been explained often enough that 'character-criticism' is a hangover from the later nineteenth century, when the novel was the dominant form in English literature and thus influenced everyone's way of looking at any literary work; that it climbed to its zenith in the days of Scott and then of Dickens, and has no business to live on into the age of *Finnegans Wake* and the post-Symbolist poets. Dramatic characters are real only in action; they do not, or at any rate should not, invite the kind of biographical fantasy that we attach to characters in prose fiction. *Und so weiter*. I know this line of argument well enough. But it seems to me that Shakespeare, who overflows the boundaries in every direction, also overflows this one. His plays differ very widely in the extent to which he rounds out the characters as a novelist might. We feel this instinctively, and no amount of preaching will alter that feeling.

Virtually all influential academic critics, in the last few decades, have turned against this tradition of Shakespearean criticism, itself largely entrenched within the older academicism. And not only academics. We find a successful novelist and dramatist like Mr J. B. Priestley saying, in his printed lecture *The Art of the Dramatist* (1956) that 'the professors' are still at their work of obfuscation.

'The professors almost persuade us that dramatists are not concerned with theatres and audiences. There are no longer any parts to be acted. The characters become historical figures, real people. "Now what", the

professors ask, "was Hamlet doing during those years?" As if we were all
private detectives employed by King Claudius! When and where, they
wonder, did the Macbeths first meet? And so it goes on. They cannot – or
will not – grasp the fact that Hamlet has no existence between the two stage
directions *Exit Hamlet* and *Enter Hamlet*, that the Macbeths never had a first
meeting because Shakespeare never wrote a scene about it. The dramatist's
characters exist in their scenes and nowhere else.'

Well, I am not a professor, but this seems to me to settle some intricate
questions a little too summarily. What is the nature of imaginative creation?
What are we doing when we think of Hamlet? When we see Othello strangle
Desdemona on the stage, do we believe he is really strangling her? If not,
what do we believe? That we are watching an actor and actress, who will
soon be cleaning off the greasepaint and putting on ordinary clothes to take
a taxi home? If 'a dramatist's characters exist in their scenes', if they can be
said to *exist* at all, why should we not have a sense of them as existing in a
continuum of experience? Surely anyone who has ever created an imaginary
character knows that it can only be done by living with that character for
long periods, getting the feel of a whole lived life behind the much smaller
area in which we show the character actually doing and suffering. The novel,
with its flash-backs and leisurely accumulation of detail, can, if the novelist
so wishes, supply a great deal of background of the kind postulated by the
question, 'What was Hamlet doing during those years?' The drama cannot.
But it is not, to me, self-evident that the imaginative process involved, for
either writer or spectator, is so very different; or that it is different in kind at
all.

At the time when Shakespeare wrote *Much Ado* he was just moving into
that phase of his work in which we find most of his really solid
character-creations. In the next five or six years he was to give us Brutus,
Hamlet, Macbeth, Cleopatra. After that, the interest in three-dimensional
character lapses and the plays become 'romances', dream-like, openly
symbolic. Clearly, one of the activities of his mind, during that period, was
the kind of character-building which we associate mainly with the novel.
This was the period when everything was rushing along at once, when
Shakespeare, at the full torrential flood of his energies, was novelist, poet
and dramatist combined. The three 'golden comedies', *Much Ado*, *As You
Like It* and *Twelfth Night*, were a springboard for this great leap. Above all
else, they are plays, and plays on a definite theme: self-knowledge as
manifested in the making of choices and particularly in courtship. But they
are also great dramatic-lyrical poems. And they are also novelistic in that
they tell credible stories about fully imagined, realistic characters.

At least, the other two mature comedies are all these things. Only in *Much*

Ado, the first of the series, the springboard to a springboard, is the balance missing. In it, the poetic element is absent; the dramatic and the novelistic elements are unusually strong. Shakespeare's mind was very like a river in spate. If it found one channel blocked, it would hurl itself with greater and greater force through the channels that remained. Dramatically – except for a stumble or two in the Hero-and-Claudio plot – *Much Ado* is more expert than the other comedies. Novelistically, if I may be permitted the term, it stands beside *Hamlet*: another play in which the whole is eclipsed by the brilliance of the parts.

As much as any novelist, Shakespeare, while writing this play, delighted in the depth and solidity of his characters. This delight comes out even in the purely mechanical business of the hoaxing of Beatrice and Benedick. Two eavesdroppings, two faked conversations, are contrived in that cuckoo-clock manner with which Shakespeare had enjoyed pleasing his audience ever since *Love's Labour's Lost*. But if we compare the hoodwinking of Benedick in II.iii, with the hoodwinking of Beatrice in III.i, we see that there is a considerable difference between the two scenes and that the difference springs from character. The men, in hoping to entangle Benedick with Beatrice, are simply diverting themselves; they may share in the general recognition that Beatrice and Benedick are meant for each other, they may even be aware of the warmth of feeling that already unites them, but they are not primarily interested in these things. Their main object is merriment. Hero, on the other hand, when she addresses Ursula on the subject of Beatrice's haughtiness, is engaged in the essential business of her life. Except for the pretence of being unaware of Beatrice's presence, there is no deception in her speech at all; she genuinely wants to caution Beatrice against the witty aggressiveness that is likely to spoil her life, and she genuinely finds it impossible to do so face to face.

> If I should speak,
> She would mock me into air; O, she would laugh me
> Out of myself, press me to death with wit!
> Therefore let Benedick, like cover'd fire,
> Consume away in sighs, waste inwardly:
> It were a better death than die with mocks,
> Which is as bad as die with tickling.

She speaks feelingly because she is quite certain that her account of the situation is the true one; and so it is. Beatrice, like Olivia in *Twelfth Night*, is offending against one of the supreme laws of Shakespeare's world; namely, that girls exist to make wives for men and mothers for children. Olivia, by clinging to her grief for a dead brother and refusing the love of Duke Orsino, is flying in the face of nature by refusing the function and the fulfilment that

71

nature offers her. The other characters see this, and gently but firmly the play eases her out of this impossible position and brings her to the altar. In exactly the same way, Beatrice is clinging to something which she thinks of as a protection – her wit – which is in fact not protecting her at all but pushing her out of reach of happiness.

Why do Beatrice and Benedick communicate by witty squabbling? In its characteristic way, the play suggests a biography behind them, and we gather that they have been close at some previous time and that they have fallen out, without, however, falling out of love with each other. This is indicated in II.i.

> *Don Pedro* Come, lady, come; you have lost the heart of Signior Benedick.
> *Beatrice* Indeed, my lord, he lent it me awhile; and I gave him use for it, a double heart for his single one: marry, once before he won it of me with false dice, therefore your Grace may well say I have lost it.

The high-spirited girl chooses to speak in riddles because she has no mind to speak openly of her troubles and sufferings in this proud, hard-hearted company; but what she means by saying that she gave Benedick 'a double heart for his single one' is plain enough; and the allusion to 'false dice' seems to indicate some suspicion that Benedick deceived her; a suspicion, perhaps, as groundless as Claudio's suspicion of Hero.

Starting from this misunderstanding, the two of them have got trapped in a psychological box. Their need for each other is intense, but they can express it only by quarrelling; a situation we have all seen many times in life, but not very often, I think, in literature, and certainly never as skilfully shown as here. The initial difficulty is heightened by the fact that their verbal defences are so highly developed; left to themselves, they will fence and fence their lives away; cleverness will be their undoing unless the much less clever characters who surround them come to their aid with heavy-handed facetiousness which breaks down the elaborate rhythms of their mating-dance. As Hero plainly tells the listening Beatrice, cleverness has no place in the business of selecting a partner.

> So turns she every man the wrong side out;
> And never gives to truth and virtue that
> Which simpleness and merit purchaseth.

To give to truth and virtue the love and respect that are 'purchased' by simplicity and merit – this, Hero thinks, is all that is necessary for happiness, and the play agrees with her. Dogberry, who has climbed to a position of respect among his fellow-townsmen by virtue of his age and his sufferings as well as his upright ways – for he is 'a fellow that hath had losses' – describes himself with honest, wrathful pride as 'one that hath two gowns, and everything handsome about him'. This is echoed in Benedick's speech in the closing minutes of the play, when he renounces his pride in superior powers of repartee. 'Dost thou think I care for a satire or an epigram? No: if a man will be beaten with brains, a' shall wear nothing handsome about him.'

I am sure this echo is intentional; cleverness is rebuked although it is enjoyed. The constables are not clever, but they restore the harmony that has been upset by quick-witted schemers; if a man will only give up judging people, himself included, by their cleverness, he will be an honest man, like Dogberry, and have everything handsome about him.

This may seem a pawky moral to find in so glittering a play, but it is in line with the import of all Shakespearean comedy; the verbal pugnacity of Beatrice and Benedick is a more attractive fault than the moping of Orsino and Olivia or the artificial disillusion of Jaques; all the comedies deal with the correction of faults that obstruct life, and what they tell us is that human beings, in spite of all the difficulties that beset them, are unquenchably vital and must, somehow, find the strength to go on being unquenchably vital. All the rest is vain expense of breath, mere to-ing and fro-ing, much ado.

[1967]

D. J. PALMER

As You Like It
and the idea of play

Now in myth and ritual the great instinctive forces of civilized life have their origin: law and order, commerce and profit, craft and art, poetry, wisdom, and science. All are rooted in the primeval soil of play.

(J. Huizinga, *Homo Ludens*, 1949)

Here nowe I recke not much, to passe over untouched, how no maner acte, or noble deede was ever attempted, nor any arte or science invented, other, than of whiche I might fully be holden first author.

(Erasmus, *The Praise of Folie*, translated by Sir Thomas Chaloner, 1549)

I

There is only enough story in *As You Like It* to send the main characters to the Forest of Arden and finally to bring most of them out again. Once in the forest, the action virtually dispenses with narrative plot. Rosalind, for instance, no longer requires her disguise when she has found her father, whom she came to seek, and Orlando as well; but she delays the discovery of her identity for as long as she can. Like the other sojourners in Arden, she passes the time (although there seems nothing to wait for) by playing games. The heart of the comedy might be described as a demonstration of man's natural propensity for play.

We first hear of Arden in the opening scene, when Charles the wrestler describes how Duke Senior and his companions live in exile: 'They say he is already in the Forest of Arden, and a many merry men with him; and there they live like the old Robin Hood of England. They say many young gentlemen flock to him every day, and fleet the time carelessly, as they did in the golden world.' It seems as though life has become a pastime for the Duke and his followers, as though they have passed out of reality into a story-book world. A legend of Merry England is merged with the classical myth of the Golden Age, and even in the word 'flock' there is a hint of pastoral associations. Yet this is only by report, as the repetition of 'they say' reminds us. Hearsay distances reality, and is itself the way in which legends come into being. We are left uncertain, therefore, whether this idyllic picture of life in Arden is the creation of the Duke and his followers or of Charles and his informants.

As a world of make-believe, however, it certainly reflects a sharp contrast with the stern realities of court life, where instead of a society of 'merry men' there is the conflict of brother with brother. As Duke Frederick usurped his brother's throne, Oliver now plots against Orlando, and immediately after Charles' description of the pastimes pursued in Arden we hear talk of another kind of play: 'You wrestle tomorrow before the new Duke?' Wrestling makes sport out of conflict, yet Oliver has a sinister design to turn Charles' match with Orlando into a game to be played in deadly earnest.

The juxtaposition of these two images of play is followed in the second scene by Celia's persuasion of her cousin to shake off melancholy and 'be merry':

> *Rosalind* From henceforth I will, coz, and devise sports. Let me see; what think you of falling in love?
>
> *Celia* Marry, I prithee, do, to make sport withal; but love no man in good earnest, nor no further in sport neither than with safety of a pure blush thou mayst in honour come off again.
>
> *Rosalind* What shall be our sport, then?
>
> *Celia* Let us sit and mock the good housewife Fortune from her wheel, that her gifts may henceforth be bestowed equally.
>
> *Rosalind* I would we could do so . . .   (I.ii.20–31)

Their sport is in devising sport, experimenting with the exhilarating possibilities of play, and casting around for some suitable object for their wit and mockery. At this point Touchstone joins them, and the advent of the professional fool adds another dimension to the treatment of life as a game. The fool's wit is intelligence at play, delighting in its own caprice, and extending by inverting them the contrary values of folly and wisdom.

Before we reach Arden, therefore, we are given some anticipation of the nature of play, and of the equivocal relations between fiction and reality, game and earnest, folly and wisdom. Each of the different kinds of pastimes presented in these first two scenes is a response to a society broken by violent enmities: Duke Senior and his companions turn their exile into a make-believe life of good fellowship; the wrestling match between Charles and Orlando is a projection of the hostility between the two brothers; while the games of wit that Celia and Rosalind play with Touchstone make sport out of adversity ('Nature hath given us wit to flout at Fortune', as Celia says). Play may be seen as a civilising impulse to create a better world, or as a way of releasing energies restrained by civilised life. Significantly, in a world that has been reduced to barbarism, where violence and cruelty are real enough, there is little use for play: the wrestling match turns into a murder-plot, and the fool is put to silence. Wrestling is a fairly primitive form of sport, in any case ('Is there yet another dotes upon rib-breaking?' says Rosalind, determined out of perverse humour to stay and watch a sport not fit for ladies). But while it reflects what has become of courtly tastes and values in the ascendancy of Duke Frederick, it also suggests by analogy the element of ritualised conflict that exists in wit-combats and games of mockery. Similarly, the pastoralism of Duke Senior's way of life in Arden, as Charles describes it, is both primitivist and civilising.

If poetry and drama are themselves forms of play, Shakespeare is also playing games with his own art in *As You Like It*. His critical intelligence and creative imagination are held in perfect equilibrium as he sports with style through parody and burlesque, and finds in the pastimes of Arden primitive analogues to the spirit of comedy. The forest itself, as we are several times reminded, is both literally and figuratively 'this wide and universal theatre', the wooden circle into which we are drawn, like fools at the call of 'Ducdame', and the 'abandoned cave' that we leave when the comedy is over.

I I

After Charles' picture of the exiled Duke and his 'merry men' fleeting the time carelessly, it comes as something of a surprise when we first encounter the Duke of Arden to find him indulging a vein of serious philosophising:

> Now, my co-mates and brothers in exile,
> Hath not old custom made this life more sweet
> Than that of painted pomp? Are not these woods
> More free from peril than the envious court?
> Here feel we not the penalty of Adam,
> The seasons' difference? – as the icy fang
> And churlish chiding of the winter's wind,
> Which when it bites and blows upon my body,
> Even till I shrink with cold, I smile and say
> 'This is no flattery; these are counsellors
> That feelingly persuade me what I am'.
> Sweet are the uses of adversity . . .   (II.i.1–12)

The climate, too, is apparently less hospitable than Charles' comparison with the golden world led us to anticipate. But it is only the nature of the game that is different: this is just as much an exercise in make-believe as playing at Robin Hood. The Duke is using imagination to convert the harshness of existence in Arden into a blessing in disguise; the struggle for survival in a hostile world becomes a benevolent schooling in self-knowledge. It is not the philosophical truth of the Duke's propositions that require assent, but his willingness to look on the bright side. So Amiens responds, not with 'How wise, how true, how noble', but with

> Happy is your Grace,
> That can translate the stubbornness of fortune
> Into so quiet and so sweet a style.   (18–20)

The only moralist in evidence is the winter's wind, whose 'churlish chiding' is in marked contrast with the 'sweet' style of the Duke. He speaks here as a poet, a maker of fictions, even necessary fictions.

But discarding this role for another, the Duke abruptly changes his tune by proposing another pastime, and one that matches the cruelty of nature which has just been his theme:

> Come, shall we go and kill us venison?

The victim of adversity would now reverse roles; but he recollects himself immediately and returns to his vein of fanciful reflection:

> And yet it irks me the poor dappled fools,
> Being native burghers of this desert city,
> Should, in their own confines, with forked heads
> Have their round haunches gor'd. (22–5)

By attributing rights of prior occupation to the deer, and conflating their 'forked heads' with those of the huntsmen's arrows, the Duke puts man and beast on the same level, and relates bloodsport to the barbarism of the world that has expelled him.

This is the attendant lord's cue to report Jaques' meditation on the 'poor sequestered stag'. It echoes the Duke's own sentimentalising of misfortune so well that we can recognise Jacques and the Duke as complementary figures, even though the Duke's 'sweet' style and his love of fellowship are antithetical to Jaques' bitter raillery and solitariness. The wounded deer was a commonplace emblem of affliction and melancholy retirement, and the familiar Elizabethan pun of hart/heart, which lies just below the threshold of this image, enables it to be extended to conceits about amorous suffering, as we shall see. For his part, by identifying with the forlorn beast Jaques dissociates himself from his comrades-in-exile:

> Thus most invectively he pierceth through
> The body of the country, city, court,
> Yea, and of this our life; swearing that we
> Are mere usurpers, tyrants, and what's worse,
> To fright the animals, and kill them up
> In their assign'd and native dwelling-place. (58–63)

Hunting now provides the metaphor for another pastime played between Jaques and the ducal party. His invective 'pierceth through/The body . . . of this our life' like a wounding arrow, but it causes amusement instead of pain, for the Duke and company treat Jaques as fair game for their mockery. The scene ends as the Duke goes to see Jaques like a sportsman stalking his quarry:

> Show me the place;
> I love to cope him in these sullen fits,
> For then he's full of matter.

Again, in introducing Jaques through the attendant lord's account, the technique of report has been used to arouse anticipation and to present action at an ironic distance.

The first scene in Arden reflects the equivocal nature of play as a series of reversible roles: the victim of misfortune is also its agent, man and beast change places, the usurped becomes the usurpers, the hunters hunted, the critic a butt of his adversaries. Men are feelingly persuaded what they are, not by 'churlish chiding', but by the contrary parts they play in their games. And these games are a bitter-sweet mixture of whimsical sentiment and wanton cruelty.

III

Play in Arden takes the form of a series of encounters, seemingly at random, for the suspension of narrative progression produces a sense of timelessness. Scenes must follow each other in linear succession, but the effect created is also that of simultaneity as we are taken from 'one part of the forest' to 'another part of the forest', in the words that eighteenth-century editors used for their scene-headings. Indeed within Arden there is no constant impression of different locations; although logically we must suppose that the Duke's encampment, Rosalind's cottage, and the trysting-place of Touchstone and Audrey lie at a distance from each other, the play as conceived for the Elizabethan stage calls only for a forest setting. The sense of meandering through the forest, of paths that cross by chance, and of a corresponding dislocation in the time scheme, is essential to the feeling of liberation in the free activity of play.

It is curious, therefore, that time occupies so much attention in Arden. In the original golden world of pastoralism, there was no time; spring was eternal. Arden, however, is subject to 'the penalty of Adam,/The seasons' difference', and characters are aware of the passing of time. But since 'there's no clock in the forest', as Orlando says, the sense of time is relative, and Rosalind replies, 'Time travels in divers paces with divers persons'. Despite Orlando's assertion, Touchstone has brought a timepiece with him, for Jaques describes the fool drawing 'a dial from his poke':

> And, looking on it with lack-lustre eye,
> Says very wisely 'It is ten o'clock;
> Thus we may see' quoth he 'how the world wags;
> 'Tis but an hour ago since it was nine;
> And after one hour more 'twill be eleven;

And so, from hour to hour, we ripe and ripe,
And then, from hour to hour, we rot and rot;
And thereby hangs a tale'.

If this melancholy rumination is an antecedent of Macbeth's despairing
reflections on the 'petty pace' that creeps through 'tomorrow and tomorrow
and tomorrow', it is also a tale told by an idiot. Touchstone is mocking the
sense of futility produced not by time itself but by the way time is spent, in
fruitless moralising. 'Pastime', on the other hand, is the way in which those
who devise sports 'lose and neglect the creeping hours of time'. Rosalind, for
instance, is well aware that love is subject to time: 'men are April when they
woo, December when they wed; maids are May when they are maids, but
the sky changes when they are wives'. But the purpose of play is to *fleet* the
time carelessly', to make time pass quickly, as in Marvell's response to
'time's winged chariot': 'Thus, though we cannot make our sun / Stand still,
yet we will make him run.' Since 'life is but a flower', in the words of the
song, sweet lovers must 'therefore take the present time'. There is nothing
leisurely about Rosalind's life in Arden; 'woman's thoughts run before her
actions', and in addition to her impatience and restlessness, the headlong
dash of the prose she speaks is that of a wit moving so fast that the tongue
and breath can scarcely keep up with it:

> Good my complexion! dost thou think, though I am caparison'd like a man, I
> have a doublet and hose in my disposition? One inch of delay more is a South
> Sea of discovery. I prithee tell me who is it quickly, and speak apace. I would
> thou could'st stammer, that thou might'st pour this conceal'd man out of thy
> mouth, as wine comes out of a narrow-mouth'd bottle – either too much at once
> or none at all. I prithee take the cork out of thy mouth that I may drink thy
> tidings. (III.ii.180–89)

IV

The mating game is of course the comedy's principal pastime, and like the
other encounters in Arden those between the lovers have a certain
combative quality which recalls the wrestling at the beginning of the play.
Indeed Orlando and Rosalind fall in love in wrestling terms. The conqueror
of Charles confesses that 'my better parts are all thrown down' at his first
meeting with Rosalind, and she acknowledges a similar defeat:

> Sir, you have wrestled well, and overthrown
> More than your enemies. (I.ii.233–4)

It is only one of the many perversities in love that losers are also winners (as
in Juliet's paradox, 'learn me how to lose a winning match').
After this preliminary but decisive bout between Rosalind and Orlando,

their mock-courtship in the forest is like a further series of rounds in which roles are again reversed. As Orlando was the unknown youth who overthrew Charles, he now finds himself outplayed by 'Ganymede'. Rosalind exploits the advantage of her disguise not only to take the initiative in wooing but to floor her partner in the lists of love (until she is herself literally floored by the sight of Orlando's bloody napkin). The analogy between love and fighting is continued in Rosalind's comparison of the encounter between Celia and Oliver with 'the fight of two rams and Caesar's thrasonical brag of "I came, saw, and overcame" '.

The wrestling match was a game played in deadly earnest, and the treatment of love as a contest between adversaries is a means of using play to explore the cruelties and antagonisms inherent in sexual relationships. Similarly the bawdiness of the comedy confronts aspects of sexuality denied by romantic or Petrarchan attitudes; as the hunting song puts it,

> The horn, the horn, the lusty horn,
> Is not a thing to laugh to scorn, (IV.ii.17–18)

but we do laugh at the old jest about cuckoldry, because we are inclined to joke about what is otherwise embarrassing. So Touchstone's impromptu jingle parodying Orlando's bad verses reflects in its indecent wordplay the use of game to release repressed realities:

> If a hart do lack a hind,
> Let him seek out Rosalinde.
> If the cat will after kind,
> So be sure will Rosalinde . . .
> He that sweetest rose will find
> Must find love's prick and Rosalinde. (III.ii.91–102)

The point of 'love's prick' is felt by Silvius as 'the wounds invisible / That love's keen arrows make', as he sublimates the pain of unrequited passion into extravagant conceits. Though Silvius the fictions of the Elizabethan sonneteers are taken to their furthest extreme and reduced to absurdity, in Shakespeare's own game with contemporary poetic fashions. But Silvius himself is not disabled by the wounds of mockery, embracing his folly and wallowing in Phebe's scorn. Their 'pageant truly played' is a sado-masochistic farce, another variation of that sexual conflict called love. Yet at the point of Phebe's greatest cruelty, when she would employ Silvius thanklessly in her own suit to 'Ganymede', the game ceases to be quite so funny, and Silvius' devotion becomes for one brief glorious moment entirely moving instead of merely silly:

> So holy and so perfect is my love,
> And I in such a poverty of grace,

> That I shall think it a most plenteous crop
> To glean the broken ears after the man
> That the main harvest reaps.

But the poignancy topples over into absurdity again:

> Loose now and then
> A scatt'red smile, and that I'll live upon.   (III.v.98–103)

Such a moment illustrates the precarious poise between playful and serious values in this comedy, and Shakespeare's ability to turn artifice inside out. 'The truest poetry is the most feigning'.

Of all the love-games played in the forest, Rosalind's counterfeiting with Orlando is the most sophisticated and double-edged. It is essentially equivocal because Rosalind has three *personae*, as herself, as 'Ganymede', and as 'Ganymede-playing-Rosalind', and we often cannot tell with which voice she is speaking. 'Ganymede' is an inversion of Rosalind's true identity both sexually and as an enemy of love: 'Love is merely a madness; and, I tell you, deserves as well as dark house and a whip as madmen do; and the reason why they are not so punish'd and cured is that the lunacy is so ordinary that the whippers are in love too. Yet I profess curing it by counsel' (III.ii.368–72).

As the free play of a sportive disposition, assuming attitudes for their amusing possibilities rather than their truth, Rosalind's wit has something in common with the teasing disinterestedness of Touchstone's mockery, and her disguise is another version of the fool's motley. But at the same time, since we know 'how many fathom deep in love' she is, the constant scepticism directed towards love's young dream verges on the melancholy disillusion of Jaques. The distinguishing feature of her wit is that, unlike Jaques who is always in earnest and Touchstone who never is, Rosalind/Ganymede is poised in ambivalence:

> The poor world is almost six thousand years old, and in all this time there was not any man died in his own person, videlicet, in a love-cause. Troilus had his brains dash'd out with a Grecian club; yet he did what he could to die before, and he is one of the patterns of love. Leander, he would have liv'd many a fair year, though Hero had turn'd nun, if it had not been for a hot midsummer-night; for, good youth, he went but forth to wash him in the Hellespont, and, being taken with the cramp, was drown'd; and the foolish chroniclers of that age found it was – Hero of Sestos. But these are all lies: men have died from time to time, and worms have eaten them, but not for love.
> (IV.i.9–95)

This is the literary game again, turning artifice against itself in mockery of poetic fictions. But if there is a joyful exuberance in the demolition of the 'foolish chroniclers', felt through the running-on of the clauses, the last sentence invites a pause and a slight change of tone. One can almost detect a certain wistfulness in the dying fall of the conclusion, 'but not for love', as though Rosalind sighs behind 'Ganymede's' back. Her enthusiasm for play reflects both security and insecurity in love:

> Rosalind Now tell me how long you would have her, after you have possess'd her.
> Orlando   For ever and a day.
> Rosalind Say 'a day' without the 'ever'. No, no, Orlando; men are April when they woo, December when they wed; maids are May when they are maids, but the sky changes when they are wives. (IV.i.127–33)

At moments such as these, there is a precarious balance between wit and feeling, between the delightful make-believe and the uncomfortable reality.

As for Orlando, for most of the time in these scenes he is little more than Rosalind's 'feed' and the butt of her wit. Her treatment of her lover, whose charm hardly lies in his mental agility, betrays a latent sexual aggression which sometimes rises to the surface:

> Rosalind Make the doors upon a woman's wit, and it will out at the casement; shut that, and 'twill out at the keyhole; stop that, 'twill fly with the smoke out at the chimney.
> Orlando   A man that had a wife with such a wit, he might say 'Wit, whither wilt?'
> Rosalind Nay, you might keep that check for it, till you met your wife's wit going to your neighbour's bed.
> Orlando   And what wit could wit have to excuse that?
> Rosalind Marry, to say she came to seek you there. You shall never take her without her answer, unless you take her without her tongue. O, that woman that cannot make her fault her husband's occasion, let her never nurse her child herself, for she will breed it like a fool!
> (IV.i.144–57)

In those unenlightened days, before Women's Lib was afoot, such an attitude was accounted shrewishness. Rosalind was sufficiently peremptory when she encountered it in Phebe: 'Down on your knees, / And thank heaven, fasting, for a good man's love' (III.v.57–8), but her own treatment of Orlando bears a close resemblance to that belligerence she falsely attributes to Phebe's style:

> Why, 'tis a boisterous and a cruel style;
> A style for challengers. Why, she defies me,
> Like Turk to Christian. (IV.iii.31–3)

If Rosalind's wit frequently leaves us guessing how far she believes what she says, it also seems at time to run away with her: 'the wiser, the waywarder'. 'We that have good wits', says Touchstone, 'have much to answer for: we shall be flouting, we cannot hold'. Her disguise is not merely the assumption of another personality; it serves as a liberation and extension of her true self, licensing what feminine modesty and a sense of decorum would else inhibit. Her game with Orlando is a lesson in awareness for each of them, a rehearsal for encountering with resilience the adversities that lie ahead. Yet, if she is being cruel only to be kind, there is no doubt that she also enjoys the sport, and that she proves herself as capricious as 'that same wicked bastard of Venus, that was begot of thought, conceived of spleen, and born of madness, that blind rascally boy'. The truths that are spoken in jest flout not only at romantic illusions but at the painful realities as well. Nevertheless, if love has its limitations, so does the play-world of Rosalind's wit. She seems willing to prolong the game for ever, but when Orlando hears that his brother and Celia are betrothed without fussing about such preliminaries as courtship, he loses interest in make-believe, finding 'how bitter a thing it is to look into happiness through another man's eyes'. The game must come to an end when he 'can no longer live by thinking'.

V

As commentators on the world of play around them, Jaques and Touchstone are complementary figures, the one transparently foolish in his wisdom, the other opaquely wise in his fooling. In a comedy composed of mutually balancing elements, where the qualities of correspondence and antithesis are as evident in the encounters between the characters as in the disposition of the scenes or the characteristics of the prose style, Jaques and Touchstone are symmetrically related. Jaques himself recognises this kinship of opposites in his ambition for motley, though his description of his meeting with the fool is another example of the dramatic use of report to gain ironic distance:

> When I did hear
> The motley fool thus moral on the time,
> My lungs began to crow like chanticleer
> That fools should be so deep-contemplative.   (II.vii.28–31)

The encounter might have been staged, but instead the joke is enriched at Jaques' expense by having him relate what is patently a parody of his own 'deep-contemplative' moralising, while he himself remains oblivious to the irony: 'O that I were a fool!'

Jaques might be described as the one character in Arden who lacks the capacity for play, since he refuses to join any of the pastimes around him. In another sense, however, to this detached observer of the passing scene life has indeed become no more than a play, as he declares in his speech on the

Seven Ages of Man. 'All the world's a stage', and he is its spectator. Yet nobody takes him at his own valuation, because there is a self-conscious preciosité about his melancholy that smacks of affectation: 'it is a melancholy of mine own, compounded of many simples, extracted from many objects, and, indeed, the sundry contemplation of my travels; in which my often rumination wraps me in a most humorous sadness' (IV.i.14–18). Jaques is suspected by his fellow-exiles of playing a game, and ironically he is made a subject for their sport; even Orlando gets the better of him. But Jaques comes into his own at the end of the comedy, by sustaining his part after they have abandoned theirs. He will remain in Arden while they return to court, and his consistency lends a certain authority to his wry benedictions. As he awaits the next party of 'convertites', Jaques the spectator is the only character who refuses to believe that the comedy is over.

If Jaques is paradoxically at home in exile, Touchstone is out of his element in Arden, wasting his sharpness on the desert air and the rustics, 'like Ovid among the Goths'. True to his name, his wit serves to bring out the nature of those he encounters, particularly through parody. He seems only to exist as a witty echo of those around him, turning all experience into a disinterested love of word-play. His encounter with Corin is typical:

> Corin   And how like you this shepherd's life, Master Touchstone?
> Touchstone   Truly, shepherd, in respect of itself, it is a good life; but in respect that it is a shepherd's life, it is nought. In respect that it is solitary, I like it very well; but in respect that it is private, it is a very vile life. Now in respect that it is in the fields, it pleaseth me well, but in respect it is not in the court, it is tedious. As it is a spare life, look you, it fits my humour well; but as there is no more plenty in it, it goes much against my stomach.   (III.i.11–20)

Touchstone's wit is evasive. He remains perfectly uncommitted, sceptical of every point of view. His motley is so impenetrable that we wonder whether there is any identity at all beneath it. And his relationship with Audrey especially brings out this opaqueness: it is impossible to be certain whether he is happy or cynical, infatuated or merely contemptuous in his intentions towards her: 'I press in here, sir, amongst the rest of the country copulatives, to swear and to forswear, according as marriage binds and blood breaks. A poor virgin, sir, an ill-favour'd thing, sir, but mine own; a poor humour of mine, sir, to take that that no man else will' (V.iv.53–7). One can understand Jaques' concern for Touchstone, and bafflement at intelligence seemingly wasting itself in this way: 'O knowledge ill-inhabited, worse than Jove in a thatched house!' Perhaps his function is no more than that of the professional fool, to expose others but not himself.

Yet delightful as it is there remains a sense of limitation in Touchstone's inability to do anything except in play, forever hedging his bets.

Before the lovers are united in Hymen's bands (the ceremonials of the theatre doing service for those of the church), it is Touchstone who rounds off this comedy of pastimes with his account of how a quarrel may be translated into a courtly game:

> O, sir, we quarrel, in print by the book, as you have books for good manners. I will name you the degrees. The first, the Retort Courteous; the second, the Quip Modest; the third, the Reply Churlish; the fourth, the Reproof Valiant; the fifth, the Countercheck Quarrelsome; the sixth, the Lie with Circumstance; the seventh, the Lie Direct. All these you may avoid but the Lie Direct; and you may avoid that too with an If. I knew when seven justices could not take up a quarrel; but when the parties were met themselves, one of them thought but of an If, as: 'If you said so, then I said so'. And they shook hands, and swore brothers. Your If is the only peace-maker; much virtue in If. (V.iv.85–97)

Like the Lie Direct, the confusions of make-believe are finally resolved with an If, as Rosalind reveals herself:

Duke Senior	If there be truth in sight, you are my daughter.
Orlando	If there be truth in sight, you are my Rosalind.
Phebe	If sight and shape are true,
	Why then, my love adieu!
Rosalind	I'll have no father, if you be not he;
	I'll have no husband, if you be not he;
	Nor ne'er wed woman, if you be not she.

And Hymen unites the lovers in similar style:

> Peace, ho! I bar confusion;
> 'Tis I must make conclusion
>   Of these most strange events.
> Here's eight that must take hands
> To join in Hymen's bands,
>   If truth holds true contents.

In the world that now lies before them, subject to time and the stubbornness of fortune, there is indeed much virtue in vows made with If. 'If' is the provisional assent that play requires of us.

[1971]

TERENCE EAGLETON

Language and reality
in *Twelfth Night*

At the opening of *Twelfth Night*, Orsino describes his love for Olivia in terms which directly recall some of the paradoxes of language and illusion in other Shakespearian plays:

> O spirit of love, how quick and fresh art thou!
> That, notwithstanding thy capacity
> Receiveth as the sea, nought enters there,
> Of what validity and pitch soe'er,
> But falls into abatement and low price
> Even in a minute. (I.i)

Orsino's love has the destructively creative quality of the language of Richard II and the *Macbeth* witches, and the illusions of Puck: it absorbs and transforms reality into its own image, levelling its values to its own standard and thus rendering all experience arbitrary and interchangeable. The free-ranging, ocean-like quality of excessive love is the ground of its own negation: its capacity to receive all experience is equally its inability to discriminate between the intrinsic values of particular items. Excessive love, like disembodied or elaborate language, is a self-generating subjectivity detached from physical reality and therefore illusory: like the illusions of Oberon and Richard II it dominates reality, shaping it to its own form and granting it validity only within these terms, negating the experiences from which it draws positive substance. Unrequited, melancholic love intensifies this process: it is self-consuming, as Orsino is pursued and consumed by his own desires. When love, like language and created illusion, ceases to be closely structured by the physical situations which render it intelligible, its relation to these situations becomes paradoxically both parasitic and imperialist: it feeds off a real condition which it simultaneously creates, and can then be seen as an embodied contradiction, a self-cancelling encounter of negative and positive life.

The complex relations of language and reality is a common theme in *Twelfth Night*. Language in the play, as in Gaunt's use of metaphor in *Richard II*, can shape reality creatively, disclosing through linguistic connection a previously obscure truth:

> Viola   And what should I do in Illyria?
>   My brother he is in Elysium.
>   Perchance he is not drown'd – what think you, sailors?
> Captain It is perchance that you yourself were saved.
> Viola   O my poor brother! and so perchance may he be. (I.ii)

The Captain catches up Viola's use of 'perchance' and gives it a slightly different emphasis, which Viola then takes up with a sense of new insight, using the word a second time with both her own original emphasis and the Captain's new meaning in mind.

This creative-exploratory use of language can be contrasted with the verbal fencing of Sir Toby Belch and his companions. In these exchanges language constantly overrides reality, ceaselessly spawning new meanings which grow, not from the substance of an argument, but from previous verbal resonances themselves unrooted in reality. Language detaches itself from reality and takes flight as a self-creating force, controlling rather than articulating the course of a conversation until reality comes to exist almost wholly at a verbal level, only tenuously connected to actual experience:

Sir Andrew	Fair lady, do you think you have fools in hand?
Maria	Sir, I have not you by th' hand.
Sir Andrew	Marry, but you shall have; and here's my hand.
Maria	Now, sir, thought is free. I pray you, bring your hand to the butt'ry bar and let it drink.
Sir Andrew	Wherefore, sweetheart? What's your metaphor?
Maria	It's dry, sir.
Sir Andrew	Why, I think so; I am not such an ass but I can keep my hand dry. But what's your jest?
Maria	A dry jest, sir.
Sir Andrew	Are you full of them?
Maria	Ay, sir, I have them at my fingers' ends; marry, now I let go of your hand, I am barren. (I.iii)

The progress of this exchange is shaped wholly by verbal resonances, each giving rise to another. The puns and allusions collide, countercross and interact rapidly, and one significant element in the wordplay is the quick, confusing switches from physical fact to metaphor. Maria converts Aguecheek's metaphor of 'hand' into fact, then unifies fact and metaphor in the image of the hand drinking at the buttery-bar; Aguecheek latches onto the metaphor and is then further confused by Maria's ambivalent use of 'dry' to apply both to her own language and Aguecheek's hand; when Augecheek settles on the first meaning at Maria's instigation, Maria reverts to apply the term to physical fact – his hand – but in a metaphorical way. Maria's language absorbs and appropriates reality for its own purpose, without ever submitting to the contours of fact itself: her speech is an area of free, fluid existence ('thought is free') beyond the rigidities of stable definition, an area within which elements of experience can be endlessly interchanged, combined and devalued to create fresh absurdities and arbitrary connections.[1]

Metaphor, then, can operate creatively or destructively: by breaking down the limits of settled definition it can extend one reality into illuminating connection with another; it can also break down defined reality into a purely negative freedom, disclosing insights and relations held at a sheerly verbal level beyond the boundaries of actuality and therefore incapable of interacting with known reality to reveal fresh truth. The breakdown of creative connection at the level of normal discourse is a corollary of this mode of communication:

> *Sir Toby*   He's as tall a man as any's in Illyria.
> *Maria*   What's that to th' purpose?
> *Sir Toby*   Why, he has three thousand ducats a year.   (I.iii)

Verbal dexterity is effective only at the level of its own self-generated illusion: brute reality can expose it for what it is, as an elaborate nothing, a substanceless patter:

> *Sir Toby*   Approach, Sir Andrew. Not to be abed after midnight is to be up
>   betimes; and 'diluculo surgere' thou know'st –
> *Sir Andrew* Nay, by my troth, I know not; but I know to be up late is to be up
>   late.
> *Sir Toby*   A false conclusion! I hate it as an unfill'd can . . .   (II.ii)

For Belch, reality consists in proving contradiction and illusion, and Aguecheek's simple-minded assertion of the self-evident offends his sensibility. Yet Aguecheek's mode of discourse is paradoxically similar to Belch's: to affirm that things are what they are, to resist elaboration, is a tautology equivalent in its own realm to the contradictions which Sir Toby discerns. A tautology is as self-contained and self-created as Belch's own language: reality itself shares the quality of illusion.

The issue of language and reality emerges directly in Viola's conversation with the Clown in Act III Scene i. The Clown acknowledges himself as a 'corrupter of words': 'To see this age! A sentence is but a chev'ril glove to a good wit. How quickly the wrong side may be turn'd outward! . . . I can yield you (no reason) without words, and words are grown so false I am loath to prove reason with them.' Reason – reality – can be expressed only in language and yet is falsified by language; without language there can be no reason yet with language there can be none either – to speak or keep silent is equally illusory. The Clown is aware that language and experience are so intertwined that to manipulate words is to distort reality:

> *Viola*   . . . they that dally nicely with words may quickly make them wanton.
> *Clown*   I would, therefore, my sister had had no name, sir.
> *Viola*   Why, man?
> *Clown*   Why, sir, her name's a word; and to dally with that word might make
>   my sister wanton.

Yet the power of language to shape reality to itself, a power which involves the absorption of reality into speech, highlights paradoxically the distance of language from reality: ' . . . in my conscience, sir, I do not care for you. If that be to care for nothing, sir, I would it would make you invisible' (III.i). Language draws real substance into itself and becomes a self-contained, substitute reality confronting a nothing – the vacuum left by the reality it has assimilated. Because it confronts nothing, and nothing cannot be changed, it is impotent to affect it: the Clown's rejection of Viola as nothing cannot in fact make her invisible.

Before the Clown leaves Viola he manages to extract from her two coins, and the connection of money and language is significant. The Clown's response to Viola's first coin is to ask for another:

> *Clown* Would not a pair of these have bred, sir?
> *Viola*   Yes, being kept together and put to use.
> *Clown* I would play Lord Pandarus of Phrygia, sir, to bring a Cressida to this Troilus.

The Clown personifies the coins, endowing them with real, generative life, reducing himself simultaneously to a neutral go-between, a mediating element. The relation of money (symbol) to human life (reality) is inverted, as it is in *Richard II*: the coins, like language, 'breed' by their own independent life, becoming the controlling masters of a human reality which exists as a parasite upon them. Human life is objectivised and inanimate life subjectivised in a single movement, as language, inanimate symbol, sucks life from real human existence and reduces it to a corpse, an inanimate nothing. In both cases, money and language control, and yet cannot control, reality: they dominate and determine it as a superior power, yet since their mode of domination is to absorb reality into themselves, they are merely regulating themselves.[2]

The duping of Malvolio is a similar instance of the controlling power of language. Malvolio is driven to false and illusory action which he believes real by a language-created illusion – the letter written by Toby and his friends – which has all the force of reality. Malvolio's laborious tracing out of letters, words and meanings is an image of a man falling under the false power of language, viewing language as a completely adequate motivation to action. His behaviour before Olivia is purely linguistic and therefore illusory, with no ground in fact: the letter determines and controls his physical existence, as in the text of the letter itself Olivia is presented as saying that 'M.O.A.I. doth sway my life', shown as under the power of inanimate strokes of the pen. As a result of the illusion, Malvolio the servant overreaches his role to become a self-created master, as language itself, the servant of human life, becomes its tyrant. The letter which Belch later presses Aguecheek to write, challenging Viola to a duel, reveals a similar confusion of language and reality:

> Taunt him with the license of ink; if thou thou'st him some thrice, it shall not be amiss; and as many lies as will lie in thy sheet of paper, although the sheet were big enough for the bed of Ware in England, set 'em down; go about it. Let there be gall enough in thy ink, though thou write with a goose-pen, no matter. About it. (III.ii)

The interchange here of symbol and reality is parallel to the similar interchange in Maria's puns. The physical yet symbolic act of writing becomes itself a substitute for physical activity, so that metaphor constantly blurs into fact: the greater the physical size of the paper the greater the insults will be, the gall is almost literally in the pen despite the physical fact that the pen may be a goose-pen.[3]

The illusory, interchangeable quality of language in the play, its capacity to absorb and regulate the substance of human reality, has a direct parallel in the action of the drama itself: in the illusions, switchings and mistakes involved in the adoption of human roles. Throughout the play, roles adopted as conscious illusions backfire and begin to control reality itself, to a point where the frontier of reality and illusion is dangerously obscured. Olivia and Orsino are both 'actors', self-consciously fostering roles of lover and beloved which are objectively false but seen by the actors themselves as real; the roles, like language, actually regulate their owners' physical behaviour, providing them, as in a play, with strictly delimited 'texts', given functions and attitudes, from which their personal action must never deviate. Each character's role depends on the role of the other, in an act of collaborative illusion: Orsino's identity as a rejected lover feeds off Olivia's identity as the cold beloved, and vice versa, in a reciprocal movement of negative and positive creation. Viola is then drawn within the illusion, through her adoption of an illusion of disguise to further her real aim of serving Orsino; she is made to act the part of one actor (Orsino) to another actor (Olivia) in a way which conflicts with her own genuine identity (her love of Orsino). Viola, like the Clown with his coins, is reduced from real human existence to the status of a neutral mediator between two illusions: in the scene where she presents Orsino's claims to Olivia she operates merely as an embodied verbal message, a metaphor connecting two separate realities. Her role in this scene is to live at a sheerly linguistic level, eliminating her own authentic desires; she is an actor who must confine herself to a given text, with no reality beyond this:

Olivia Whence came you, sir?
Viola I can say little more than I have studied, and that question's out of my
part. (I.v)

When Viola asks to see Olivia's face she is told that she is 'now out of (her)
text'; the face which is then shown is equally a defined and static illusion, a
'picture' which can be itemised in mechanical detail, as Viola's set speeches
are a similar categorisation of elements.

The consequence of Viola's entering the reciprocal illusion of Orsino and
Olivia is the creation in Olivia of a reality – her love for Viola – which breaks
beyond the illusion and yet is similarly illusory – she does not know that
Viola is a woman. Both Viola and Olivia define themselves and each other in
roles which contradict their personal reality, weaving a network of illusion
which neither dare break: their conversation is false for each, yet each
considers it real for the other. Viola's enforced role as mediator for Orsino is a
kind of self-cancellation: she is placed in a 'double-bind' situation where to
secure Orsino's love is to further his love for Olivia and therefore destroy his
love for herself. Either way she will come to nothing: her original, conscious
adoption of the illusion of disguise to win Orsino's love is turned against
itself, controlling rather than nourishing her real aims. Viola's own
substance of identity is at odds with her role as linguistic mediator in
precisely the way that language, in the play, falsifies human reality. Olivia is
placed in a similarly impossible position: in rejecting Viola at the level of
linguistic mediator she must harm herself by rejecting her also as the 'man'
she loves. Since Viola has fully assimilated this personal reality into her
assumed role when she confronts Olivia, the language and substance cannot
be separated out.

The story of Malvolio brings together similar themes and images into a
significant pattern. Malvolio, like Macbeth, overreaches a defined social role
at the instigation of inauthentic language and becomes himself inauthentic,
illusory: his bid for a higher freedom is a self-enslavement, leading to
physical imprisonment in a suffocatingly narrow dungeon which is at once
materially cramping and, because pitch dark, a kind of nothingness, an
absence of all material experience. By confining himself so strictly to the false
role which Sir Toby creates for him, in order finally to overreach and negate
it (he obeys 'every point of the letter', as Viola talks precisely within her text),
he plunges himself into a prison which is a cynically apt image of his real
condition: a space so narrow and enclosed that it is at once positively
limiting and, in its darkness, a negation which allows his imagination free
and impotent range beyond it. The prison, that is, is simply a grotesque
intensification of Malvolio's previous existence, disclosing its deepest
reality: his positive and pedantic self-confinement to a narrow social role –

brought out in the solid, laborious quality of his language – and the self-negating, overreaching ambition which paradoxically accompanied it, are pressed in prison into caricatures of themselves, and the essential relation of these positive and negative aspects exposed within a single condition. Malvolio falls both below and above the level of true identity: he restricts himself inhumanly to a rigid social role, and simultaneously allows his imagination free and ludicrous range beyond it.

The scene where Sir Toby and the Clown visit Malvolio in his prison brings the confusions of illusion and reality to their highest peak. The Clown disguises himself as a curate, and in doing so exposes four levels of illusion: he is a Clown (and thus, as we shall see later, a kind of illusion) disguised in the illusion of a curate, a role itself often illusory ('I would I were the first that ever dissembled in such a gown'), visiting Malvolio in a prison whose darkness – itself a nothingness – renders the disguise superfluous, doubly unreal. This particular interaction of illusion and reality discloses the nature of the whole situation: Belch and his companions trap Malvolio in a created illusion aimed to reveal the reality of his character (a reality itself defined by illusory ambition), and then treat the illusion as real, bringing rational criteria to bear on it to torment Malvolio into a further sense of unreality. The Clown refuses to treat Malvolio's answers to his questions as 'real', attributing them to a devil inside the illusory facade of Malvolio's personality, treating Malvolio's physical reality as a disguise for a diabolic (and therefore illusory) reality behind it. Because Sir Toby and the Clown have themselves set, and can control, the terms of the illusory game in which Malvolio is trapped, they can turn any of his answers against him as proofs of his madness, offering a question or remark which he grasps as real and then withdrawing it as illusory:

> Clown   What is the opinion of Pythagoras concerning wild fowl?
> Malvolio   That the soul of our grandam might haply inhabit a bird.
> Clown   What think'st thou of his opinion?
> Malvolio   I think nobly of the soul, and no way approve his opinion.
> Clown   Fare thee well. Remain thou still in darkness: thou shalt hold th'
> opinion of Pythagoras ere I will allow of thy wits.   (IV.ii)

Malvolio cannot win: whatever answers he advances will be absorbed, neutralised and turned against themselves by the rules of the illusion. It is his word against the Clown's, and because the Clown controls the conventions of the game Malvolio will always lose:

> Malvolio   I am not mad, Sir Topas. I say to you this house is dark.
> Clown   Madman, thou errest. I say there is no darkness but ignorance; in
> which thou art more puzzled than the Egyptians in their fog.
> Malvolio   I say this house is as dark as ignorance, though ignorance were as
> dark as hell . . .

Within the framework of an illusion which has carefully excluded real fact, truth is a matter of who can destroy the other linguistically. The Clown frames his questions to create 'double-bind' situations for Malvolio, blocking off certain aspects of reality and loading his language to produce the replies he wants:[4] 'But tell me true, are you not mad indeed, or do you but counterfeit?' The possibility that Malvolio is neither mad nor counterfeiting but sane and ill-treated is carefully excluded from the question; whatever Malvolio replies can then be used to his detriment. When Malvolio attempts to prove his sanity by comparison with the Clown's – 'I am as well in my wits, fool, as thou art' – the Clown, by exploiting the ambiguity of 'fool', as both a social title and a character-description, denies his own sanity and therefore Malvolio's: 'Then you are mad indeed, if you be no better in your wits than a fool'.

Illusion, then, both defines a man falsely and negates as false any criterion beyond itself to which appeal can be made: it is a kind of language which, by collapsing and controlling reality within itself, can adjust it endlessly for its own purposes. Illusion and language create a structure whose roles operate to control, not only the experience within the structure, but any possible experience outside it. By setting up the language and the illusion in a particular way, all experience is controllable and any assault on the structure can be deflected, as Malvolio's answers are deflected and distorted. Language, money, illusion, are only parts of reality, but parts which can encompass and regulate the whole.

Just as, in *A Midsummer Night's Dream*, Titania, herself an illusion, is trapped by Oberon into the further illusion of loving Bottom, so in this play Andrew Aguecheek, who helps Belch to ensnare Malvolio, becomes himself the victim of a Belch-created illusion, when he is induced to duel with Viola. Belch's manipulation of the duel is a striking instance of illusion creating reality: by mediating illusory information about each other to Viola and Aguecheek, Belch creates a situation in which each of the duellers thinks himself unwilling and the other willing to fight. The supposed mediator is in fact the creator and controller of the event: by deluding each character about the other, Belch can make something from nothing, fashioning a positive – a fight – from two negatives.[5] By falsely defining each character to the other, Belch induces each to fight under the sway of this false image; by pretending to take his own created illusion as a real drama in which he is a minor participant, he produces a positive quarrel which is also a negation, one without cause or substance. In Viola's case, the illusion of the duel is simply a further illusion into which her original illusion of disguise has led her: it interlocks with the illusion brought about by the confusion of her with her brother Sebastian. In Aguecheek's case, the duel serves to expose the disparity evident throughout the play between his language and action, his real condition and his illusions about it: '. . . besides that he's a fool, he's a great quarreller; and but that he hath the gift of a coward to allay the gusts he hath in quarrelling, 'tis thought among the prudent he would quickly have the gift of a grave' (I.iii). Aguecheek's language and action are mutually cancelling: he is a contradictory embodiment of language and action, and the point of the duel is to bring him to recognition of this reality. Sir Toby persuades him first that language is an adequate substitute for reality: '. . . so soon as ever thou seest him, draw; and as thou draw'st, swear horrible; for it comes to pass oft that a terrible oath, with a swaggering accent sharply twang'd off, gives manhood more approbation than ever proof itself would have earn'd him' (III.iv). By creating this illusion, he can draw Aguecheek into the further falsity of the duel, a real action which reveals his negativity.

The positions of Belch and the Clown in this general confusion of reality and illusion, false role and language, are especially significant. Belch refuses all limit, all definition:

> *Maria*   . . . you must confine yourself within the modest limits of order.
> *Sir Toby*   Confine! I'll confine myself no finer than I am.   (I.iii)

His rejection of definition is a refusal of external limit, of imposed convention; a play where false versions of identity are being continually offered, he escapes relatively unscathed, defining others rather than suffering definition. Yet his rejection of restraint is not made in terms of an absolute freedom to become all, to appropriate all roles and experiences; it is made simply in terms of a freedom to be himself, to live within his own limits, confining himself to precisely what he is. His presentation in terms of physical sensuality, of the body, underlines this fact: like Falstaff, his overriding of social order springs from an achieved stasis, a bodily fullness which breaks order not by reaching beyond it but by ignoring it in favour of a stolid self-containment, by falling below rather than above it.

The Clown is in some senses the opposite of Belch, in some ways a parallel figure: they are positively related as polarities. The Clown, like Puck, is roleless, a negative, disembodied presence within and yet beyond the conventions of human community, all-licensed and thus a limitless nothing, a merely linguistic mode of existence, fast-talking but inactive. He is beyond community-rules because he questions all codes, all definitions, dissolving them into the paradox and contradiction of his free, fluid speech; yet he is also within the community because this negativity is sanctioned by the social role of Clown. Like Puck, his role is to be roleless; his positive and defined function in society is to criticise all function, all positivity. Olivia's rebuke to Malvolio, whom the Clown's wit offends, suggests the degree to which the fooling is sanctioned: 'There is no slander in an allow'd fool, though he do nothing but rail; nor no railing in a known discreet man, though he do nothing but reprove' (I.v). The emphasis here is on 'allow'd' and 'known': once it is recognised that the fool's formal function is to rail – that he draws positive identity from this negativity – he can be tolerated: his social role both lends him defined reality and, by containing his wit, neutralises it to the level of play, of illusion. The Clown is himself aware of this process, as his ambivalent use of the word 'fool' signifies. As we have seen already in his taunting of Malvolio, the Clown creates paradox by using the word in two senses, as professional occupation and character-judgement:

> Olivia   Take the fool away.
> Clown   Do you not hear, fellows? Take away the lady . . . The lady bade take
> away the fool; therefore, I say again, take her away.   (I.v)

The Clown goes on to justify 'fool' as a judgement on Olivia, thus validating his reversal of her command. He dissolves the defined status of 'fool' – the social meaning – into the reality of human foolishness, thus showing the social status to be illusory – he, the Fool, has wisely revealed foolishness in what seemed reality – and therefore ironically exposing his own (illusory) role as more real than reality itself.

The truth implicit in his word-play is that to be a Clown is to be simultaneously real and illusory, positive and negative. The Clown is a 'corrupter of words' and as such the supreme focus of society's unreality, reflecting it back to them: he is thus both more real than others, disclosing what is ultimately true of them, and less real, since his own foolery is the function of an arbitrary social role before it is a genuine personal characteristic. He exists in so far as he is 'allow'd', as Fool, by society, given a social function which, because the negation of all function, is self-cancelling and illusory. Yet he is more real than others because *consciously* a fool, adopting this negative role with grim and positive realism: 'Those wits that think they have (wit) do very oft prove fools; and I that am sure I lack thee may pass for a wise man' (I.v).

Viola recognises this truth also:

> This fellow is wise enough to play the fool;
> And to do that well craves a kind of wit . . .
>   This is a practice
> As full of labour as a wise man's art;
> For folly that he wisely shows is fit;
> But wise men, folly-fall'n, quite taint their wit.   (III.i)

The Clown is therefore more real than Orsino and Olivia, who are fools without knowing it; he is a good actor who, like Viola herself, consciously adopts an illusory role and remains undeceived by his own acting. The Fool is thus wiser than the fool: the more of a fool he is, the better Fool he makes and thus the less foolish he becomes, the more he fulfils a particular, settled definition without overreaching it into absurdity. The greater his clowning, and thus his illusion, the more real a man he becomes. The Clown, unlike Macbeth and Malvolio, can combine a complete social definition with complete freedom: total linguistic liberty is the constitutive element of his sanctioned role. He fuses the self-containment of Olivia and Orsino with the self-squandering liberty of Sir Toby Belch, achieving that synthesis which is implicit in the ideal (rather than, in this play, the reality) of the *steward*, who preserves and dispenses in careful balance. The Clown's sanity – his reality – springs from the fact that he fulfils a settled role consistently, and it is the lack of such consistency in the play as a whole which suggests that illusion and insanity are general conditions. Consistent role-playing allows conjunction and communication, a reciprocal confirmation of identity and thus of sanity; inconsistent role-playing creates insanity, unreality, as the general confusion of identities at the end of the play suggests. In this situation, the Clown's ironic self-awareness, his insight into the confusion, is a negative mode of sanity.

In the whole action of the play, then, illusion, role and language connect into a single pattern. The switching and interchange of human roles is a kind of living pun and metaphor, a blurring of the symbols through which reality is expressed in a way which casts radical doubt on the consistency of that reality. Hamlet's advice to the Players, to suit the action to the word and the word to the action, cannot be sustained: language overwhelms and manipulates action, draining reality until it finds itself in danger of collapsing into nothing under the weight of its own excess. If language is in this sense articulate unreality, social role shares the same quality: they, too, define reality falsely, detaching themselves from the real purposes they were fashioned to sustain into a self-contained realm of illusion where they set up relations between themselves in isolation from real experience, thwarting and obscuring it. The final irony, as in *A Midsummer Night's Dream*, is that this whole process occurs within a play which is itself, as the subtitle suggests, a kind of illusion, a momentary sport; when Fabian remarks that he would condemn Malvolio's behaviour as 'an improbable fiction' if he were to see it on stage, the play pauses to reflect on its own illusory nature, becoming for a moment less real than the characters it presents. When Viola confronts Olivia with Orsino's love, the effect, once the illusion of the whole play is held in mind, is one of an overlapping series of unrealities: Viola, an actor playing an actor playing an actor, presents the case of one actor playing an actor to another actor playing an actor. The relations of illusion and reality touch a peak of complexity which is equalled only later, in some of the mature tragedies.

[1967]

Notes

1   Cf. Falstaff in *Henry IV Part II*: 'A good wit will make use of anything. I will turn diseases to commodity.' (1.22).
2   Cf. the Clown's own connection between language and money when he remarks that words have been disgraced by *bonds*. Cf. also the quarrel between Antonio and Viola in Act III Scene iv, which is created and controlled by money: the purse which Antonio gave to Sebastian as a symbol of trust and friendship becomes humanly divisive, as (from Antonio's mistaken viewpoint) the 'purse-bearer', the servant, becomes the master, overstepping his role.
3   This interchange of animate and inanimate occurs in several minor images in the play. Physical objects are themselves symbolic – they have meaning, like signs, only in terms of what they do – but can be endowed with a constant human existence: Belch wishes that his boots should 'hang themselves in their own straps' (I.iii), Malvolio, at the moment he is endowing the symbolic shapes of written language with life, begs leave of the wax of the letter for breaking it.
4   Cf. also the exchange between Fabian and the Clown, Act V Scene i:

Fabian   Now, as thou lov'st me, let me see his letter.
Clown   Good Master Fabian, grant me another request.
Fabian   Anything.
Clown   Do not desire to see this letter.
Fabian   This is to give a dog, and in recompense desire my dog again.

The Clown frames his remark so that Fabian cancels out his own request: Fabian's generosity is turned against itself, by the Clown's verbal dexterity.
5   Cf. the Clown, Act V Scene i: 'Marry, sir, (my friends) praise me and make an ass of me. Now my foes tell me plainly I am an ass; so that by my foes, sir, I profit in the knowledge of myself, and by my friends I am abused; so that, conclusions to be as kisses, if your four negatives make your two affirmatives, why then, (I am) the worse for my friends and the better for my foes.' Negative criticism induces by negation positive self-awareness.

R. L. SMALLWOOD

All's Well that Ends Well at the Royal Shakespeare Theatre

In the third scene of Trevor Nunn's masterly revival of *All's Well that Ends Well* (the first at Stratford for fourteen years) the Countess's steward, Rynaldo (played by Bert Parnaby) reports to his mistress his discovery of Helena's love for Bertram. As he reaches his account of the soliloquy he has overheard, he takes a small notebook from his pocket to verify his memory of Helena's words, a gesture vividly expressive of his anxiety to be truthful, and accurate, and loyal, which calls forth the Countess's tribute to his 'honest care'. It is a small point in a comparatively minor role, but in its immediate establishment of character it typifies the attention to detail, the honest care, of the production as a whole.

All's Well that Ends Well is a difficult and puzzling play. Like a number of earlier directors (most obviously Tyrone Guthrie at Stratford in 1959), Trevor Nunn has shifted its period in an attempt to come to terms with its troublesome juxtaposition of folktale romantic plot and realistic characterisation. Lavish costumes, and a more substantial set than has been seen on the Stratford stage for some years, evoke a period, early in the twentieth century, of fragile grandeur and lingering tradition soon to be destroyed by war. Surprising numbers of extras supply the Countess's household with maids and servants, the court with young lords 'sick for breathing and exploit' and ladies to dazzle in ball gowns, and the episodes in Florence with soldiers and nurses for the wounded and with waitresses for the café in which Bertram's attempted seduction of Diana takes place.

John Gunter's permanent set of glass and elegant white metal appears first as a conservatory but proves astonishingly versatile as, with the help of various moveable screens and curtains, and a generous assortment of furniture, it is transformed into a fencing school, a gaming saloon, a ballroom, a railway station, a field hospital, or a café. These transformations are often accompanied by the images and sounds of travel: characters are restlessly, tiringly, on the move, often seen carrying suitcases, and we hear the rush of trains and the roar of primitive motor cars, emphasising the frequent shifting of the action between Rossillion and Paris and the wars in Florence. The contrasts build up our sense of Rossillion as a haven of stillness and calm, of Chekhovian grace, presided over by the quiet dignity and love of the Countess, haunted by the songs of birds and the sound of wistful piano music.

Guy Woolfenden's music, indeed, offers a constant enhancement of the

98

brilliant array of visual images that director and designer have devised: the poignant piano melody which begins at Rossillion and accompanies Helena on her yearning quest for Bertram's love through France and Italy; the exuberant polka which explodes on to the stage at the court ball celebrating the King's recovery; the Italian victory anthem lustily sung by Bertram's troops in recognition of his success as 'general of our horse'; and the splendidly buoyant march, with the full RSC Wind Ensemble parading about the stage in figures of eight, led by a prancing standard-bearer in an episode of such joyful panache that it provokes the urge for immediate enlistment and wholly justifies the excitement of the ladies of Florence who observe it so keenly.

The updating gives to the war scenes an immediacy which they can rarely have had before: in a scene dominated by the flash and bang of exploding shells Bertram receives his unexpectedly exalted command for the very good reason that all other possible candidates have obviously perished, while the singing and drinking and sexual adventuring that go on in the war-zone café frequented by off-duty soldiers create a powerful sense of the reality of the war to which Bertram flees rather than endure marriage to Helena. The urgent planning of the notorious 'bed trick' by Helena and the widow, seated at one of those uncompromisingly ordinary and familiar café tables, throws into sharp relief the contrast between this stock plot device of Elizabethan romantic storytellers and the desperately real determination with which Shakespeare's heroine pursues her love. The pride of her claim to her right as a wife, and the humiliation into which she is forced in order to prosecute it, are intensely felt, issuing forcefully in her later reflection: 'But, O strange men! / That can such sweet use make of what they hate / . . . so lust doth play / With what it loathes for that which is away.'

The production's constantly thoughtful and illuminating overall conception is peopled by a series of outstanding performances. In her long-awaited return to the Stratford stage Dame Peggy Ashcroft brings to the role of the Countess ('the most beautiful old woman's part ever written', as Bernard Shaw declared) a graciousness and understanding that form a centre of stability and humanity in the play, radiating kindness and generosity to servants and retainers as well as to courtiers and monarch. For her son and adopted daughter her love has a poignancy derived from a sense of its powerlessness to help or influence. 'Even so it was with me when I was young', she confesses as she contemplates Helena's love for Bertram, conveying in the remark a sense of shared emotion so keen that one not only knows how sympathetically aware she is of what it feels like to be in love, but also finds oneself suddenly wondering whether she too once loved above her station in yearning for a Count of Rossillion. Her sense of despair as she learns of Bertram's repudiation of Helena is movingly set against the fierceness of her love for these difficult young persons: 'Which of them both / Is dearest to me I have no skill in sense / To make distinction.'

As those other two representatives of the play's older generation, the King and Lafeu, John Franklyn-Robbins and Robert Eddison capture precisely the sense of mellow dignity and tolerant understanding which are in such contrast to the behaviour of the young. As the King, numbed by despair at his 'past-cure malady', John Franklyn-Robbins begins as a pathetically lonely figure. We see him first, while his young courtiers vault and fence, in a wheelchair, unconsolable even by the simple truth of Dumaine's reassurance 'You're loved, sir'. It is entirely credible that this self-pitying invalid should for so long resist Helena's medicinal allurements until, overwhelmed, and then restored to health, by her insistent faith in her more-than-human power, he becomes her immovable champion. Robert Eddison's Lafeu is a coolly perceptive but fundamentally compassionate observer of human behaviour with a devastating precision in his use of language, above all in the ruthless verbal demolition job he performs on the astonished Parolles, his icy contempt beautifully tempered by a touch of amused tolerance that prepares us for his later forgiveness.

Stephen Moore's Parolles, be-scarfed and be-medalled, cigar-smoking, noisy, clubbable and vapid, is another remarkably fine achievement. Even the comparatively minor roles of the brothers Dumaine make a powerful effect in the performances of Peter Land and Philip Franks, blond and Rupert-Brookeish, moving from the eager immaturity of their first appearance, in flying-officer uniform, trying to convince the King that their love is adequate compensation for his suffering, through their experiences of war, to the moral earnestness of their desire to expose Parolles and the quiet and sombre realisation of the truism (and the truth) that 'the web of our life is of a mingled yarn, good and ill together'.

It is perhaps in the roles of Diana and Lavatch that Trevor Nunn's setting and search for realistic and detailed characterisation meet most difficulties; only in the case of Lavatch have these been fully resolved. Diana's most important characteristic is largely summed up in her name and in the younger Dumaine's description of her as 'of a most chaste renown'. But since her mother keeps a lodging-house which in this production turns out to have a café attached, it apparently follows that the daughter must support the family enterprise by singing saucy French songs to the soldiers. The role is brilliantly performed by Cheryl Campbell, the archness of her resistance to Bertram's wooing perfectly calculated to inflame him further, but there is something a little implausible about her naïve surprise as she recalls that 'my mother told me just how he would woo', while her personality in Florence makes for a somewhat awkward transition to the dignified and enigmatic role she has to play in the final scene.

The updating of the play makes it impossible to present Lavatch as the bauble-carrying jester presumably conceived by Shakespeare (though in an awkward no-man's-land between witty fool and foolish wit). Guthrie's response to the challenge was to duck it completely by cutting the role; Trevor Nunn and his actor rise to it splendidly. Geoffrey Hutchings presents us with a family retainer long tolerated about the estate, bent and humped, a countryman who combines simplicity and shrewdness and who enjoys the amused affection of the Countess and repays it with a devotion and trust that make of their relationship one of the warmest and most moving in the play. For the first time one understands why she trusts him as her messenger to court, and in her brushing of his coat, adjusting of his scarf, and affectionate pat on his head as he kisses her hand in farewell, are summed up the gracious tolerance and understanding towards which so much in the play aspires but which its central pair of characters find so elusive. And in Lavatch's frequent movement between sexual and religious obsessions (between 'Isbel the woman' and 'the house with the narrow gate') is paralleled at a comic level the duality of Helena.

Harriet Walter makes an impressive attempt at the difficult role of Helena. From her pathetic hope, as Bertram utters his farewells in the opening scene, that he will find something affectionate to say to her, to her reaching out, in the play's final lines, to take the hand he withdraws at the last moment, she constantly suggests her unswerving and involuntary love for this unpleasing young man. In her first scene with the Countess there is a passionate directness about her avowal of love, and a sense of religious mystery in her belief that 'there's something in't / More than my father's skill', a sense that she rekindles in her interview with the King. Miss Walter is less successful, perhaps, in conveying the sort of radiance that elicits the latently sexual imagery of Lafeu's response to her, while a danger that (like Antonio in *Much Ado About Nothing*) we may know her by the waggling of her head is a distraction in some of her soliloquies. In that moving avowal of unselfish love that ends the first half of the play, however, she achieves her most telling effect in her realisation of failure ('Whoever shoots at him, I set him there') and, to the ominous hooting of an owl, steals away, as her husband stole away a couple of scenes earlier.

Mike Gwilym's Bertram powerfully conveys Parolles's assessment of him as 'a foolish idle boy, but for all that very ruttish'. Gwilym is not an actor who easily suggests a self-conscious nobility and his abhorrence at the idea of marriage to the poor physician's daughter is seen, therefore, to come from sexual rather than snobbish motives, making Helena's quest seem all the more forlorn. The sequence in which he humiliates her by coldly ignoring her request for a farewell kiss and, after her departure, gleefully flings his arms around Parolles, memorably demonstrates his callousness and immature emotional dependence on his companion. It is a remarkable moment, as is his rejection of Helena before the King and the assembled court in the first of the three elaborate, climactic scenes (the others being the exposure of Parolles and the finale) around which the production is built.

The first, the choosing scene (II.iii), is full of music and dance, from the sprightly flourish of young courtiers in the opening polka, through the statelier, but still joyful, rhythm of the newly-restored, resplendently-uniformed King leading Helena in this production's version of a 'coranto', to the series of delightfully-patterned elimination dances in which Helena arrives at her choice of Bertram. The outburst of contempt and disgust that Bertram spits out as the election lights on him shatters this mood of gaiety. Helena watches initially in a stunned silence which one wishes conveyed a more acute sense of embarrassment, but as Bertram's disdain achieves more hurtful expression a splendid theatrical climax is created out of the panic of her withdrawal – 'That you are well restored, my lord, I'm glad. / Let the rest go' – and the King's enraged insistence – 'My honour's at the stake'.

The exposure of Parolles (IV.iii) is another brilliantly contrived theatrical spectacle, the blindfolded figure slumped in a chair in the widow Capilet's café, surrounded by his captors, quaking as a fork is scraped on a metal tray to suggest the sound of torture instruments, flinching at first as a cigarette is thrust into his face by the interpreter and then dragging on it gratefully. Stephen Moore presents us with a wretched, whining figure, very anxious to please with the accuracy of the military details he reveals, revived a little by the pleasure of hearing his warning letter to Diana read aloud, and only briefly dismayed by the revelation that he has been exposing his cowardice to his own compatriots. The biting sarcasm of the interpreter's exit, uttered with all the NCO's contempt for the disgraced officer – 'I am for France too; we shall speak of you there' – and the lingering glance of realisation and disgust (and self-realisation and self-disgust) from Bertram, leave Parolles to face the seemingly devastating truth about himself. The detachment and resilience that Stephen Moore conveys in his determination that 'simply the thing I am shall make me live' achieve their proper effect of surprise and even exhilaration.

It is right that the production should remind us of this crushing of Parolles with a plot when we reach the exposure of Bertram in the final scene. Mike Gwilym begins the scene glib and cocksure, but as his lies become more frantic he gulps his wine with growing desperation. The servants are ordered to withdraw as the revelations become more compromising, while the poise and dignity of Diana make an increasingly salutory contrast with Bertram's contemptible and self-degrading attempts to sully her reputation. Bertram is seated on a stool downstage for the solemn reappearance of Helena to solve Diana's riddles. Restored from supposed death she stands motionless, framed in a doorway upstage, the melody which has haunted her appearances throughout the play heard in a new variation as the servants and Lavatch press back in to see the spectacle. After a few moments the statue moves and advances towards Bertram. The evocation of the ending of *The Winter's Tale* is, however, quickly undercut. 'Both both. O Pardon!', says Bertram, reaching out towards the outstretched hand of the slowly advancing Helena. But just as their hands are about to touch he withdraws his and it is Helena's restoration to the King and the Countess that produces the tears of joy from Lafeu and Parolles. Bertram's and Helena's hands do join briefly at last as he promises, again conditionally, to 'love her dearly, ever, ever dearly'. The Countess and the King leave the stage together, seeming to make literal Lafeu's prophecy from the beginning of the play, 'you shall find of the King a husband'; the younger Dumaine eagerly accompanies Diana; Parolles has his arm on the shoulder of a somewhat reluctant Lafeu; there is even a joyful reconciliation between one of the soldiers and one of the housemaids. But the mood of the final exit of Bertram and Helena remains subdued. The production began with a graceful circling dance of a young couple in silhouette, before the opening scene of Bertram's departure from Rossillion. Here, after the final scene of his return, Helena and Bertram seem about to begin a similar dance, answering our wonderings about the identity of those first two dancers. But the dance does not quite manage to start, and the couple walk slowly from the stage, side by side but not quite hand in hand; and we are left wondering. 'All yet *seems* well, and if it end so meet . . . ': it is the last of this production's succession of splendid achievements to capture perfectly that combination of timid hope and threatening uncertainty with which the play concludes.

[1982]

NICHOLAS BROOKE

Reflecting gems and dead bones: Tragedy versus history in *Richard III*

I

The theatrical success of the role of Richard himself has tended to obscure the fact that his play presents any important critical problems. It was a very early play, the earliest of those which have consistently held the stage; and if it seemed dull in parts, or inconsistent, or in any way puzzling, that was easily accounted for by Shakespeare's immaturity. The fact that it is a work of outstanding technical virtuosity, in words and stagecraft, has not always been given the stress it needs; still less that the elaborate patterns worked out in it give it an exceptionally firm sense of structural unity.[1] It was treated in the eighteenth century as a tragedy, and compared (unfavourably, of course), with *Macbeth*; in the nineteenth century it was hardly allowed the tragic dignity, but rather regarded as melodrama, a prototype for *The Red Barn*, and fit matter for Lewis Carroll's parody. But the play thus criticised was scarcely the one that Shakespeare wrote: Colley Cibber's version was first acted at Drury Lane in July 1700, and though the proportion of Shakespeare's words gradually increased, Cibber's arrangement of material dominated stage versions until very recently indeed.[2] It concentrated exclusively on Richard himself; omitted scenes in which he did not appear, minimised Margaret's role (which was often cut entirely), and drastically pruned the formalised patterning of language which is so conspicuous a feature of the play, on the grounds that it was undramatic. This selective procedure is still often followed, most notably in Sir Laurence Olivier's film. And although the critics usually did read Shakespeare's text, their attention was for two centuries as selective as the actors'.

Recent critical history, and even more recent theatrical history, have however offered us a totally different view of the play, stressing the elements which Cibber excised: the tendency to ritual, the formalised staging and language, are held to be devices for binding together and rounding off the epically conceived sequence of moral-history plays about the Wars of the Roses. This attitude is not altogether irreconcilable with Cibber's activities, for it likewise assumes that the play is not viable as an independent unit, but is only intelligible when played in series with its predecessors. The dominant role of Richard can be assimilated if he is seen as the instrument of divine retribution on a guilty society; but the notion that his career has any significance as tragedy is nowadays rarely expressed. The usual attitude seems to be that the play results from a rather uncomfortable fusion of two distinct purposes: a formal conclusion to the series on the one hand, and a lively melodrama about Richard himself on the other.

I am not concerned to deny that the formal aspects of the play develop from 2 and 3 *Henry VI*, nor that it is intended to conclude an impressive sequence. But it does not seem to me to be dependent on that sequence for its own quality, and it does seem to me to have its own most interesting unity. I want to argue in this essay that the play, once deprived of its moral-history, was deprived of any adequate opposition to Richard; so that his stature, which Cibber might seem to have enhanced, was in fact diminished, and the decline from tragedy to melodrama became inevitable. On the other hand, concentration on the moral-history has tended to divert attention from the centrality of Richard's disturbing vitality in the play, and so has tended also to produce an unintelligent and boring play. My assertion is, therefore, that the two aspects of the play require each other, and that the contrast between them is not a technical accident which Shakespeare should have been concerned to minimise, but an important structural device, elaborated to its maximum effect in the use of contrasting linguistic and dramatic modes, with a consequence which can properly be called tragic.

I I

Such a contrast is by no means new in this play. As the series of Histories moves towards its conclusion, we become aware of a mounting weight of ritual on the stage; an echoing series of scenes in patterned form and patterned speech lead on from 2 and 3 *Henry VI* into the highly formalised structure and writing of *Richard III* itself. This mounting tide of ritual is punctuated by actions of violence – battles, murders, executions; a sequence which itself becomes by repetition a pattern, a kind of anti-ritual of chaotic violence, which is inclined towards grotesque comedy in Richard's famous comment on Hastings: 'Chop off his head – something we will determine' (III.i.193).[3] Simultaneously, as the actions of men accumulate in destruction, the lamentations of women mount in chorus from the solo voice of Margaret in Act I to the assembly of weeping dowagers in Act IV:

> I had an Edward, till a Richard killed him;
> I had a Harry, till a Richard killed him:
> Thou hadst an Edward, till a Richard killed him;
> Thou hadst a Richard, till a Richard killed him.   (IV.iv.40–3)

And so on – as we may easily feel – for far too long. Too long because, amongst other reasons, we cannot for the life of us remember who all these

Nicholas Brooke

Henrys and Edwards were, though we remember well enough who the Richard is that concludes every line. The theory runs that seeing *Richard III* in series with the other Histories would give this jingle new significance, for we should then know all the references. This I do not believe; not simply because in practice (e.g. at Stratford in 1964) it hardly works out that way, but because it seems to me that the form of language itself precludes such precise intelligence. Even if we have studied the cast lists and the genealogical table and carried our knowledge fresh to the performance of this scene, as Margaret speaks we shall forget the detailed identifications: the names roll on in ritualised accumulation until their whole weight is laid on the single focus, Richard:

> From forth the kennel of thy womb hath crept
> A hell-hound that doth hunt us all to death.   (47-8)

The ritual repetition piles up the roll of the accusing dead in *un*particularised accumulation to convert Richard from his natural state of man into that of a sub-human figure of evil. In this process the identical names fit easily; it is the more singular titles that are awkward to assimilate. We forget the Harrys and the Edwards; but Rivers, Vaughan and Grey stick out. Shakespeare absorbs them adroitly into the anonymous pattern by an exceptional use of rhyme:

> And the beholders of this frantic play,
> Th' adulterate Hastings, Rivers, Vaughan, Grey . . .   (68–9)

The jingling rhyme distracts attention from the names and makes even them part of the sing-song litany, the generalised accumulation of death.

This technical device clinches the function of language I have been dwelling on: it is to generalise and to de-humanise the sense of events; not to recapitulate our knowledge of detail, but to transcend the detail in creation of a larger pattern in which individuals lose their independence and identity. Just as the litany of the church overwhelms us with the *number* of evils from which the good Lord should deliver us, rather than calls our attention to their separate identities. One aspect of the rhetoric of the play finds its climax here, not in imitation of Seneca, but in echo of liturgical forms, such as the ancient 'Ubi sunt' theme to which Margaret proceeds:

> Where is thy husband now? where be thy brothers?
> Where be thy two sons? wherein dost thou joy?   (92–3)

And so on.

I have somewhat laboured this rather obvious point, because awareness of it seems to me necessary to what I want to say about the play. It is this aggregation of events into a generalised momentum which seems to me to represent the fundamental sense of 'history' in the play; and it is this development which links it most closely to *Henry VI*. None of Shakespeare's histories, not even 1 *Henry VI*, is a mere chronicle; but *Richard III* is the most remote of them all from mere chronicling. The events are there, but in unfamiliar proportions, so that (for instance) the murder of Clarence is more conspicuous than that of the boy princes. Interpretation is always more prominent than event: Richard's coronation is not shown, so that the stress remains on the blasphemous parody of election by which he reaches the throne. History, the legacy from the earlier plays, becomes an order of chaos, a ritual of destruction that grows in power until it destroys the destroyer, Richard himself. Strictly speaking it is not Margaret and her pupils who destroy Richard, it is Richmond; and Richmond is something which they decidedly are not, an unequivocally 'good' character. But it is quite impossible to see him as Richard's 'mighty opposite' in the dramatic conflict of the play: the force that builds up against Richard till his fall becomes inevitable is not Richmond, but the ritual of history, the swelling chorus of a more-than-human force. Richmond is a tertium quid, the inheritor of the new land when the conflicting forces have destroyed each other.

History, therefore, becomes imaginatively felt as an impersonal force rolling on beyond the lives of individual men, who are thereby belittled and cannot achieve the stature of a tragic figure. It is against this weight that Richard's personality is pitted, with impressive wit and force. The conflict in the play becomes therefore almost a matter of conflicting genres, for the historical and the tragic as shown here represent radically contrasting ideas of value – history has no place for tragedy, and in the end we must balance one against the other. It is for this reason that I have called this essay 'tragedy *versus* history'.

III

The first need is to explore the technical means by which Richard is thus isolated from the ritual sense of the play, in order to define the significance of this isolation. For it is not, I think, simply a matter of his being a different character; nor is our response to him a simple matter. One way of accounting for our fascination with so repulsive a figure is indeed simple enough: it is psychologically fairly obvious that while we can delight in the machinations of a clever dog who cocks a snook at all rectitude, authority and religion, we can simultaneously be complacently satisfied when he is properly punished in the end. This is a simple and familiar ambivalence; but how Shakespeare establishes this double delight, and what he constructs out of it, call for more precise attention to the play, and particularly to the different kinds of utterance found there.

I have pointed to the generalising ritual patterns of words in IV.iv; that is the furthest the play goes in formality of speech. In contrast, I quoted also Richard's 'Chop off his head', a shockingly *informal* treatment of an (obviously) serious matter. Opposite as those two utterances are, it is Margaret's which is closer to the play's norm, which is more insistently rhetorical than that of any other; ejaculations of the flexibility of private speech are almost confined to Richard himself. Even with him they are not common, but by virtue of their repeated surprise come to seem characteristic of his personality. Accepting his mother's blessing in II.ii, he continues aside:

> and make me die a good old man!
> That is the butt-end of a mother's blessing:
> I marvel that her grace did leave it out. (109–111)

It is not a gentlemanly tone, but it adds a dimension to the scene, not only by its caustic wit, but also by momentarily introducing a mundane level far from the rhetorical pitch at which the scene has been proceeding. The effect is the same in III.v when Richard recalls his mother as he plans to rumour her adultery:

> Yet touch this sparingly, as 'twere far off,
> Because, my lord, you know my mother lives. (92–3)

The sentiment is hardly touching, because it is so inevitably ironic: but the possibility of sentiment is glanced at, more sharply than in all the wailing of the queens.

This punctuation of rhetorical formality with sudden penetrations of the mundanely human adds, by itself, a whole critical dimension to the play; and it is something peculiarly associated with Richard himself. He makes the contrast felt in the end of I.i:

> Which done, God take King Edward to his mercy,
> And leave the world for me to bustle in! (151–2)

God versus the world, formal language versus 'bustle'; and, one may now add, the formal structure of the play versus Richard. That awareness is sustained in I.ii, the tour de force of the wooing of Anne. The whole is a supreme triumph of rhetoric, superbly varied in pace as the balancing lines are longer or shorter, and varied too by the contrast of long solo speeches. But to call it a triumph of rhetoric is not to deny its psychological plausibility: the grieving widow trapped into a reversal of feeling is a familiar and well-attested theme, and Richard's performance is built on that. He intensifies her hatred until he achieves the peripeteia, the bewildered reversal into acceptance of his totally repulsive suit. It *is* convincing; but it is also a performance. And it must be a very good performance, or it does not work. The words are virtuoso, so must the acting be. The tendency of all Richards that I have seen is to do what Lamb condemned in Cooke's performance: to make the underlying villainy obvious all the time.[4] That is what Olivier did, and the scene lost all power. But the full descriptive notes which survive on Kean's performance make it clear that he did not do this.[5] He made the scene brilliantly persuasive, the charm real, and he triumphed. So that when he was alone on the stage after Anne's departure, and blew the gaff on his performance, the audience felt a sense of shock. A shock, of course, not of total surprise, but of recognition, of what had been always known yet almost forgotten.

Almost forgotten, but never quite: the scene was always rhetorical in an obtrusive if brilliant way. A spectacle of persuasion, not quite persuasion itself, however brilliantly based on psychological observation. This is what is made clear in Richard's soliloquy:

> Was ever woman in this humour wooed?
> Was ever woman in this humour won?   (I.ii.227–8)

These lines are a parody of the rhetorical performance he has just given, and the point is enforced by the characteristically abrupt switch to direct speech which follows: 'I'll have her; but I will not keep her long' (229). The abrupt change of utterance makes a sharp critical comment on the whole mode of the scene; in a way, on the whole play. The rhetorical mode in which *Richard III* is so ostentatiously written, and the formal structure which matches it, are not the result of Shakespeare uncritically doing his best in a given theatrical fashion (Senecan or otherwise): the rhetorical mode is known and placed, both for its splendour and its falsity, within the play. The distance which I have noted in general terms between Richard's interjections and the general tone of the play, can here be seen as directly critical exposure. A distinction is felt which is finally made explicit in Margaret's advice on how to curse:

> Think that thy babes were sweeter than they were,
> And he that slew them fouler than he is:
> Bett'ring thy loss makes the bad causer worse:
> Revolving this will teach thee how to curse.   (IV.iv.120–3)

The relationship between rhetoric and reality could not be more plainly stated; that the words are put in Margaret's mouth confirms her as the only antagonist comparable to Richard himself. Elsewhere the agent of this critical exposure is, almost always, Richard alone; and this fact as much as any other sets him apart from the other actors and, what is more, sets him in a favourable light to other people's disadvantage. It is not a question of whether he is better or worse than other people, but simply that he is more real.

This sense of him makes everyone else mere actors in a play. It is one aspect of the rhetorical mode that it confines the actors within its limitations, from which only Richard and Margaret stand apart. In a sense this is ironical, because Richard himself is the supreme actor. From the actor's point of view, this is not one role, but many: the ardent wooer, the honest blunt puritan at the court of King Edward, the witty uncle with his nephew York, the devout scholar with his clerical tutors, and so on – it is a long list. It is this protean quality which makes him so theatrically brilliant, provided that the actor, like Kean, gives every role its full value, and does not, like Cooke, attempt the super-subtlety of reducing them all to one.

This condition in Richard's part has a further consequence. In *his* performance, the difference between 'being' and 'acting' is very clear; and it is when he is with others on the stage that he is acting, as (each in their single roles) so are they. Thus, as I said, it is with him alone that a dimension of reality is felt. It follows that his relation to the audience – to us – is essentially different from anyone else's and this is established in his very first speech, in the unusual manner of opening a play with the solo appearance of the leading actor.

Unusual, that is to say, for Shakespeare. Marlowe had opened *The Jew of Malta* and *Dr Faustus* with soliloquies from the heroes; but each of their speeches follows a prologue, so that they are already within the play. Richard's speech is itself a prologue as well as a soliloquy from the hero, though to some extent it shifts from the one into the other; from: 'Now is the winter of our discontent / Made glorious summer by this sun of York' into: 'But I, that am not shaped for sportive tricks . . . ' (14). This is not, however, soliloquy in the sense of the speaker talking to himself: it is an address to the audience, not so much taking them into his confidence as describing himself. This mode of initial self-description is, of course, taken over here from the old tradition of the morality play. But it is a mistake, I think, to suppose that Shakespeare uses it simply because this is an early play following familiar conventions. He did not do it in any other play, nor did his contemporaries; nor does he follow it in this play with similar speeches for any other character. In other words, this should be seen as a deliberately bold technique used for specific purposes in establishing the distinctive character of *this* play.

The first effect to note is that it supplies, very economically, a traditional role for Richard from the moralities, that of the Vice: a sardonic humorist, by origin a kind of clown, who attracted to himself the attributes of anti-Christ bent on the mocking destruction of accepted virtues: a singularly welcome figure whenever virtue becomes tedious or oppressive; but one in whom the audience's delight is always coupled with condemnation. This, of course, is Richard's role as he claims in III.i:

> Thus, like the formal Vice, Iniquity,
> I moralize two meanings in one word. (82–3)

The Vice was commonly the star of a morality play, what the audience most wanted to see. His entry, or his cue rather, was used as the moment for passing the hat round. He had, like other kinds of clown, a special relationship with the audience, a kind of sly ironic confidence insinuated between them and the other players; and this is also Richard's. Like most ironists, he secures the audience 'on his side', and yet involves us even further when (again like most ironists) he betrays our trust, and turns out to be way beyond us, leaving us embarrassed as Baudelaire did: 'Vous! hypocrite lecteur: mon semblable! mon frère!' Our condemnation of his evil is involved in recognition of our brotherhood with it.

This relationship between Richard and the audience is given a special emphasis because, as I said, he alone is given the morality address, he alone has any direct contact with the audience at all. It follows that, in the technical construction of the play, Richard is set apart from the other actors, not just in character, nor just in mode of speech, but also in theatrical mode. Everyone else is distanced from the audience, is in a sense taking part in a play within a play of which Richard is the presenter. We are forced to know them as actors acting, just as, when Richard joins them, he is (more obviously) an actor acting; and the consequence of this alienation (the Brechtian term is appropriate) is a carefully imposed limitation on the sympathy or approval that other figures can have. The audience can never become closely involved with Anne, or Elizabeth, Hastings or Buckingham. It is this critical detachment which is enforced in the unusually sustained rhetorical language of the play. The result is that the whole play is set in a perspective which I have compared to that of a play within a play: we have, continually revived by Richard's rare but very telling asides, a double view of what is happening: we view the patterns of formal development for themselves, and we know them for an artefact, a coldly formal order *imposed* on the warmer but less orderly matter of human life. If this alienation were less marked, we could more easily detach ourselves from Richard in sympathy for his victims.

IV

The actual patterns evolved in the play are not one but several, which is why its structure, though felt to be highly organised, always proves difficult to describe. In fact, it is rather in the multiplicity of patterns, and thus in the sense of patterning as such, that the stress on order is felt so strongly. The simplest is the sequence of little tragedies, the falls of princes, from Clarence, through Rivers, Vaughan and Grey, to the more extended hubris of Hastings, Buckingham and finally the fall of Richard himself. This is not merely a sequence, because all the others form part of the structure which Richard builds up against himself. I said that he is aligned with the Vice, who was a kind of clown; but here the clown has become a tragic figure, a serious protagonist. In this translation he is, of course, linked with Marlowe's representatives of the ambition for human self-sufficiency, the will to domination; and specifically with the brilliantly evil figure of the Machiavel. Richard is the condemned outsider, rising to supreme power by sheer force of will. In doing so he steadily intensifies his own alienation from other men, and develops, with his own rising power, simultaneously the force that will destroy it. At the moment of his highest triumph, the grasping of the crown, the messengers of disaster come crowding in with news of rebellion and desertions; and his last ally, Buckingham, withdraws his support. That this is fatal for Buckingham does not make it less so for Richard: his isolation must eventually unite all men against him.

That highly moral tragedy of self-destruction is continuously present at a human, political level, pointed by the occasional commentary from citizens (II.iii) and the scrivener (III.vi). It is distinct from, but very closely associated with, the even more moral pattern of supernatural condemnation which Richard challenges: in the last Act it is not only the living who oppose him, but the ghosts of his victims as well. The staging of the last Act, with tents for Richard and Richmond symmetrically opposed on the stage, is again highly formalised, and again borrows its form from the moralities.

In fact, the first and last Acts, formally echoing each other, provide a framework for the play as a morality on conscience. This is made clear in I.iii, when the play is shifted from the preliminary demonstration of Richard's intention and skill in action to the larger scope of a crowded court scene, dominated by the malignant prophetess, Margaret. Margaret emerges here as Richard's opponent, but her curse falls upon everyone present as well as on him; yet she is not a figure of either virtue or goodness. The other figures, Elizabeth and her family, Buckingham, Hastings, have not the independence which I defined as Richard's, nor the half-supernatural power of Margaret, to which I shall return; they are thus more remote, and less in stature. But they are all guilty. The world in which Richard operates is guilt-ridden. On this state of affairs Clarence provides a commentary in his famous speech about his dream, in I.iv, leading to the vivid image of jewels scattered on the bottom of the sea:

> Some lay in dead men's skulls; and in the holes
> Where eyes did once inhabit there were crept,
> As 'twere in scorn of eyes, reflecting gems,
> That wooed the slimy bottom of the deep,
> And mocked the dead bones that lay scatt'red by.   (29–33)

This strange, and very potent, image recurs elsewhere in Shakespeare, most vividly in *The Tempest*:

> Full fathom five thy father lies;
>   Of his bones are coral made;
> Those are pearls that were his eyes . . .   (ed. Alexander. I.ii.396–8)

Here, in *Richard III*, it involves a kind of imaginative poetry not found elsewhere in the play, and so has seemed to many critics intrusive and irrelevant. But the shining brilliance set in dead men's skulls on the slimy bottom seems to me too perfect an image of the play to be set aside: I would rather take this as a kind of choric speech, commenting on the state of things represented in the previous scene. Clarence proceeds from it to a discussion of guilt, accused by his conscience and the ghosts of his victims, which clearly anticipates the guilt and accusing ghosts of Act V. The difficulty of seeing this as a choric speech is that Clarence speaks it only of his own experience, its general application is not made immediately apparent. This, I think, is a technical clumsiness, akin to the problems raised at the end of Act II of *Titus Andronicus*, when Marcus speaks a poem similarly commenting on the play, but maladroitly adapted as a speech to his niece. Shakespeare here avoids that particular embarrassment, but at the expense of detaching this poetry too far from the general situation to which it most effectively applies.

The pattern of guilt and conscience is extended in comic prose in the grotesque hesitations of Clarence's murderers, and re-emerges in the main action with Edward's futile efforts to promote reconciliation and goodwill. If Richard's detachment from the main play can sometimes set him in a favourable light, we have also to see that he achieves his domination precisely by repudiation of his conscience which returns to torture him in Act V.

In seeing this morality-pattern of guilt and conscience reflected in a profoundly imaginative image we move perhaps deeper into the heart of the play, certainly further from the social and political level of the patterns examined before. Clarence's dream is of a classical, and therefore mythological, hell; for Richard later it is translated into a Biblical and therefore theological damnation. At that point it catches up and includes other manifestations of a dimly-perceived supernatural order behind the events. I said that Richard piles up the opposition against himself, but I did not then refer to one aspect of this which contributes a conspicuous pattern of its own, the accumulation of dispossessed ladies. Elizabeth, the Duchess of York, and Anne come together in a cumulative series of scenes as a chorus of grief and denunciation, in a language which develops from the normal rhetoric of the play towards the ritual patterning I quoted from IV.iv, when at last they unite with Margaret to exorcise the devil.

Margaret thus forms the focus of the most conspicuous pattern of all (made conspicuous by the most obviously patterned language); a pattern which alone decisively involves events beyond what are presented in this play, for Margaret serves both as remembrancer of the past and prophet of the future. Thus, as I said, Margaret alone shares with Richard the distinction of being detached from the other figures in the play. But her detachment is of a different kind: whereas Richard seems more humanly real, Margaret's affiliation is more supernatural. Her presence is a fiction of Shakespeare's, for historically she died in France before most of the events of this play took place. And some awareness of this seems to be carried into her presence, which could well be called ghostly, even though not quite literally. Richard, perhaps better, describes her as a witch, for her predictive powers are certainly not holy. But she *is* a ghost, in another sense, from the earlier plays. This does, of course, serve to link the plays together, but it does more than that: it provides a sense of pattern, larger than single lives or generations, which comes to include all the specific events of this play, for they are predicted in Margaret's prophetic speech in I.iii, of which the rest of the play is simply a fulfilment.

This returns me finally to the point from which I began: to the reflection that in this play History, in the person of Margaret, represents a crushing weight of retribution. A pattern which becomes a vast ritual of destructive vengeance; and the closer it approaches to ritual, the stronger become its associations with the supernatural. This supernatural order emerges in Act V as a manifestation of the Divine Will, destroying Richard and substituting the unequivocally angelic Richmond. So that in the end the ironist himself is subject to a greater irony, that he has functioned as an instrument of destruction in the world of guilt.[6] This divine pattern is explicitly Christian; one cannot help reflecting that it is, at the same time, repulsive.

V

What emerges in this revelation of a Christian order behind the seeming chaos of human affairs is a final sanction to the formal structure and the formal language of the play. The rhetorical norm which can rise to the forms of ritual establishes this sense of predestination on which the whole theory of Tudor history is built. It provides a framework in which men and women become mere actors, but it provides also a fitting ceremonial conclusion to the sequence of plays. Its obtrusiveness in the play, however, accounts for more than this, not simply because of the multiplicity of other patterns I have discussed, but also because this final development of the formal Order in the series of plays produces its own anti-body, Richard himself.

Every point I made to show Richard's dissociation from the body of the play tends also to dissociate him from the orderly pattern. And when one remembers that this included a critical awareness of rhetorical falsity, and a human dimension that is his alone, one can glimpse, I think, why this play does in the end move us with some sense of tragedy. Within this gigantic machine of order there is no place for the human will; we are oppressed by the same sense of helplessness as can be induced by a rolling mill, or the rolling weight of the ocean. Mankind, here, is no more than dead skulls on the slimy bottom of the deep; and if any jewel shines in the eyeless socket, it is not Richmond, but Richard himself. To be good, is to submit to the crushing weight; the only resistance possible is the way of deliberate evil. I said that Richard derived his role from the Vice of the moralities; there is a sense in which he becomes in the end Mankind as well (though not, of course, Everyman): the human representative, bolder than ourselves, resisting oppression, and being destroyed. The world not only seems, but is, the poorer for his loss.

Which is, of course, a perverse conclusion, however true. Shakespeare's histories have been shown to be supremely orthodox in the pattern they display; but it seems to me that in *Richard III* Shakespeare admits the challenging scepticism of Marlowe to a place in his play, and in so doing discovers the tragic dilemma of his own orthodoxy: the orderly predestinate scheme destroys the dignity of man. The result is in no sense a sentimentalising of Richard. It is, however (as A. P. Rossiter insisted), supremely ambivalent: a simultaneous perception of two utterly different and opposed scales of value, the historical and the tragic. The sense of History and the sense of Order here become synonymous: even at the political level history is larger than the individual man; at the metaphysical pitch mankind loses all significance. Such a view of history is hostile to any sense of tragedy. But in this play the one does not eclipse the other: they are clearly distinguished and simultaneously developed into maximum contrast and conflict. The tragic conflict, what lifts the play above melodrama or the mere narrative of a well-merited fall, is not offered within the character of Richard, but in the character of the play itself, in the conflict of dramatic modes that it presents. And in this we may see the morally and physically deformed Richard as an image of the tragic enfeeblement of man.

Nicholas Brooke

Notes

1 This has been fully argued by A. P. Rossiter in *Angel with Horns* (1961).
2 See Clifford Leech: 'Shakespeare, Cibber, and the Tudor myth', in *Shakespearian Essays*, ed. A. Thaler and N. Sanders, *Tennessee Studies in Literature*, (1964).
3 Quotations are from the *New Cambridge Shakespeare*, ed. J. D. Wilson (1961).
4 See *Lamb's Criticism*, ed. E. M. W. Tillyard (1923), pp. 52–3.
5 See *Oxberry's 1822 Edition of King Richard III, with the Descriptive Notes Recording Edmund Kean's Performance Made by James H. Hackett*, ed. A. S. Donner (1959).
6 See A. P. Rossiter, *op. cit.*

[1965]

D. J. PALMER

Casting off the old man: history and St Paul in *Henry IV*

Biblical quotations abound in Shakespeare's two *Henry IV* plays, and most of them are made by Falstaff, whose allusions, as Richmond Noble says, 'are the aptest in the whole of the plays'.[1] They are also, of course, singularly profane in Falstaff's mouth, and his 'damnable iteration' of Scripture, we may suspect, is a relic of his former identity as Sir John Oldcastle, the name of Prince Hal's riotous companion in that execrable play, *The Famous Victories of Henry the Fifth*. It seems that after borrowing the name of his fat knight from the older play, Shakespeare subsequently rechristened him as Falstaff out of deference to the family feelings of Oldcastle's Elizabethan descendant, Lord Cobham.[2] For the historical Oldcastle, as the Epilogue in Part Two tells us, 'died a martyr, and this is not the man'. He was in fact a Lollard burned at the stake for his faith during the reign of Henry V, and honoured by the more zealous Protestants of Shakespeare's day as one of the early heroes of their cause. A familiarity with the Bible was therefore particularly, if scurrilously, appropriate to the first Sir John, and no doubt this irreverent representation of his ancestor as a pseudo-puritan offended Lord Cobham as much as the imputation of cowardice.

Prince Hal, however, knows his Bible at least as well as Falstaff, and in the concluding couplet of his soliloquy at the end of the first tavern scene,

> I'll so offend to make offence a skill,
> Redeeming time when men think least I will,   (I.ii.209–10)[3]

editors have noted the echo of St Paul's Epistle to the Ephesians: 'Take hede therefore that ye walke circumspectly, not as fooles but as wise, Redeeming the time: for the days are evil' (5:15–16).[4] The aptness and full significance of this allusion, however, remain to be explored. Preserving an essential distinction between the fool and the wise man, Hal's resolve 'to make offence a skill' parallels Falstaff's virtuosity in avoiding reproof by turning offence into an ingenious and apparently harmless display of wit, while Hal's promise to redeem the time follows Falstaff's mock-determination, 'I must give over this life, and I will give it over' (I.ii.92). The soliloquy clearly has an important dramatic function: it distinguishes the Prince at the beginning of the play from the wild youth that others, including Falstaff and the King, suppose him to be, and in so doing it puts an entirely new complexion

117

upon the traditional legends of the riotous Prince, such as those represented on the stage in *The Famous Victories.*

As Falstaff says, but in two senses that he is not aware of, 'the true prince may, for recreation sake, prove a false thief' (I.ii.149). Behind Falstaff's back, Poins and Hal plot the Gadshill robbery as a 'jest', 'for recreation sake', to prove Falstaff himself 'a false thief', that is, a liar and no thief at all. But at a deeper level in the play, the 'recreation' signifies that 'reformation' which Hal promises in his soliloquy at the end of this scene. The soliloquy therefore states the central business of both plays, to show us the process by which Hal is to redeem the time; it also insists that Hal's 'reformation' will be not so much an amendment of life, as a 'recreation' of his true identity in men's eyes. 'Never call a true piece of gold a counterfeit', Falstaff tells him at the abrupt end of the 'play extempore', 'thou art essentially made without seeming so' (II.iv.476). Moreover, this 'recreation' of the true Prince also reflects Shakespeare's artistic and historical purpose in the two plays, which are themselves presented to us 'for recreation sake'.

Hal's allusion to the words of St Paul is thus at the heart of the dramatic structure. It is no accident that the Eastcheap community is described to Hal in Part Two as 'Ephesians, my lord, of the old church' (II.ii.143), for when Hal's promise to redeem the time is eventually fulfilled at the end of Part Two, his rejection of Falstaff ('I know thee not, old man')[5] again recalls the Apostle's injunctions to the Ephesians: 'That is, that ye cast of, concerning the conversation in the time past, the olde man, which is corrupt through the deceivable lustes, And be renewed in the spirit of your minde, And put on the new man, which after God is created in righteousnes, and true holines. Wherefore cast of lying, & speake everie man trueth unto his neighbour: for we are members one of another' (4:22–5). Paul speaks of a metaphorical 'olde man', the unregenerate Adam in the self, and Hal addresses an all too substantial counterpart, but one surely well qualified to recognise the appropriateness of the text. If we can suppose so, Shakespeare's old man must have found the Biblical context as a whole particularly galling: 'Let no man deceive you with vaine wordes: for suche things commeth the wrath of God upon the children of disobedience. Be not therefore companions with them' (5:6–7); 'And be not drunke with wine, wherein is excess' (5:18).

The page in the Geneva Bible which Hal seems to have had particularly in mind bears the heading over its double columns, 'Put on the new man . . . Awake from slepe', words which must have struck a responsive chord in the imagination of the author of *A Midsummer Night's Dream* (where Bottom himself, in his garbled fashion, has occasion to recall the Apostle on the subject of dreams and visions):[6] 'Wherefore he saith, Awake thou that slepest, and stand up from the dead, & Christ shal give thee light' (5:14). So

Hal says in his rejection speech:

> I long have dreamt of such a kind of man,
> So surfeit swell'd, so old, and so profane;
> But, being awak'd, I do despise my dream.   (V.iv. 50–2)

If there is an ironic echo of this image of awakening and standing up from the dead at the end of Part One when Falstaff arises from the dead on the battlefield ('Counterfeit? I lie, I am no counterfeit: to die is to be a counterfeit', V.iv. 114), then it is also remembered in Hal's last interview with his dying father in Part Two, when he mistakes sleep for death and prematurely removes the crown to the distress of his waking father. 'Ye were once of darkenes', says Paul (5:8), and it is true that Hal was formerly one of the 'squires of the night's body' (Part One, I.ii.23), but when he assumes the crown, he will 'have no fellowship with the unfruteful workes of darkenes, but even reprove them rather' (5:11). Finally, Hal stands up from the dead, not only as his father's rightful successor, but in his renewed existence on Shakespeare's stage. [7] The history play itself is redeeming time.

Henry IV therefore owes considerably more to St Paul's *Epistle to the Ephesians* than the passing reference noted by the commentators. The use of these allusions to relate the beginning of Part One to the end of Part Two reinforces the arguments of those who regard the two plays as structurally unified although individually self-contained. The theme of time's redemption and the renewal of life also links the two plays with the comedies. In addition, it does not seem likely, as some have suggested, that Hal's soliloquy in the second scene of Part One is an interpolation inserted when Shakespeare was revising the play, since the very phrase which carries such a burden of dramatic significance, 'redeeming time', is integrated with the language of Part One as a whole, as well as being carried through to Part Two.

II

The influence of the earlier Tudor morality drama upon the structure of the *Henry IV* plays has often been observed. In treating the theme of Hal's 'reformation', Shakespeare naturally turned to the 'prodigal son' motif of the interludes, and Falstaff is actually referred to in terms of the leading comic character of the morality plays, as 'that reverend vice'. More specifically, Paul A. Jorgensen[8] has pointed out that one such interlude, *Lusty Juventus* (*c.* 1550), anticipates Shakespeare in making the same allusion to St Paul:

> Saint Paul unto the Ephesians giveth good exhortation,
> Saying, walk circumspectly, redeeming the time,
> That is, to spend it well, and not to wickedness incline.

Jorgensen also notes that this text was introduced into the Homily for Rogation Week, where many in Shakespeare's audience must have become familiar with it. But his explanation of the text 'as meaning to take full advantage of the time that man is given here on earth for salvation', however theologically correct, falls a long way short of its significance in relation to Hal's situation and purpose, because it overlooks the primary importance of the etymological association with buying and selling. Even the lines from *Lusty Juventus* paraphrase 'redeeming the time' as 'to spend it well'. Strictly the word means 'buying back', as in redeeming a debt: in the language of the pawnshop, even today, it has no theological overtones.

The marginal glosses to the text in the Geneva Bible explain the word in these terms: 'Selling all worldlie pleasures to bye time . . . In these perilous dayes & crafte of the adversaries, take hede how to bye again the occasions of godlines, which the worlde hathe taken from you.' So in his soliloquy Hal says he will 'pay the debt I never promised' (I.ii.202), and the language of settling debts is heard throughout Part One.

The days of Henry IV are indeed evil and perilous, as the King's speech opening the play makes clear. The disastrous consequences of the deposition of Richard are felt throughout the land, in 'the intestine shock And furious close of civil butchery'. In an attempt to redeem his guilt, the King has vowed a crusade to the Holy Land,

> Over whose acres walk'd those blessed feet
> Which fourteen hundred years ago were nail'd
> For our advantage on the bitter cross. (I.i.25–7)

To walk circumspectly (or rather to march 'in mutual well-beseeming ranks') in the path of his Redeemer is the vow that Bolingbroke will never redeem; the very act of usurpation was that of an oath-breaker, and the rebels know him as a man who will not pay the debt he promised.

After the succeeding tavern scene and Hal's soliloquy, the rebels are introduced, and Hotspur exhorts his companions to purge the dishonour of their complicity in the usurpation:

> Yet time serves wherein you may redeem
> Your banish'd honours, and restore yourselves
> Into the good thoughts of the world again. (I.iii.180–2)

In their very different context, Hotspur's words echo those of Hal's resolve in the soliloquy of the previous scene. Worcester finds another motive for rebellion, in self-defence rather than high principle, but he also uses the language of redemption:

> To save our heads by raising of a head:
> For bear ourselves as even as we can,
> The King will always think him in our debt,
> And think we think ourselves unsatisfied,
> Till he hath found a time to pay us home.   (I.iii. 284–8)

The first three scenes of Part One therefore establish the theme of 'redeeming time' in relation to each of the play's three worlds: the court, the tavern, the rebel camp. The talk of dues and payment heard in the tavern scenes must also be related to the major preoccupations of the play. Falstaff, for instance, 'will give the devil his due', but his other accounts must be settled by Hal on his behalf:

> Prince Why, what a pox have I to do with my hostess of the tavern?
> Falstaff Well, thou hast call'd her to a reckoning many a time and oft.
> Prince Did I ever call for thee to pay thy part?
> Falstaff No; I'll give thee thy due, thou hast paid all there.   (I.ii. 46–51)

At the end of the second tavern scene, when Hal discovers in the pocket of the sleeping Falstaff the outstanding account for that 'intolerable deal of sack', he also speaks of the money taken at Gadshill, which 'shall be paid back again with advantage' (II.iv. 528).

Thus when Hal promises his father in the interview scene of Part One to 'redeem all this on Percy's head', the appropriateness of his analogy has by this point been well established in the play:

> Percy is but my factor, good my lord,
> To engross up glorious deeds on my behalf;
> And I will call him to so strict account
> That he shall render every glory up,
> Yea, even the slightest worship of his time,
> Or I will tear the reckoning from his heart.   (III.ii. 147–52)

The interview scene closes with the King's line, 'Advantage feeds him fat while men delay', which is Falstaff's cue to begin the following scene with a reference to his fancied loss of weight ('Do I not dwindle?') suggesting also the dwindling of his role in the increasing imminence of more urgent affairs. He makes another vow of amendment, echoing that we have just heard from Hal: 'Well, I'll repent, and that suddenly, while I am in some liking' (III.iii. 5). He was, he says, virtuous once, and 'paid money that I borrowed – three or four times'. So too before the battle of Shrewsbury, Falstaff confides his fear to the Prince before launching upon his 'catechism' of honour:

> Falstaff I would 'twere bed-time, Hal, and all well.
> Prince Why, thou owest God a death. (*Exit*)

> *Falstaff*   'Tis not due yet; I would be loath to pay him before his day. What
> need I be so forward with him that calls not on me? . . . What is
> honour? A word. What is in that word? Honour. What is that honour?
> Air. A trim reckoning!
>
> (V.i.125–40)

These illustrations demonstrate how central is that Pauline phrase, 'redeeming time', to the play's concern with the proper time for settling debts of one kind or another. The very language of the play is coloured by this Biblical allusion, which in its sense of redeeming a promise relates to the many oaths that are sworn and foresworn in the course of the action, and so to the idea of honour, (honour is 'a word', but a word that should be kept), while the phrase also expresses that sense of time as a commodity spent well or ill in the play. When the days are evil, and the time is out of joint ('Find we a time for frightened peace to pant', sighs the King in the play's opening lines), the idleness of the tavern life with its 'play extempore' ('What a devil hast thou to do with the time of the day?' as Hal demands of Falstaff), is contrasted with the hasty impatience of Hotspur:

> O gentlemen, the time of life is short!
> To spend that shortness basely were too long
> If life did ride upon a dial's point,
> Still ending at the arrival of an hour.   (V.ii.82–5)

'The time will come,' Hal promises his father, and with a sense of mounting urgency in the play, the hour arrives at Shrewsbury: 'What, is it a time to jest and dally now?'. For the dying Hotspur, 'life, time's fool, And time, that takes survey of all the world, Must have a stop,' but for Hal in his triumph, 'the day is ours' at the end of Part One and his father acknowledges, 'Thou hast redeem'd thy lost opinion'.

III

'Redeeming time when men think least I will', Hal speaks not of being renewed in the spirit of his mind, but rather of renewing his reputation in the minds of others. He intends to 'falsify men's hopes', to 'show more goodly and attract more eyes'. Hotspur has a similar understanding of honour, as being restored 'into the good thoughts of the world again', though of course he has a misplaced conception of how this is to be achieved. What men think, both collectively as the world at large, and as particular individuals, is of crucial concern throughout both plays. Facing his father's suspicion that he is even in collusion with the rebels, Hal replies,

> Do not think so; you shall not find it so:
> And God forgive them that so much have sway'd
> Your Majesty's good thoughts away from me!
> I will redeem all this on Percy's head.   (III.ii.129–32)

Such a sustained association with men's thoughts suggests that for Shakespeare the word 'redeem' not only bore its etymological sense of settling a debt, but also, through a species of pun, attached itself to the meaning of 'deem'. To be restored from disgrace into men's good thoughts is thus to be 're-deemed'.

'I would to God thou and I knew where a commodity of good names were to be bought,' says Falstaff to Hal (I.ii.80), and honour and reputation in Part One have had much to do with what men call one as with what they think of one. A man is known by his name, and Falstaff is a master of giving good names to bad things:

> Marry, then, sweet wag, when thou art King, let not us that are squires of the night's body be called thieves of the day's beauty; let us be Diana's foresters, gentlemen of the shade, minions of the moon; and let men say we be men of good government, being governed, as the sea is, by our noble and chaste mistress the moon, under whose countenance we steal.   (I.ii.22–8)

The Ephesians were worshippers of Diana, and so Falstaff can argue, ' 'tis no sin for a man to labour in his vocation' (I.ii.102). Does not St Paul exhort the Ephesians to 'walke worthie of the vocation whereunto ye are called' (IV.i)?

Talk of being 'called' to a reckoning, to a 'strict account' (e.g., (I.ii.48, II.ii.49, V.i.128, all quoted above) is thus related to the importance of names and titles in the play. What a man is called by, and what he is called to, are, in the strict meaning of the word, his 'vocation', and to be worthy of his vocation as Prince is Hal's chief concern in Part One. When he reappears in the tavern after the Gadshill robbery, he shows a wry sensitivity to the names he is called by the potboys:

> I have sounded the very base-string of humility. Sirrah, I am sworn brother to a leash of drawers and can call them all by their christen names, as Tom, Dick, and Francis. They take it already upon their salvation that though I be but Prince of Wales yet I am the king of courtesy; and tell me flatly I am no proud Jack, like Falstaff, but a Corinthian, a lad of mettle, a good boy – by the Lord, so they call me – and when I am King of England I shall command all the good lads of Eastcheap. They call drinking deep, dyeing scarlet; and when you breathe in your watering, they cry "hem!" and bid you play it off. To conclude, I am so good a proficient in one quarter of an hour that I can drink with any tinker in his own language during my life.   (II.iv.3–16)

There follows the jest with Poins at Francis' expense, an episode that seems to have baffled satisfactory interpretation. But to understand the point of Hal's joke, we should note his reference to being called 'a Corinthian', for the

Corinthians, like the Ephesians, were exhorted by Paul to mend their ways, and offered advice on vocation: 'Let every man abide in the same vocation wherein he was called. Art thou called being a servant? Care not for it; but if yet thou maist be free use it rather' (I Corinthians, 7:20–1). So in stage-managing his play extempore with Francis, Hal plays upon the multiple meanings of 'vocation', calling his name, and talking of his calling, while Poins calls him to a reckoning:

Prince	Come hither, Francis.
Francis	My lord?
Prince	How long hast thou to serve, Francis?
Francis	Forsooth, five years, and as much as to –
Poins (within)	Francis!
Francis	Anon, anon, sir.
Prince	Five year! by'r lady, a long lease for the clinking of pewter. But Francis, darest thou be so valiant as to play the coward with thy indenture and show it a fair pair of heels and run from it?
	(II.iv.37–47)

In Francis, Hal is parodying himself as a fellow-Corinthian and a fellow-apprentice, and the repetition of 'Anon, anon, sir', like the stage-direction at the end of the joke, '*Here they both call him: Francis stands amazed, not knowing which way to go*', dramatises Hal's critical reflection upon his own neglect of his vocation: 'Away, you rogue! Dost thou not hear them call?' It is certainly Hal's private joke as far as both Francis and Poins are concerned, and one that expresses a very different mood from the confident, even complacent, tone of the soliloquy at the end of the first tavern scene. He is close here to the mood of Hamlet's 'O what a rogue and peasant slave am I!'

Hal's problem is to seem what he is, to be given his due, and to be called by his proper name ('Prince Hal' itself reflects an indecorous mixture of formality and familiarity). He is, in Falstaff's words, 'essentially made without seeming so', a peculiar irony for one whose title is 'heir apparent'. It is small comfort to hear from Falstaff in jest what he would claim from all men in earnest: 'By the Lord, I knew ye as well as he that made ye. Why hear you, my masters: was it for me to kill the heir apparent?' (II.iv.258–9). Unfortunately, it is only too true that Falstaff knows the Prince no better than 'he that made ye', his own father. But the 'open and apparent shame' which the Gadshill adventure was intended to fix upon Falstaff is thus turned instead upon the Prince himself.

In the self-assured vein of his soliloquy, Hal compared himself to the sun,

> That when he please again to be himself,
> Being wanted, he may be more wondered at.   (I.ii.193–4)

Ironically, this 'policy' of withholding oneself from the public eye to be the more admired is the very same argument which his father uses to reproach Hal for keeping low company (and the irony is doubled when we recall that in *Richard II* it was this Bolingbroke who courted popular favour in an undignified fashion: 'Off went his bonnet to an oyster wench'). The premises of Hal's self-justification are thus invalidated in the interview scene, and it is a much chastened Prince who now promises in the plainest terms, 'I shall hereafter, my thrice-gracious lord, / Be more myself' (IV.ii.92–3).

On Shrewsbury field, the King shamefully lends his name and identity to others to protect himself in battle, and when Douglas encounters him and supposes he is addressing yet another decoy, 'What art thou / That counterfeit'st the person of a king?' (V.iii.27–8), the question cuts deeply into Bolingbroke's dubious claim to the title. By contrast, Hal's decisive encounter with his namesake begins with a declaration of his true identity:

> *Hotspur*　If I mistake not, thou art Harry Monmouth.
> *Prince*　Thou speak'st as if I would deny my name.
> *Hotspur*　My name is Harry Percy.
> *Prince*　　　　　　　　　Why then I see
> 　　　　A very valiant rebel of the name.
> 　　　　I am the Prince of Wales. 　　　　(V.iii.59–63)

Seen on the stage, Hal is quite literally now in his true colours, bearing over his armour the heraldic insignia of the heir apparent. This transformation was earlier described in what are surely the play's most magnificent lines, spoken by Vernon in answer to Hotspur's scornful enquiry about 'the nimble-footed madcap Prince of Wales, And his comrades that daff'd the world aside And bid it pass':

> 　　　　　　All furnish'd, all in arms;
> All plum'd like estridges, that with the wind
> Bated like eagles having lately bath'd;
> Glittering in golden coats, like images;
> As full of spirit as the month of May,
> As gorgeous as the sun at midsummer;
> Wanton as youthful goats, wild as young bulls.
> I saw young Harry with his beaver on,
> His cushes on his thighs, gallantly arm'd,
> Rise from the ground like feathered Mercury
> And vaulted with such ease into his seat
> As if an angel dropp'd down from the clouds
> To turn and wind a fiery Pegasus,
> And witch the world with noble horsemanship. 　　　　(IV.i.97–110)

All the 'wild' and 'wanton' energies of youth, associated in legend with the 'madcap Prince', are here beautifully assimilated to the imagery of natural vitality, and transcended by the picture of the rider on his horse, the traditional emblem of disciplined energy and good government. Hal has 'put on the new man'.

IV

Hal's tribute to Hotspur, also reported by Vernon,

> He gave you all the duties of a man,
> Trimm'd up your praises with a princely tongue;
> Spoke your deservings like a chronicle, (V.ii.56–8)

reminds us that the chronicle, the record of history, is the final arbiter of reputation. The chronicler himself, 'redeeming time', gives honourable men their due, restoring them into the good thoughts of the world again. Shakespeare's treatment of Hal's 'reformation' in terms of men's judgements of him rather than any sudden moral conversion on his part reflects his attitude to the stories of the Prince's reprobate youth as unauthoritative material, distinct from the authentic matter of historical record. The very existence of these stories must have demonstrated to Shakespeare how prone are men's minds to invent and credit fiction and to entertain conjecture – a phenomenon which as poet and dramatist he naturally exploited, and which throughout his work was obviously one of his deepest and most abiding interests.

As Vernon says, the Prince is 'So much misconstrued in his wantonness' (V.ii.69). The lines in which Hal protests to his father,

> in reproof of many tales devis'd,
> Which oft the ear of greatness needs must hear,
> By smiling pick-thanks and base newsmongers, (III.ii.23–5)

follows Holinshed's account of the supposedly riotous youth as a fabrication, so many 'tales' and 'slanderous reports':

> Whilest these things were a dooing in France, the lord Henrie prince of Wales, eldest sonne to king Henrie, got knowledge that certeine of his fathers servants were busie to give informations against him, whereby discord might arise betwixt him and his father: for they put into the kings head, not onelie what evil rule (according to the course of youth) the prince kept to the offense of manie: but also what great resort of people came to his house, so that the court was nothing furnished with such a traine as dailie followed the prince. These tales brought no small suspicion into the kings head, least his sonne would presume to usurpe the crowne, he being yet alive, through which suspicious gelousie, it was perceived that he favoured not his sonne, as in times past he had doone.

126

> The Prince sore offended with such persons, as by slanderous reports, sought not onelie to spot his good name abrode in the realme, but to sowe discord also betwixt him and his father, wrote his letters into everie part of the realme, to reproove all such slanderous devises of those that sought his discredit.[9]

Even the word 'pick-thanks' is taken from Holinshed: 'Thus were the father and sonne reconciled, betwixt whome the said pick-thanks had sowne division.'[10]

'Let no man deceive you with vain words': it is certainly appropriate that in the tavern world, which has attached itself to history by 'slanderous report', Falstaff should be the embodiment of lies, 'gross as a mountain, open, palpable'. In his account of the men in buckram, we see the very process by which history is translated into fiction, and his 'play extempore' bears the same relationship to Shakespeare's history play as the unlicensed tales of the wild Prince do to the authentic versions of the chronicle. Falstaff habitually takes the Lord's name in vain; he also takes in vain all titles of honour: they are 'a word', no more.

It is supremely ironical, but presumably a sheer coincidence, that a play so deeply concerned with the 'commodity of good names' and 'vocation' should have run into difficulties over the name and reputation of its chief slanderer. When Shakespeare redeemed Oldcastle from the posthumous ignominy of his stage identity, he baptised the fat knight after the cowardly figure of Sir John Fastolfe, who had made a brief début in the poet's first history play, and was there condemned as one who

> Doth but usurp the sacred name of knight,
> Profaning this most honourable order.
> *(The First Part of King Henry VI, IV.i.42–3)*

Even this reincarnation was to provoke some complaint that Shakespeare had taken another good name in vain, and later in the seventeenth century Thomas Fuller tried to do for Sir John Fastolfe what Shakespeare had done for the Prince, to rescue him from ill-fame:

> Now as I am glad that *Sir John Oldcastle* is *put out*, so I am sorry that *Sir John Fastolfe* is *put in*, to relieve his memory in this base service, to be the *anvil* for every *dull wit* to strike upon. Nor is our Comedian excusable, by some alteration of his name, writing him *Sir John Falstafe* (and making him the *property* of *pleasure* for King *Henry* the fifth, to abuse) seeing the *vicinity* of sounds intrench on the memory of *that worthy Knight*, and few do heed the *inconsiderable difference* in spelling of their name. *(The Worthies of England,* 1662)[11]

The difference in spelling, however, is sufficient to achieve a certain propriety in the first syllable of Falstaff's name.

Hal keeps his promise to call Hotspur to 'so strict account That he shall render every glory up', and in his defeat Hotspur surrenders his 'proud titles' to the Prince. But what is the nature of the honour so won by Hal at the end of Part One? There is little glorification of Hal's victory; it is rather the hollowness of Hotspur's conception of honour 'that is stressed. Hal's generosity to his dead enemy is certainly noble:

> Thy ignominy sleep with thee in the grave
> But not remembered in thy epitaph. (V.iii.100–1)

But far from coveting the admiration of men's thoughts at the end of the play, Hal is contemptuously acquiescent in Falstaff's demand to be given the official credit for Hotspur's fall:

> For my part, if a lie may do thee grace,
> I'll gild it with the happiest terms I have. (V.iii.156–7)

The Prince, one feels, is more genuinely concerned about his personal relationship with his father, and more deeply affected by the pointless death of the young Hotspur; he is content to let the rest go, just as he orders Douglas to be set free without claiming ransom. Hal has come a long way since the desire of the soliloquy to 'show more goodly and attract more eyes'.

In the eyes of true judgement (and in the theatre Shakespeare flatters us with this vantage point), such a refusal to court public esteem will commend itself all the more favourably. 'Nothing confutes me but eyes, and nobody sees me', says Falstaff, even as we watch him desecrate the body of Hotspur. If honour lives only in men's eyes and opinions, it is a very ambiguous and unstable commodity, as Hal has now learned:

> An habitation giddy and unsure
> Hath he that buildeth on the vulgar heart. (Part Two, I.iii.89–90)

When the days are evil, where does true judgement of honour reside? This, however, is where Part Two takes up the story.

V

Lord Cobham, and Thomas Fuller too, might well have turned against the poet himself Rumour's words in the Prologue to Part Two:

> Upon my tongues continual slanders ride,
> The which in every language I pronounce,
> Stuffing the ears of men with false reports. (6–8)

Indeed, with an aggressive swipe worthy of Ben Jonson, and striking the discomfiting note which is characteristic of this play, Rumour identifies 'the still-discordant wavering multitude' with his present theatre-audience:

> But what need I thus
> My well-known body to anatomize
> Among my household? (20–2)

Here in the theatre Rumour recognises his home, the place where men's judgements and imaginations are exercised upon the illusions they see and hear. Rumour is the presiding spirit of Part Two, and Falstaff is his Apostle: 'Lord, Lord, how subject we old men are to this vice of lying' (3.2.294). But the course of the play is to fulfil the words of that other Apostle, 'that ye cast of, concerning the conversation in time past, the olde man, which is corrupt through the deceivable lusts . . . and put on the new man': 'Wherefore cast of lying, & speake everie man trueth unto his neighbour: for we are members one of another' (Ephesians, 4:22–5).

With Hotspur gone, the prevailing mood of Part Two is set by its old men: Northumberland, Falstaff, the Lord Chief Justice, that other Justice, Shallow, and of course the King himself. There is much talk of sickness and death, and the time is burdened with memories of the past and anticipations of things to come. As the Archbishop of York says, 'The commonwealth is sick of their own choice . . . What trust is in these times? . . . Past and to come seems best; things present worst' (I.iii.86–108). Even more than was the case in Part One, the days are evil, and 'we are time's subjects' (I.iii.110).

Hal's reappearance in the tavern, after his personal triumph at the end of Part One, is a reversion that defeats our expectations, in a play full of false anticipation. The 'weary' Prince who makes his entrance in 2.2. is a very different figure from the buoyant confident youth who promised to redeem the time in Part One, and who there seemed about to 'witch the world with noble horsemanship'. He now appears oppressed, in accord with the disenchantment of this old men's world, and bitter in his self-reproach. 'What a disgrace is it to me to remember thy name', he says unflatteringly to Poins, whose equally bald rejoinder raises the very question in our minds concerning Hal's apparent relapse after his achievement on Shrewsbury field: 'How ill it follows, after you have laboured so hard, you should talk so idly! Tell me, how many good young princes would do so, their fathers being so sick as yours at this time is?' (II.ii.27–30). Stung by the reproof coming from such a quarter, Hal's reply goes to the heart of the play's concern with slanderous rumours, opinion, and men's judgements:

Prince   Marry, I tell thee it is not meet that I should be sad, now my father is sick; albeit I could tell to thee – as to one it pleases me, for fault of a better to call my friend – I could be sad and sad indeed too.
Poins   Very hardly upon such a subject.
Prince   By this hand, thou thinkest me as far in the devil's book as thou and Falstaff for obduracy and persistency: let the end try the man. But I tell

> thee my heart bleeds inwardly that my father is so sick; and keeping such vile company as thou art hath in reason taken from me all ostentation of sorrow.
>
> *Poins*   The reason?
> *Prince* What wouldst thou think of me if I should weep?
> *Poins*   I would think thee a most princely hypocrite.
> *Prince* It would be every man's thought; and thou art a blessed fellow to think as every man thinks.   (II.ii.37–54)

With the death of the King imminent, a sudden display of grief from his successor would be construed as hollow indeed, particularly in one whose former estrangement from the court was on every tongue of Rumour. The very depth of Hal's genuine feelings for his father, far more than a mere politic concern of the Prince for his reputation, cannot tolerate the prospect of such an imputation being put upon the most intimate relationship of his life. But this is indeed what happens later in the play, when Hal's misprision of his father's sleep leads to the King's misprision of Hal's motives for removing the crown:

> *Prince* I never thought to hear you speak again.
> *King*   Thy wish was father, Harry, to that thought.
>   I stay too long by thee, I weary thee.
>   Dost thou so hunger for mine empty chair
>   That thou wilt needs invest thee with my honours
>   Before thy hour be ripe?   (IV.v.92–7)

In Part One, Hal's vow to redeem the time signified the need to recover an essentially personal esteem, to be recognised for what he is, 'heir apparent'. In this sequel, the course of time is to lead him, not to his true name and vocation, but to a new name and vocation as King. Now 'redeeming time' signifies a duty to the nation as a whole, for the time is out of joint, and the sick commonwealth must be rejuvenated, the divided realm reunited as 'members one of another':

> *King*   Then you perceive the body of our kingdom
>   How foul it is; what rank diseases grow,
>   And with what danger, near the heart of it.
> *Warwick* It is but as a body yet distempered
>   Which to his former strength may be restored
>   With good advice and little medicine.   (III.i.38–43)

The Hal of Part One fulfilled his vow by defeating young Hotspur; in Part Two, it is the old man who must be cast off, though not in the sense that the King suspects.

'You that are old consider not the capacities of us that are young', as Falstaff says (I.ii.165). The old indeed totally misjudge the young, and in harbouring very similar expectations of Hal, one in fear and the other in hope, both the King and Falstaff misconstrue the times to come:

> The blood weeps from my heart when I do shape
> In forms imaginary, th' unguided days
> And rotten times that you shall look upon
> When I am sleeping with my ancestors.
> For when his headstrong riot hath no curb,
> When rage and hot blood are his counsellors,
> When means and lavish manners meet together,
> O, with what wings shall his affections fly
> Towards fronting peril and oppos'd decay! (IV.iv.58–66)

But Hal's youth has no more 'headstrong riot' in it than the youth of Justice Shallow: 'Jesu, Jesu, the mad days that I have spent! and to see how many of my old acquaintance are dead!' (III.ii.32–3). Time past and future lives in 'forms imaginary', and Shallow's wonderful reminiscences ('every third word a lie', says Falstaff) exemplify how natural it is to turn history into mythology and legend.

The consciousness of time in Part Two is developed into the idea of history itself, as the play looks both before and after, through the long memories of old men and through their anticipations of the future. In this respect the dialogue between the King and his wise counseller Warwick in III.i is of central significance. Reflecting ruefully upon the former allegiances of Richard's time between men now bitter enemies, the King sees 'the revolution of the times' as merely the flux and mutability of Nature, in which man is helplessly and unpredictably tossed and turned by 'necessity':

> how chances mock,
> And changes fill the cup of alteration
> With divers liquors! O, if this were seen,
> The happiest youth, viewing his progress through,
> What perils past, what crosses to ensue,
> Would shut the book and sit him down and die. (III.i.51–6)

In his reply Warwick advances a different conception of history, not as some impersonal, inscrutable decree in 'the book of fate', but as an essentially human process, analogous to Nature's laws of organic growth rather than to lawless mutability:

> There is a history in all men's lives,
> Figuring the natures of the times deceas'd;
> The which observ'd a man may prophesy,
> With a near aim, of the main chance of things
> As yet not come to life, who in their seeds
> And weak beginning lie intreasured.
> Such things become the hatch and brood of time;
> And by the necessary form of this . . . (III.i.80–7)

131

D. J. Palmer

Warwick's point of view lends quite a different significance to the idea of historical 'necessity'; instead of being mere victims of blind circumstances, as the King supposes, men can and must direct their lives by reaping advantage from experience. It is Warwick who later correctly prophesies that

> The Prince will, in the perfectness of time,
> Cast off his followers; and their memory
> Shall as a pattern or a measure live,
> By which his Grace must mete the lives of other,
> Turning past evils to advantages. (IV.iv.74–8)

Hal's progress through both plays demonstrates that life is not 'time's fool', as Hotspur believed, but a meaningful and purposeful relationship between past and future. What will appear to Hal's contemporaries (and to legend) as a sudden and unpredictable 'revolution of the times' has been presented to us a wise use of time on Hal's part, and also a process of developing wisdom and insight from the moment of that over-simplified, over-confident view of things expressed in the soliloquy at the beginning of Part One. Hal is to inherit a usurped crown and its attendant evils, that have driven his father into his grave, and he is to succeed, not by 'indirect crook'd ways' but by the 'plain and right' inheritance of the 'hatch and brood of time' from 'the times deceas'd'. Youth does not usurp age, although age may often suppose so, and feel itself cast off. In the larger design of the play, and of Nature, time is redeemed as youth matures, and assumes the burdens which age can carry no more. Shakespeare's reading of history in Part Two, like that of Warwick, is related to the wider perspectives of natural processes.

When at his father's death Hal puts on the new man with 'this new and gorgeous garment, majesty', he is royally proclaimed by a stage-direction which indicates his change of name, habit, and company: 'Enter KING HENRY THE FIFTH, *attended*'. In losing his father he has also cast off the old man:

> And, Princes all, believe me, I beseech you,
> My father is gone wild into his grave,
> For in his tomb lie my affections;
> And with his spirits sadly I survive,
> To mock the expectation of the world,
> To frustrate prophecies, and to raze out
> Rotten opinion, who hath writ me down
> After my seeming. (V.ii.122–9)

Such sad mockery of expectation is seen in the rejection of Falstaff, which we have been led to anticipate from the very start, but which we actually witness with a feeling of regret, for in banishing the old man, as in burying his father, Hal has also cast off his youth.

Notes

1   Richmond Noble, *Shakespeare's Biblical Knowledge* (1935), p. 169. An indispensable but far from complete treatment of the subject.
2   See Introduction to *The First Part of King Henry IV* (new Arden Shakespeare), edited by A. H. Humphreys (1960), pp. xxxix-xlii.
3   Quotations of Shakespeare's text are from *The Complete Works*, edited by Peter Alexander (1951).
4   Quotations from the Bible are from *The Geneva Bible: A Facsimile of the 1560 Edition* (1969).
5   'I know you not' is also the Bridegroom's reply to the foolish virgins (Matthew, 25:12).
6   'The eye of man hath not heard, the ear of man hath not seen, man's hand is not able to taste, his tongue to conceive, nor his heart to report, what my dream was' (4.1.20–2). Cf. I Corinthians, 2:9.
7   A well-known Elizabethan tribute to the power of the history play to restore the dead to life and so to redeem the time is Thomas Nashe's allusion to Shakespeare's *Henry VI Part One* in *Pierce Penilesse His Supplication to the Divell* (1592): 'How would it have ioyed braue *Talbot* (the terror of the French) to thinke that after he had lyne two hundred yeares in his Tombe, hee should triumphe againe on the Stage, and haue his bones new embalmed with the teares of ten thousand spectators at least, (at seuerall times) who, in the Tragedian that represents his person, imagine they behold him fresh bleeding?' Quoted in E. K. Chambers, *William Shakespeare: A Study of Facts and Problems* (2 vols., 1930), II, p. 188.
8   Paul A. Jorgensen, *Redeeming Shakespeare's Words* (1962), pp. 52–69.
9   Humphreys, *ed. cit.*, p. 177.
10   *Ibid.*, p. 179.
11   Quoted in Chambers, II, p. 244.

[1970]

BARBARA EVERETT

Romeo and Juliet:
the Nurse's story

The heroine of *Romeo and Juliet* enters the play late. Not until the third scene of the first act is she called onstage by her mother and her Nurse, who are also appearing here for the first time. The latter part of this scene is given to Lady Capulet's brisk and formal announcement of an offer for her daughter, with Juliet's timid and obedient response. All the earlier part of it is dominated by the Nurse, and her reminiscences of the past set the tone for the first appearance of the only three really important women in this romantic and domestic tragedy. Lady Capulet's conventional niceties make their point too, but it is the Nurse who holds the stage. Indeed, her 'moment' seems to have an importance in the play as a whole which has not been recognised. It demands to be looked at in a little detail. At Juliet's entry, mother and Nurse are discussing her age:

> Lady C. She's not fourteen.
> Nurse   I'll lay fourteen of my teeth –
>   And yet, to my teen be it spoken, I have but four –
>   She's not fourteen. How long is it now
>   To Lammas-tide?
> Lady C. A fortnight and odd days.
> Nurse   Even or odd, of all days in the year,
>   Come Lammas Eve at night shall she be fourteen.
>   Susan and she – God rest all Christian souls! –
>   Were of an age. Well, Susan is with God;
>   She was too good for me. But, as I said,
>   On Lammas Eve at night shall she be fourteen;
>   That shall she, marry; I remember it well.
>   'Tis since the earthquake now eleven years;
>   And she was wean'd – I never shall forget it –
>   Of all the days of the year, upon that day;
>   For I had then laid wormwood to my dug,
>   Sitting in the sun under the dove-house wall;
>   My lord and you were then at Mantua.
>   Nay, I do bear a brain. But, as I said,
>   When it did taste the wormwood on the nipple
>   Of my dug, and felt it bitter, pretty fool,
>   To see it tetchy, and fall out with the dug!
>   Shake, quoth the dove-house. 'Twas no need, I trow,
>   To bid me trudge.
>   And since that time it is eleven years;
>   For then she could stand high-lone; nay, by th' rood,
>   She could have run and waddled all about;

> For even the day before, she broke her brow;
> And then my husband – God be with his soul!
> 'A was a merry man – took up the child.
> 'Yea', quoth he, 'dost thou fall upon thy face?
> Thou wilt fall backward when thou has more wit,
> Wilt thou not, Jule?' And, by my holidam,
> The pretty wretch left crying, and said 'Ay'.
> To see, now, how a jest shall come about!
> I warrant, an I should live a thousand years,
> I never should forget it: 'Wilt thou not, Jule?' quoth he;
> And, pretty fool, it stinted, and said 'Ay'.

Lady C. Enough of this; I pray thee hold thy peace.
Nurse Yes, Madam. Yet I cannot choose but laugh
> To think it should leave crying and say 'Ay'.
> And yet, I warrant, it had upon its brow
> A bump as big as a young cock'rel's stone –
> A perilous knock; and it cried bitterly.
> 'Yea', quoth my husband, 'fall'st upon thy face?
> Thou wilt fall backward when thou comest to age;
> Wilt thou not, Jule?' It stinted, and said 'Ay'.

Juliet And stint thou, too, I pray thee, nurse, say I.
Nurse Peace, I have done. God mark thee to his grace!
> Thou wast the prettiest babe that e'er I nurs'd;
> An I might live to see thee married once,
> I have my wish.

The one detail in these rich ramblings that has earned examination is the earthquake. There were real earthquakes in England in the 1580s, and one in 1580 big enough to be long memorable; and some have hoped that the Nurse's allusion might date the play. But this is perhaps to fail to grasp the very special milieu set up in these passages. The Nurse's mind has its precision, but not one such as to make her sums trustworthy. There is even a slight oddity about the figures involving the infant Juliet, since to have been only just weaned, and to be only just 'waddling' about, at rising three years, seems backward even for rustic Tudor non-gentry babies. Mathematical computations clearly increase the Nurse's dither.

'Dither' may be said to be the point of this speech. We can look in it, that is to say, for human interests and purposes even if we cannot trust its figures; indeed, the figures may be there simply to divert us from looking for the wrong thing. The Nurse's speech is a highly original piece of writing. It is perhaps Shakespeare's first greatly human verse speech, so supple in its rhythms that its original text – the Good Quarto – prints it as prose. Indeed, this looseness of rhythm, when added to the idiosyncrasies of the thought-processes as far as logic and mathematics are concerned, has increased the suspicions of some scholars about the authenticity of the whole; suspicions which can only be met by setting forth clearly a justification for it.

In part we can explain what the Nurse says here in terms of 'character' interest. In Brooke, the main source, the heroine's old Nurse holds forth to Romeus about Juliet as a small baby, and tells how she 'clapt her on the buttocks soft and kist where I did clappe', in a moment of coarse and genial humour that Shakespeare is perhaps remembering and adapting. And Brooke too has 'beldams' who

> sit at ease upon theyr tayle
> The day and eke the candlelight before theyr talke shall fayle,
> And part they say is true, and part they do devise . . .

The Nurse is a product of this comfortable and recognisable world. Shakespeare has taken Brooke's sketch of a conventional character-type and given it a dense human solidity; moreover, later in the play the Nurse will find herself in a further dimension, a moral context that defines and painfully 'places' her. In this, her opening speech, a mere something given by the story-situation is first and most massively 'rounded out', and there are also perhaps hints of that moral context to come. Her role as Nurse, her comfortable humanity, and her limitations of vision are all revealed in the references backward to Juliet's babyhood, and in the profuse mindlessness which is the medium of narration.

On the other hand, such a character need not have been quite as comical as the Nurse: and something important is contributed to *Romeo and Juliet* by the fact that she and her counter-poise Mercutio are each, in their opposed ways, exceptionally funny. She is a 'natural' and he is a 'fool', and this fact makes a good deal of difference to the way we respond to their two 'straight men', the hero and heroine of the play. Romeo and Juliet are two romantic children, but we take them – or should take them – absolutely straight; and we might fail to do so if it were not for the obliquity, or folly, that characterises their constant companions. That is to say, from the beginning what the Nurse has is more than personality: it is function; and by function she is a 'natural'. The presence of Bottom in *A Midsummer Night's Dream*, a companion piece to this play, serves to suggest that the discourse of Shakespeare's fools and especially of his naturals will provide insight even – or most – where it appears to be failing to provide information. There is a kind of insight early achieved in the Shakespearean comic mode which can shift the comic up and away from the limits of the satirised or satirising and into a medium which is a form of truth; or perhaps one ought to say, which is *another* form of truth. If a fat middle-aged woman congenitally disposed to muddle is made, by function, into a fool licensed to speak profound nonsense, then she may undercut the rational and move into an area of more primitive and powerful (though more elusive and dangerous) utterance. The Nurse's speech is followed by Lady Capulet's thin and superficial conventionalities, and these latter help to intensify by retrospective contrast the crude depth achieved by the Nurse.

I would argue that the major function of the Nurse's speech is to provide a *natural* context for the motif of 'death-marked love' which governs the play. Such intimations of mortality as occur here hardly rise to tragic dignity. But it is commonly agreed that *Romeo and Juliet* makes tragedy out of the lyrical and comical. The Nurse's jokes operate well within that region of the 'painfully funny' which comes fully and deeply into being at the death of Mercutio. Indeed, one might call Mercutio's death-scene, with the astonishing death-blow given unheralded to the irresponsibly free and funny young man, a perfect match or counter-poise in a harsh vein to what is set forth here with a rough tenderness. What the Nurse says at this early point acts as a semi-choric commentary, helping to build up the background of suggestions which in the earlier part of the play act as an unconscious persuasion stronger than the explicit feud-motif in accounting for the catastrophe. It might be objected that this would demand an audience impossibly acute, able at once to laugh at the Nurse, relish her 'character', and respond to the more impersonal connotations of what she says. But it must be pointed out that for the original theatre audience this charmingly comical account of a marriageable girl's infancy was narrated on a stage hung everywhere with black. The reference to 'Juliet and her Romeo' at the end of the play certainly makes it sound a story already very familiar, almost fabulous; but even those not familiar with the tale could hardly fail to observe that a death was likely at some point to take place: that they were assisting at a tragedy. They could not be wholly unprepared to hear, at the very least, a touch of painful irony in the lines that close the Nurse's affectionate apostrophe:

> Thou was the prettiest babe that e're I nursed;
> An I might live to see thee married once,
> I have my wish.

'Married once' just about covers Juliet's case. It seems worth while to look at the Nurse's speech in rather closer focus than it has received.

The passage falls into three sections: the first concerned with Juliet's age and birthday ('On Lammas Eve at night shall she be fourteen'), the second with the child's weaning and the third with the child's fall. First things first: the birthday. Lammas Eve is 31 July and so an appropriate date (as the New Penguin editor has pointed out) for a heroine named from July. But there

137

may be a particular resonance in the festival date, which is thrice repeated, with an effect as much of ritual as of wandering memory. The Christian feast of Lammas took the place of what was possibly the most important of the four great pagan festival days, the midsummer feast. 'Lammas' itself meant originally 'loaf-mass', the sacrament at which were offered loaves made from the first ripe corn, the first fruits of the harvest. One therefore might expect Lammas Eve to carry, for an Elizabethan consciousness, mixed and fugitive but nonetheless suggestive associations, both with Midsummer Eve and with harvest festival. Such associations would be appropriate. For *Romeo and Juliet* is a summer tragedy as its companion-piece, *A Midsummer Night's Dream*, is a summer comedy. *Romeo and Juliet* so consistently evokes different aspects of high summer, both inner and outer weather, that Capulet's 'quench the fire, the room is grown too hot' (at I.v.29) (apparently borrowed from the wintry season in which this part of Brooke's poem takes place) is often noted for its discordance with the general 'feel' of the play. We are told that the furious energies of the fighting, fornicating and witticising young men are in part to be explained by the season of 'dog-days': 'now is the mad blood stirring'. The relation of hero and heroine embodies a different, more tender aspect of summer: the lyrical sense of a time that 'Holds in perfection but a little moment' (Sonnet 15). In the balcony scene,

> This bud of love, by summer's ripening breath
> May prove a beauteous flow'r when next we meet . . .

but in the tomb, 'Death . . . hath suck'd the honey of thy breath'. Then at the end of the play, these 'midsummer' associations are replaced by an image in which the golden statues are something much more like first fruits:

> As rich shall Romeo's by his lady's lie –
> Poor sacrifices of our enmity!

A reference to Lammas, then, may carry a proleptic suggestion both of the fall that follows the midsummer equinox in the course of nature and of the sacrificial offerings of first-fruits. And there is a further point to be made, concerning Elizabethan idiom. The expression 'latter Lammas' was used to mean 'Never' – a time that will never come. The more sombre, if tender side of these hints is strengthened by the Nurse's references to Juliet's dead foster-sister, Susan. 'Susan is with God: / She was too good for me.' In Shakespeare's time, so pitifully small a proportion of babies born survived their first six years that this reminder of a massive infant death-rate brings closer to Juliet the whole context of fatality. Not very many years will separate the deaths of the two girls. And the Nurse's 'She was too good for me' is one way of interpreting the meaning of the destruction of Romeo and

Juliet themselves, and it is one that is offered as a possibility by the play as a whole.

It would be unwise to argue, from all this, that a perceptive mind ought to take the hint that Juliet is unlikely to reach or much pass the age of fourteen: or to urge that an audience ought somehow to feel *consciously* that the ludicrous argument about the precise extent of Juliet's past holds ironical premonitions of the absence of her future. But the twice-repeated 'Lammas Eve' line holds between its repetitions the dead Susan; and the conjunction of birthday with deathday lingers in the mind. The effect is not irrelevant to a tragedy in which Juliet reaches maturity with a suddenness and brevity both splendid and shocking.

To speak of maturity here is to bring up the whole question of Juliet's age, on which the passage turns in a more than merely nominal sense. The figure 'fourteen' is obtruded upon our attention so as to make it scarcely forgettable. Shakespeare is choosing an age which makes his heroine two years younger than the already very young heroine in Brooke's poem. In both stories the age of the heroine seems to have more to do with romance than with ordinary bourgeois reality.[1] Marriage at sixteen or fourteen, let alone the Nurse's 'Now, by my maidenhead at twelve year old', cannot be taken as a reflection of ordinary Elizabethan facts of life. It may be that Shakespeare was availing himself of the notion of 'hot Italy', where girls matured far earlier than in his own cooler clime, but for that the original sixteen would presumably have served. It seems important that Capulet should give the impression that Juliet is a little young for marriage –

> She hath not seen the change of fourteen years;
> Let two more summers wither in their pride,
> Ere we may think her ripe to be a bride

and that Lady Capulet should apparently contradict this later:

> By my count,
> I was your mother much upon these years
> That you are now a maid.

Considering all this, we may say that Juliet's age is important, and that the question is brought up by Lady Capulet and elaborated by the Nurse as a way of giving a good deal of information about the play's heroine, though not exactly of a chronological kind. Shakespeare is utilising a characteristically poetic sense of time. On the one hand (he seems to insist) there is nothing abnormal about Juliet's marriage at her present age; on the contrary, given that we are moving in a romantic world, the event is a part of a great cycle – both natural and ceremonious or customary – that occurs generation after generation. On the other hand, the choice of an age slightly young even by romantic standards achieves the sense of extremity, of a painful too-soonness: Juliet is a 'rathe primrose', a 'fairest flower no sooner blown than blasted'. Juliet is so young indeed that the figure of fourteen seems to suggest a coming-to-maturity that accompanies the simple physical process of puberty itself: Juliet is at a threshold. (Such hints are paralleled in Romeo's case by the adolescent fits of passion, and the rapid change of affection, which characterise him). That Juliet is said – with some iteration – to be fourteen, is a way of establishing that she is at an *early* age for a *natural* process of maturity. Or, to put it another way, our sense of the tragedy entails both a sharp recognition of unripeness, of a pathos and gravity recognisably childish, and an acknowledgment that the grief experienced is itself 'full, fine, perfect'.

The fact that the tragic process involves a maturation brings us back to the Nurse's speech. The first of the two incidents she recalls concerns Juliet's weaning; which we may now call, in view of that movement to maturity involved with the whole tragic action, Juliet's *first* weaning. The interesting fact about the earthquake that ushers in this first movement of the narrative is not (or not only) that several such actually happened in England in the last decades of the sixteenth century, but that in this speech one happens at the same time as the weaning. This particular specimen is a poetic and not a historical event and it takes place within a context of its own. On the one hand there is the earthquake, a natural cataclysm of extraordinary magnitude, such as people remember and talk about and date things by: something quite beyond the personal – really unstoppable: it shook the dovehouse. On the other hand, there is the dovehouse, symbol – as Shakespeare's other references to doves reveal – of mildness and peace and affectionate love; and there is the Nurse, 'Sitting in the sun, under the dovehouse wall'; and in the middle of this sun and shelter, framed as in some piece of very early genre painting, there is the weaning of the child. The most domestic and trivial event, personal and simply human as it is, is set beside the violently alien and impersonal earthquake, the two things relating only as they co-exist in a natural span (or as recalled by the wandering mind of a natural); and because they relate, they interpenetrate. The Nurse's 'confused' thought-processes contemplate the earthquake with that curious upside-downness that is merely the reflex of those who communicate most with very small children and who speak as though they saw things as small children see them. Her 'Shake, quoth the dovehouse!' has not been quite helpfully enough glossed, presumably because few Shakespeare editors are sufficiently acquainted with what might be said to a very small child about an earthquake. It does not simply mean, as has been suggested, 'the dovehouse shook'; it allows the unfluttered dovecote to satirise the earthquake, as in a comical baby mock-heroic – to be aloof and detached from what is happening to it. Thus, if the dovecote gains a rational upper hand and superior tone over the earthquake, the same kind of reversal occurs in that the weaning produces an (if anything) even more formidable storm in the small child, a cataclysmic infant rage satirised by the unfluttered Nurse:

> To see it tetchy, and fall out with the dug!
> Shake, quoth the dovehouse. 'Twas no need, I trow,
> To bid me trudge.

In this last phrase a fairly simple dramatic irony and pathos will be evident. Since Juliet's marriage is the subject of discussion, it is nearly time for her to 'bid the Nurse trudge' once and for all. The situation recurs in the later scene in which the young woman shows that she no longer needs support:

> Go, counsellor!
> Thou and my bosom henceforth shall be twain . . .

and helps to bring out the different pathos of the unnatural which is also latent in the situation. And the two kinds of pathos meet and fuse when Juliet is finally forced to stand free.

> I'll call them back again to comfort me.
> Nurse!– What should she do here?
> My dismal scene I needs must act alone.

But there is faintly but suggestively shadowed under this straightforward dramatic irony a different kind of irony. Throughout this whole first-act speech Shakespeare creates a poetic medium for which the Nurse's 'muddled old mind' is something of a subterfuge, as Clarence's drowning vision in *Richard III* justifies itself by the conventions of dream. Because the Nurse is stupid she stands outside what she sees, endowing it with a curious objectivity. She has no moral opinion or judgment on the events that, as she pensively contemplates them, detach themselves from her and animate themselves into a natural history of human infancy. Confused and unjudged, earthquake and weaning interpenetrate in the past, sudden event with slow process: the earthquake becomes necessary, a mere process of maturing, and the weaning of a child takes on magnitude and *terribilità*, it shakes nature. The Nurse does not know the difference; and this not knowing becomes, in the course of the play, her innocence and her guilt. She has this in common, to Shakespeare's mind, with 'Mother Earth' herself, who is similarly unaware of vital differences:

> The earth that's nature's mother is her tomb;
> What is her burying grave, that is her womb.
> And from her womb children of divers kind
> We sucking on her natural bosom find . . .

The account of the weaning is less 'muddled' than so designed as to give the Nurse impressive associations such as recur much later and in the far more famous image, 'the beggar's nurse, and Caesar's'. The Nurse, lively and deathly as she is, with 'wormwood to my dug', is Juliet's natural context, the place she starts from (and Capulet's pun is relevant here: 'Earth hath swallowed all my hopes but she; she is the hopeful lady of my earth.'). Bidding the Nurse 'trudge' is the effort, one might say, of the horizontal man to be a vertical one – the human move to surpass the mere milieu of things.

The Nurse's second anecdote adds a brief, ludicrous but nonetheless shrewd comment on that hunger for verticality, the perils of standing 'high-lone'. The ironic and pathetic notes of the earlier part of the speech modulate here into something brisk and broadly comic; hence the introduction of the 'merry man', the Nurse's husband, as chief actor – a replacement of surrogate mother by surrogate father, which explains the slight fore-echoes of the relationship of Yorick and the gravedigger with Hamlet. Yet even here there is more than the merely anecdotal. The iterations, like those in the first part of the speech, are not circumscribed by the effect of the tedium of folly; there are echoes of the wisdom of folly too.

> 'Thou wilt fall backward when thou has more wit,
> Wilt thou not, Jule?' And, by my holidam,
> The pretty wretch left crying, and said 'Ay'
>
>   'Wilt thou not, Jule?' quoth he;
> And, pretty fool, it stinted, and said 'Ay',
>
> 'Wilt thou not, Jule?' It stinted, and said 'Ay'.

Such iterations are as close to the rhythm of ritual as they are to tedium. And they are a reminder of the presence in this play of what Yeats called 'custom and ceremony', of the ordered repetitions that frame the life of generations:

> Nay, by my maidenhead at twelve year old . . .

> I was you mother much upon these years
> That you are now a maid . . .

>   I have seen the day
> That I have worn a visor and could tell
> A whispering tale in a fair lady's ear . . .

> Now old desire doth in his death-bed lie,
> And young affection gapes to be his heir . . .

This feeling for age-old process is perhaps caught up into a casual phrase of the Nurse's, a warm appreciation of the old man's unsubtle joke:

> I warrant, an I should live a thousand years,
> I never should forget it.

Involved with the husband's repetitions, one might say, is the rhythm of an existence unchanged in a thousand years. Under Juliet's particular gift, in the action that follows, for saying 'Ay' to a situation, lies any small child's easily-observed habit of hopefully saying 'Yes' to anything; and under that – so the Nurse's speech suggests – lies a resilience and resurgence in nature itself.

All in all, there is considerable density of reference in the Nurse's speech. And this density is not in itself affected by the explanation we find for it: whether we choose to talk of a tissue of inexplicit conceptions within the mind of the artist himself, or whether we like to think of it as some more conscious artistry that expects a more conscious response, does not matter. The degree of deliberation that ever exists on Shakespeare's part does not seem a fruitful critical issue: it contains too many questions impossible to answer. What one can say is that the Nurse's speech presents an image of Juliet's past that happens to contain, or that contains with a purpose, a premonitory comment on her future. It alerts and reminds the audience of what is to come as do the far more formally deployed curses of Margaret in *Richard III*. But here an interesting and important complexity occurs. Margaret's curses are choric and impersonal in function: she speaks almost as Clio, the Muse of History. But the Nurse is a character in a romantic tragedy, and approaches the impersonal only insofar as a fool may. The degree of impersonal truth in her account remains a lively question. To ask whether the natural is true might have seemed in itself a not unnatural question to an Elizabethan; for Edmund, who made Nature his Goddess, was an unnatural bastard who played his brother and his father false. Both the Nurse and her vision of things are (we might say) true but not necessarily trustworthy. It is for this reason that one may call her account 'the Nurse's story'; something that offers fascinating and rich glimpses of the centre of the play from an angle that is an angle merely. She presents the play's major subjects and events – love and death – in an innocent and natural language, that of earthquakes and weaning and a fall backward. In her first story the earthquake comes out of the summer heat randomly, but not meaninglessly, for the catastrophe has scale – is a date in nature: and so with love and death. A weaning is a stage, from milk to the stronger meat of existence; so also with love and death, if we take it that it is the death of eros in agape, and of youth in manhood which is in question. In her second reminiscence, the old man's joke reduces the complicated interwoven events of the play to a 'fall backward': and in the phrase, a childish accident, Adam's maturing sin, sexuality and tragic death are all involved. In the connotations of the phrase, a child's innocence and an age-old blame blend with the potent romantic and erotic myth of love and death as inseparable companions, and make it startlingly harmless: romanticism grows into 'something childish but very natural'.

Through 'It stinted, and said "Ay" ' significance and appropriateness move, as through the whole of the Nurse's speech; and they are of a kind whose resonances are not easily pinned down. The action that follows certainly pins down the Nurse: what she comes down to is a randy and treacherous advocacy of bigamy. In this light we can look back and find her account of things, for all its humanity, lacking in full meaning and dignity. The Nurse's sense of 'need' ('Twas no need . . . To bid me trudge') does not cover a large enough human span, and the old man's consolations (' 'A was a merry man – took up the child') are clearly slightly outgrown even by an intelligent three-year-old. And yet something remains to be said. If we find some difference between the vision of *Romeo and Juliet* and that of Shakespeare's more mature tragedies, this difference might be in part put down to the effective predominance in the former of 'the Nurse's story'. Her speech establishes a natural milieu in which earthquake and weaning, a fall and a being taken up so balance that the ill effects of either are of no importance; and insofar as what she says relates to the rest of the play, it helps to suggest that the same might be true of love and death. And there seems to be a peculiar echo of her procedure in all the rhetorical doublings and repetitions of the play and especially in the paradoxes of the love and death speeches. The play's structural doublings, too, are curious, and perhaps deserve to be more often noted than they are. Romeo loves twice, once untruly and once truly; Juliet dies twice, once untruly and once truly. In any such doubling there is a point of contrast (the first love and death were illusory, the second real) but there is bound to be in implication a point of similarity also: if the first was mere game, so may the second be. Whatever the relation of the two in terms of logic, when acted out the doubled events create an imaginative equivalence.

This sense of a final equilibrium in which there is recompense for loss is in fact established as early in the play as possible, in its Prologue: which closes its doubling and paradoxical account of the feud with

> The which if you with patient ears attend,
> What here shall miss, our toil shall strive to mend.

By the end of the play it is possible to have a stubborn expectation, against all rationality, that love and death are going to 'cancel out', that Romeo and Juliet have been merely 'Sprinkled with blood to make them grow'. The image is horticultural (and is used by Bolingbroke at the end of *Richard II*). Such an image is not wholly inappropriate to a play in which Romeo lightly accuses the Friar of telling him to 'bury love' and the Friar sharply answers 'Not in a grave / To lay one in, another out to have'. The expectation that the young lovers will 'rise again' is fairly equivocally met. Their survival owes more to art than to nature: they are no more than golden statues. Yet *Romeo and Juliet* is one of the first of Shakespeare's many plays whose peculiar quality is to make distinctions between art and nature seem false: 'the art itself is nature'. It is perhaps no accident that Mercutio and the Nurse, the play's fool and natural, turn out to be the most fertile of storytellers.

Note

1   These remarks are indebted to Peter Laslett's discussion of the relatively late age of puberty and of marriage in Elizabethan bourgeois society in his valuable sociological study *The World We Have Lost*.

[1972]

A. W. BELLRINGER

Julius Caesar : room enough

I

Julius Caesar is best regarded as an example of Polonius's category 'tragical-historical'. The tragedy is inherent in the historical situation: it is Rome's in the same sense that in the history plays the tragedy is England's. But Roman politics are significantly different. *Julius Caesar* cannot simply be read as a cautionary tale for the times, warning dissatisfied subjects against the folly of killing the king. Any relations with Elizabethan politics are tangential rather than analogous. Ancient Rome is not just a monarchical nation-state, but the whole expanse of conquered Europe. She is also a small city with a peculiar political tradition. From this contradiction comes the tension of 'the times' which largely determines the fates of the individuals in the play. As Robert B. Heilman has argued, 'the antecedent fact is the public situation – . . . the apparent development of a political dictatorship – and we see the private life in this context'.[1] It is a mistake to look for a tragic hero here. There is no scope and no worked out role for greatness.

Shakespeare's interest in Roman history seems to have been twofold. He is concerned literally with analysing a transfer of power, with dramatising errors and their results, with demonstrating what was practical. But he is also taken up with firm sentiments, with admiration for sacrifice, with regret for passing ideals, and conversely with distaste for a sterile ethic. The result is an appropriate poetic style, dignified and clear, rarely persuasive, capable of giving away the speaker without satire, and yet suggesting a certain hollowness.

Obviously he took his lead from his source. Plutarch, though republican in his sympathies, concluded that in Caesar's time absolute rule was a necessity for Rome. The aristocratic cause was upheld merely by those who refused to recognise the inevitable. The republic, once dominant in Italy by virtue of its coherent inner structure and intelligent policies, had now as a result of territorial expansion become ineffectual. The noble virtues which had worked in the early days, frankness of dealing, openness in negotiation, respect for the consensus, were no longer relevant. They were the marks of patriotism and honour in a governing class imbued with the strong sense of legality which allows for compromise between contending interests under the pressure of limited national aims. Plutarch regretted their obsolescence. The need now was for control, but the glamour had departed; these are the points that Shakespeare's drama undoubtedly makes. His play is coolly distanced aesthetically. The experience it enacts is of a saddening, almost chilling kind. Rome is in an unfavoured, graceless state. There is some personal pathos, but no individual tragic focus. The play is an episode in a larger action, and is open-ended in the sense that it conveys the idea that it can all happen again, in a slightly altered form. The death of Caesar is central only chronologically. The theme is the emergence of another Caesar. There are even signs of yet another civil war.

Width of reference, spaciousness both geographical and historical, is indeed a poetic characteristic of *Julius Caesar*, not perhaps with the excess of *Antony and Cleopatra*. But the dispersal of forces is essential in the earlier play too. Antiquity is made to evoke its own antiquity once removed, but the effect is not the paradox of making the scene seem more contemporary. The sense of the past within the past is not simply a device, but is thematically crucial, since the play turns on the issue of the relevance of that remoter, small Rome to the Rome of Caesar. As usual the opening scene concisely indicates what is to be salient and gives us an advantage of hindsight before any of the main characters has appeared. Two disintegrating forces have destroyed republican stability and threaten to overturn the existing tradition entirely. Inside the city there is the populace, never likely to be organised into more than an instrument, but exhibiting a kind of 'murderous innocence' and dangerously inconsequential in its ideas and loyalties. Beyond the city the unimaginable extension of the frontiers has put power into the hands of generals, whose armies have warred against each other. Civil wars pre-date the conspiracy, which is itself as much Pompey's revenge as the battle of Philippi is Caesar's. Military power, answerable only to these ambitious generals, of whom Caesar is the greatest, but still only one in a series, is complemented by the manageable riotousness of the citizens, to the detriment of conventional institutions, particularly the senate. The opening exchanges of the play, humorously selfish as they are, soon turn to menace. The commoners, unlike Dekker's shoemakers, get no joy from their holiday for the occasion is unworthy of it. They are seen to vanish from the stage 'tongue-tied in their guiltiness' at the thought of the plague that must light upon their ingratitude to Pompey. They are at first upbraided by the tribune for appearing on a working day without the signs of their crafts; the tradesmen are lost in the mob. The puns glance at the theme of mending what is bad and recovering what is in danger. The disorderliness and irresponsibility of the people are, however, not emphasised till Marullus vehemently denounces them.

> You blocks, you stones, you worse than senseless things!
> O you hard hearts, you cruel men of Rome,
> Knew you not Pompey?

The speaker is Pompey's man and his partisanship crude. We rather feel it is the misfortune of the cruel men of Rome to have experienced both Pompey and Caesar in turn. Marullus's righteous distinction between a valid triumph, in which the tributaries 'grace in captive bonds' the chariot wheels of the victorious Pompey, and an invalid one, in which Caesar, the conqueror in a civil war, comes victorious over his rival's 'blood', that is, Pompey's heirs, is far from impressive. The tribunes' outspokenness has already the quality of a forlorn protest, and their courage in disrobing the images of Caesar's trophies looks futile. But at the end of the scene Flavius's words,

> These growing feathers pluck'd from Caesar's wing
> Will make him fly an ordinary pitch,
> Who else would soar above the view of men
> And keep us all in servile fearfulness,

though impracticably sanguine, express an ominously sane sense of Caesar's own delusions, as well as a fear of his unpredictability. The first grim moment in the play is when we hear from Casca in the next scene that 'Marullus and Flavius for pulling scarfs off Caesar's images, are put to silence'. It is the unmistakeable sign of arbitrary power in a society where it is dangerous to think too much.

Reminders that Pompey is still to be revenged are unexpectedly prominent in *Julius Caesar*. Caius Ligarius's original offence with Caesar, we are told, was that of 'speaking well of Pompey'. After the assassination Brutus does not refrain from pointing out that Caesar 'now on Pompey's basis lies along, / No worthier than the dust!' Anthony in his speech to the people adds the lurid detail that Pompey's statue 'all the while ran blood' as Caesar fell, presumably out of sympathy, but also possibly accusingly. Even more striking is the reference in the last act when Cassius in his moment of partial belief in ill omens calls Messala to witness that against his will,

> (As Pompey was) am I compell'd to set
> Upon one battle all our liberties.

The interest in these passages does not lie in the question of whether Pompey could plausibly be seen as a champion of 'liberties' rather than just as a proto-Caesar. The significance is that the fighting into which the action of the drama visibly deteriorates at the end is not the unprecedented result of a unique crime, but is the reversion after an interlude to a state of affairs which was, and is, as is hinted by Octavius's differences with Antony, to continue, normal, until the man of destiny inaugurates his empire. The play ends suitably with a war-act in which the 'bloody sign of battle is hung out' and Octavius, or as he calls himself, 'another Caesar' asserts his superiority over Antony and fulfils his ambition of succeeding where his uncle failed. 'I was not born to die on Brutus' sword.' The boasts and confusions of the battle-scenes are not, however, as in *Troilus and Cressida*, left to amount to ironic farce. In *Julius Caesar* the disorder represented on the stage by a succession of clumsy combats and nasty suicides confronts us with that condition of 'hazard' in the remote regions of the Roman world on which the militarists continuously depend. The ending establishes an oppressive continuous present, 'this losing day' of the defeated Brutus's bitter boast. The drastic instant solution attempted by the conspirators loses significance, for slaying has become 'a deed in fashion'. As J. F. Danby points out, Antony's moral tribute to Brutus is in effect a testimony to the hollowness of the triumvirs' victory. 'The problems implicit are only made more urgent by this false resolution' (*Shakespeare's Doctrine of Nature*, 1949, p. 145). Octavius has the last word, less generous than Antony's, but proper in a deadly way.

> Within my tent his bones to-night shall lie,
> Most like a soldier, order'd honourably.

His tent has become the place of honour. The unimaginative injunction at the close can hardly engage the audience's assent: 'let's away, / To part the glories of this happy day.' For can glories be parted so happily? One's mind turns to what has been lost, unity, civility, scrupulosity, and what was a commonwealth of sorts.

II

I mean by this the old Roman Republic, to whose values Shakespeare's verse affords a resonance thinner than, but still comparable with, his pastoral idealism elsewhere; in their desperate vulnerability these virtues are emphatically stressed. For whatever Horatio may have felt about

> the most high and palmy state of Rome,
> A little ere the mightiest Julius fell,

in the play which deals with that period we are given scant evidence of security. In fact it is a clear point that Caesar's presence, though arguably more commanding and more persuasive than it seems, is unworthy of his reputation. The details that are to Caesar's disadvantage do not amount to a denigration of the historical character, but they make the hero-worship of the mob seem very blind. His domination of public life is imposing enough, but a little doubt as to his reliability makes all the strength of the republicans' case. Negatively, their logic is sound. Caesar's first entry too is surely undignified. His requirement that the unfortunate Calpurnia should be touched by Antony's fertility symbol exposes the central weakness of the monarchical system, the uncertainty of suitable succession. His pompous style with its imperious presumptions is oddly deflated by the admission that he is deaf in one ear. Also he is inconsistent, for while respecting one superstition in the matter of his wife's barrenness, he rejects the soothsayer as 'a dreamer'. In his domestic setting later Caesar makes a poorer showing than Brutus does. Though he evidently relates the disquieting features of the night to his personal circumstances (Act II, Scene ii), he concedes nothing to Calpurnia's case, based on a dream, but only, for a time, something to her 'humour'. Caesar's usage of his wife looks like a kind of proleptic royal arbitrariness (in that house we are already in a world of palace influences), especially in the light of the fact, which the next scene presents excitedly, that Brutus has confided fully in Portia and had meant it when he said,

> You are my true and honourable wife,
> As dear to me as are the ruddy drops
> That visit my sad heart.

He could trust her. Caesar's unattractiveness is partly due to his inability to drop the public mask. This might not be a serious flaw in a ruler, but the public mask in itself is also not pretty. When Caesar makes Stoical contentions like this, 'Of all the wonders that I yet have heard, / It seems to me the most strange that men should fear', he reveals the kind of self-deception that can issue in cruelty.[2] There is of course the argument that, in spite of his failings of tone, Caesar's pre-eminence can be taken dramatically for granted just as God's can in a miracle play. As for instance T. S. Dorsch suggests, Caesar's 'greatness and nobility do not need to be emphasised; they are implicit in the attitude towards him of every one else in the play'. So we can soon realise 'that the stabbing is mere senseless butchery' and admire Shakespeare for providing 'some intelligible motives for this incredible piece of criminal folly' (Arden edition, 1955, intro., pp. xxix, xxxv and xxxix). This interpretation demands a great deal in the way of silent meaningful expressions from the actor who plays Caesar, but I doubt if he could have counted on unequivocal admiration for Julius Caesar in audiences of the 1590s any more than in audiences today.[3] Ben Jonson of course complained that Shakespeare had put sayings into Caesar's mouth 'which were ridiculous', but whether his example, 'Caesar did never wrong, but with just cause', or the Folio version, possibly altered to meet his criticism, 'Know, Caesar doth not wrong, nor without cause / Will he be satisfied', is the original, neither lacks the sinister assumption of infallibility.[4] There is also the revealing phrase that Caesar drops casually, 'Caesar and his senate'. Caesar's last, unsuspecting speeches are almost thrasonical in style. The insistence on constancy in decisions suggests an authoritarian rigidity, which is virtually tautological.

> I was constant Cimber should be banish'd,
> And constant do remain to keep him so.
> . . . Hence! Wilt thou lift up Olympus?

That Caesar should stress his immobility the moment before he is struck down scarcely makes for implicit grandeur. The irony confirms one's unfavourable response when he interrupts Metellus, before any reasonable case can be made for repealing his brother's banishment, with a scornful speech. Here Caesar distinguishes himself from ordinary men, or fools, whose blood can be thawed or fired so as to 'turn pre-ordinance and first decree / Into the law of children'. He professes that he rejects the suit in order to demonstrate that he is the one man in the world he knows 'That unassailable holds on his rank, / Unshak'd of motion'. One's impression of a long-sighted *hauteur*, of an inflexibility that over-simplifies to justify prejudice, is not lessened by the knowledge that this was precisely the reaction that the conspirators had calculated on getting and had needed from Caesar. And 'so, by excluding the passions, repressing the sensitive soul, and disjoining the operational nexus of hand and heart', argues John Anson, 'Caesar, in his will to remain untouchable, threatens to occupy the whole space of the living world: . . . now a god, now a block, Caesar emerges precisely a colossus, and, as such, the incarnation of Stoic man'.[5] But the terrible event which ensues shows us his human vulnerability again; Caesar had neither the pure ruthlessness of a tyrant, nor the political sagacity to survive in a transitional period. Nevertheless there is a sense in which Caesar transcends his opponents. It is not really that he is more trustworthy, but that he thinks more broadly. If not by any means sublimely puissant, he still takes a truly high, lonely view; he thinks in terms of the northern star, the gods; his mind moves easily to the outskirts of the Roman domain where the exiles languish. He knows the magnitude and the necessary solitude of the responsibility of governing Rome, his eyes, in Yeats's phrase 'fixed upon nothing'. It is for this reason that his ghost can haunt Brutus, repeating the ominous place-name, Philippi, where the homesick republicans are to go under.

III

The way Shakespeare succeeds in maintaining sympathy with the republicans while almost analytically showing their mistakes is the most remarkable feature of *Julius Caesar*. The interest is partly that of recording the internal strains and complexities of a faction as it works itself out to defeat. Mutual loyalty, though impaired, keeps humanly alive right throughout, in contrast with the contradictions in the narrowly based alliance of the triumvirs. Brutus and Cassius, men of mixed temperaments, interact dramatically. We are not to suspect that Cassius, though most unscrupulous in his shrewdness, is *politically* insincere. He does, it is true, reinforce his influence with calumnies, but he naturally loves freedom. Nor is Brutus, on the other hand, committed entirely to open dealing. He admits in his first speech that his private worries have veiled his look, and his decision to participate in the use of force involves him in hypocrisy. A main theme is the disguise and misinterpretation of motive that must go on in a situation menaced by violence. The cross-assessments and counter-estimates, the generalisations on men and their worth, are not mere constructions of ambiguous 'characters' on Shakespeare's part, but fall essentially into a dialectic of suspicion. The overtone is one of uneasiness, where nothing but drastic evidence will serve and mistakes quickly multiply. As Cicero is made to comment,

> Indeed, it is a strange-disposed time:
> But men may construe things, after their fashion,
> Clean from the purpose of the things themselves.

This 'purpose of the things themselves' is felt in *Julius Caesar*, not as a supernatural fate, but as a power at once human, because the result of human actions in the past, and terribly inexorable. For respect for the logic of events does not mean that judgements of value are mere idealism. As Norman Rabkin says, Brutus's faults of perception 'undercut but do not vitiate the nobility of the character he demonstrates',[6] with the consequence that the coming Augustan peace is felt as peculiarly dubious. The play projects no welcome for it; the verse warms only to the values which it cannot foster.

In their discussion of principles provoked by the mob's adulation of Caesar off-stage, Brutus and Cassius define the serious Roman idea of honour. As distinct from the chivalrous honour ridiculed by Falstaff, 'the name of honour' here is associated by Brutus with what is 'toward the general good', as well as with courageous defiance of death. An honourable man puts first the interests of the whole state. Brutus's error is to conceive of 'the general' too narrowly, to concentrate on the patrician tradition of the past, on the capital city as the important arena, on a superficial experience of others as being all reasonable men of good will. It may be said that he assumes what is good for the public with a patronising disregard for what it wants, but he is not dogmatic. Honour is the subject of Cassius's story too, but his sarcasm soon establishes that Caesar's notion of honour is a purely competitive one; to 'get the start of the majestic world, / And bear the palm alone'. Cassius's attitude to Caesar is more than envy; he despises his philosophy as well as his physique. His dislike is only sharpened by the fact that Caesar's idea of political honour derives from personal sporting contests. Brutus picks up the bitterness when the second 'general shout' suggests to him applauses 'For some new honours that are heap'd on Caesar'. It is left to Cassius to clinch the point in his most important speech. A heavy emphasis is given to the dishonour in death which is in prospect if the republicans acquiesce in the court of events. This indignity he represents as an extreme disaster where manhood is crushed by an oppression that is monstrous.

> Why, man, he doth bestride the narrow world
> Like a Colossus, and we petty men
> Walk under his huge legs, and peep about
> To find ourselves dishonourable graves.

Cassius's bitter image of an autocracy where men (the vocative 'man' is not just expletive in this context) have no freedom of vision but to 'peep about' is effective, but his irony lacks a certain dimension. Caesar's power and opportunity depend on the fact that their world is no longer narrow, as Shakespeare surely means us to remember when later in the speech Cassius uses the literal epithet 'wide'. Now more rhetorical, he evokes the grand extension of Rome in time and space and yet still remains unconscious of the crucial inference.

> Age, thou art sham'd!
> Rome, thou hast lost the breed of noble bloods!
> When went there by an age, since the great flood,
> But it was fam'd with more than with one man?
> When could they say, till now, that talk'd of Rome,
> That her wide walls encompass'd but one man?
> Now is it Rome indeed, and room enough,
> When there is in it but one only man.

The word which betrays Cassius is 'walks'; he still, as the slip tells, confounds the state with the city. This defect is cleverly built into the expression of sentiments that are too obviously admirable. By setting the Colossus against a universal scale Cassius succeeds in reducing him three times to his real size, a meaning reinforced by the *pointilliste* emphasis of the verse. There are only five words in the passage quoted that are not monosyllabic.[7] The pun on Rome and room contains Cassius's contempt for the moral littleness of a society which could accept tyranny, but the ambiguities of 'room enough' are very dramatic. In the existing diffused state of the Roman dominions, could the political entity be preserved by more than one controller? Plutarch thought not. In this sense the tradition that, for Cassius, is Rome is no longer enough; it is sadly irrelevant to changed circumstances. Despite its noble antiquity the republicans' 'Rome' is empty of current significance, in hard political terms.[8] Shakespeare soon lets us know that Brutus too has missed this momentous point, when he affirms that he, in the deceptive objectivity of the third person,

> had rather be a villager
> Than to repute himself a son of Rome
> Under these hard conditions as this time
> Is like to lay upon us.

There is something of the villager in Brutus, if his outlook is parochial and nostalgic. Military power based on provincial conquest and demagogic power able to work the urban mob have made the republicans' situation more hopeless than they can admit. Nevertheless they are not presented as pathetically obsolete or ludicrously effete. Cassius, if not far-sighted, remains shrewd, and Brutus's thought has power, exerting a transforming influence in decisive scenes. But both leaders are doomed, as the supernatural omens clearly denote. Even after Cassius's boast that his strength of spirit cannot be bound by tyrants' chains, because of his freedom to kill himself, the stage direction contradicts him. *Thunder still.* The menace of fact is persistent.

IV

Act II of *Julius Caesar* is devoted mainly to the establishment of Brutus's charismatic quality. Shakespeare gives him a more positive personality than he could find in Plutarch ('a marvellous lowly and gentle person' – the Plutarch references can be found easily in the Arden edition). Cassius had said that Brutus's favour, 'like richest alchemy', will change the apparent offensiveness of the conspiracy 'to virtue and to worthiness'. Shakespeare softens the impact of the speeches in which Brutus justifies his consent of the act of assassination by framing them in dialogues with the boy, Lucius, whose innocent sleepfulness Brutus envies.

> Enjoy the honey-heavy dew of slumber:
> Thou hast no figures nor no fantasies
> Which busy care draws in the brains of men;
> Therefore thou sleep'st so sound.

His reluctance to disturb his servant is an aspect of the sensitivity which keeps him restless with scruples. His 'cause of grief' is his detestation of the means that must be used to redress 'the time's abuse'. Of the necessity of

Caesar's death he is convinced before he speaks. He does not believe that Caesar intends to be remorselessly tyrannical, but he knows that he is ambitious to be sole ruler, and that 'might change his nature', for absolute power lends itself to ineradicable abuse. If that fear is not sufficient motive, he taunts the conspirators,

> So let high-sighted tyranny range on,
> Till each man drop by lottery.

But the 'dreadful thing' of murder, which the 'moral instruments' must carry out, and the furtive, hypocritical aspects of organising it, he detests; he cannot give himself to the deed with a completely good will; his conscience worries him with nightmarish vividness. All this is creditable in Brutus (comparisons with Macbeth here are wide of the mark; Antony later admits that Brutus was not personally ambitious). Brutus's repugnance to secrecy and violence is admirably natural, but he is not, to the regret of some critics, a conscientious objector; he bravely commits himself to the assassination, though with genuine shudders. I cannot agree with L. C. Knights that Brutus is 'a man who tried to divorce his political thinking and his political action from what he knew, and what he was, as a full human person'.[9] For fullness of humanity requires a favourable political context. Brutus already felt his humanity menaced by Caesar; inactivity at this critical stage did not save Cicero from being later put to death by the triumvirs, as is emphasised. Sophisticated passivity is no viable alternative, however much one deplores what they did. Brutus's struggle to overcome his squeamishness pointedly enhances our acceptance of the 'even virtue' of their enterprise. At the same time we realise that in a world of opportunists it will only amount to a gesture. Brutus totally lacks a credible policy, imprudently trusts his opponents and makes culpable misjudgements on the course of events. That these are more than mistakes of detail we already discern in the speech in which he rules out an oath for the adherents to the faction. They need no other formality than having given their word as Romans in private, 'Than honesty to honesty engag'd', for breach of promise convicts a noble Roman of being illegitimate. Brutus's idealism is not essentially at fault, but his focus is badly blurred. His influence is impracticably conservative. His appeals invariably take the form of reminders about patrician ethical tradition. The patriotism refers to the small city-state of the past where it is conceivable to assess the nobility of 'every Roman'. The conspirators' horizon is the city-boundary, their prospect a retrospect. That distracting minute of chat in Act II, Scene i, between Decius, Cinna and Casca about the dawn, while Brutus and Cassius whisper, symbolically describes these limits; they do not know where in the urban landscape lies the east. Casca, pointing his sword, traces, like a well-informed but unimaginative weather-forecaster, the sun in March, 'a great way growing on the south' to its position in May, 'up higher toward the north'; so, he argues, 'the high east / Stands, as the Capitol, directly here'. Too soon their leaders will indeed experience 'the high east' on the provincial plains where they will face defeat, but Casca is confined to close-ups, his range foreshortened. By way of contrast, Caesar, Antony, Lepidus, and Octavius are all seasoned frontiersmen, ruthless tacticians conditioned by far-flung commands.

Cassius alone of the republicans seems to glance at the real threat, the strength of Caesar's supporters, when he urges that Antony, the 'shrewd contriver', should also be executed;

> and you know, his means,
> If he improve them, may well stretch so far
> As to annoy us all; . . .

this unspecified allusion may be to Antony's links with Octavius as well as to his rhetorical skill, but Cassius does not press his case. Brutus overrides it with his alarm that the people would condemn them for more killing than was strictly required and with his assurance that Antony would be powerless without his leader. Shakespeare means us to understand how ineptly Brutus mistakes the real centre of power, even confusing the general will with the shouts of the city-populace, but his insistence that bloodshed should be kept to a minimum is given, and carries, of course great weight. Paradoxically the blundering statement, 'Antony is but a limb of Caesar', suggests to Brutus his vital distinction between sacrificers and butchers, carvers and hewers, purgers and murderers. This speech,[10] though it has something of the sinister ring of the propagandist's set of euphemisms to modern ears, should not be read as moral self-deception on Brutus's part, as though he could believe that to regard assassination as a ceremony would lessen the amount of blood spilt. The killing is not to be ritualised so much as disciplined in order to underline to the people the republicans' control of their vicious passions, especially their wrath, by their 'hearts', that is, by a reasoned ethic based on common feeling. The speech reaches its climax in what is a profound, if bitterly ironic, truth.

> We all stand up against the spirit of Caesar,
> And in the spirit of men there is no blood.
> O, that we then could come by Caesar's spirit,
> And not dismember Caesar! But, alas,
> Caesar must bleed for it.

Against political force, whatever one's personal feelings towards those in power, there is no alternative resort but counter-force. This must be recognised, even though one must also insist on minimising the violence as much as possible. This is the point of the conspirators' 'purpose necessary, and not envious', but where Brutus's apologia falls down is in his failure to mention the guarantee of effectiveness. On any pragmatic test, their resistance to the spirit of Caesar shows up poorly. In a practical sense there is little chance that Caesar's spirit can be 'come by' after a single killing, as Antony's action confirms when, immediately after the assassination, he sends to Octavius. Brutus is only justifying what amounts to a tactic. His blindness is in not seeing that as such it could not serve. But this culpability of Brutus's is mitigated by the general foreboding which Shakespeare gives him with full seriousness of style throughout the scene, as when he undertakes to construe in his wife's presence 'All the charactery of my sad brows'. There is no undramatic dwelling on the brooding, and the scene ends briskly with a piece of striking stage-transformation. Ligarius, an actually sick man, appears, wearing a kerchief, the sign of his sickness, only to discard it on hearing that Brutus has in hand the expected 'exploit worthy the name of honour'. The feverish adherent speaks with an extravagance that is at once enthusiastic and ominous.

> Soul of Rome!
> Brave son, deriv'd from honourable loins!
> Thou, like an exorcist, hast conjur'd up
> My mortified spirit. Now bid me run,
> And I will strive with things impossible,
> Yea, get the better of them. What's to do?

This metamorphosis of Decreptitude into Resolution symbolises most economically the immense prestige of what Brutus stands for, the ancestral sanctions, the governing spirit working within the law, the civic pride. Yet the comparison with the magic of the necromancer is significantly unhappy. The accent is still that of hectic euphoria, hinting involuntarily that the question is not of what can cure a sickness, but of what is in reality dead.

After the murder the republicans assert joyfully that it is tyranny that is dead. Brutus calms their fitful fear of the mob with the ceremony, invented by Shakespeare for the occasion, of smearing their arms and swords with Caesar's blood. For Brutus the act is a sign of their common and open responsibility, but the visual indecency of its performance as a stage-spectacle convicts him here of inadequate sensitivity. Death looks ubiquitous in prospect, and there is nothing but dramatic irony in Brutus's revolutionary cry:

> Then walk we forth, even to the market-place,
> And waving our red weapons o'er our heads,
> Let's all cry, 'Peace, freedom, and liberty!'

The antique style of giving a direction and his unquestioning respect for the destination are so typical of Brutus. Subsequently in the market-place he addresses the people in a speech of quaint balances and patronising lucidity. He appears as a precise constitutionalist, sadly over-confident of his influence on events, his idealism spent in tired phrases. 'Who is here so rude, that would not be a Roman? . . . The question of his death is enroll'd in the Capitol; . . .' There could be no fitter comment on his incapacity than the total misunderstanding evident when the crowd takes up the cry, 'Let him be Caesar'. The conspirators can in fact go no further, and the point of view in the play has already shifted to take in Mark Antony, who cleverly improvises to get the situation under control. Antony had previously demanded to learn the reasons why Caesar was considered dangerous, but as soon as Brutus, against Cassius's advice, had agreed to let him speak at the funeral Antony was content not to hear the reasons: '. . . pity to the general wrong of Rome' was all that had been mentioned to him. His repudiation of the conspiracy first emerges in the episode where, left alone, he apostrophises Caesar's body with an apology for his seeming gentleness with

> . . . these butchers.
> Thou art the ruins of the noblest man
> That ever lived in the tide of times.

Antony turns Brutus's vocabulary cruelly against him in his absence. The sincerity of his loyalty to his dead leader is not in doubt, for he is determined not to do justice to the republicans. The military note predominates terribly as he foretells the merciless character of the widespread war which he is in fact willing to initiate.

> Domestic fury and fierce civil strife
> Shall cumber all the parts of Italy;
> . . . And Caesar's spirit, ranging for revenge,
> With Ate by his side come hot from hell,
> Shall in these confines with a monarch's voice
> Cry havoc . . .

The curse is pronounced with a revenger's relish. It is also appropriate that the ghost of Caesar is to retain 'a monarch's voice'. With Antony, as the moral response is at once lowered to barbarism, so the topographical range is correspondingly broadened ('these confines' are only the base from which the dogs of war are to be let slip). Octavius' servant enters to confirm that Caesar had already sent for his nephew; 'He lies to-night within seven leagues of Rome'. The phrasing, though it is unwarranted by Plutarch, seems to suggest an army pausing on the march. Plutarch says that Octavius was studying at Apollonia, tarrying for Caesar, 'because he was determined to make war with the Parthians'. It was Lepidus whose troops moved into the city of Rome the next night after the assassination. At any rate, Antony instructs the man to tell Octavius,

Here is a mourning Rome, a dangerous Rome,
No Rome of safety for Octavius yet.

The pun, an unconscious echo of Cassius's pun, again serves to keep in our imaginations the wider territorial room in which the militarists can group their forces. Shakespeare evidently wanted to hold over the entry of the soldiers till his scene had moved far from Rome. A similar, if this time incidental, effect can be noted from a passage in Antony's long demogogic speech to the people. He works on their imperialist sentiment as he displays Caesar's rent mantle.

I remember
The first time Caesar ever put it on;
'Twas on a summer's evening in his tent,
That day he overcame the Nervii.

Actually Antony had not been present at this victory over the Belgae, but powerful nostalgia for the field makes the conspirators' disloyalty seem treacherously ungrateful, and their perception of their own interests quite myopic. Once the mischief of the mob is set afoot by Antony's verbal incendiarism, which one sees as a classic example of oratorical manipulation, Shakespeare exaggerates the rapidity of events. Brutus and Cassius are reported to have fled before there is time to light the fires. Octavius and Lepidus are installed in Caesar's home, and Antony is willing to set up the triumvirate with them instantaneously, although Plutarch tells of a year's conflict between them. On the other hand the take-over of Rome by Lepidus's army is played down. The point is to dramatise that the furious mob gets no scope beyond what is implemental to the wishes of the friends of Caesar. The political aimlessness of the mob is enacted in the incident in which Cinna the poet is subjected to a disorderly catechism and then apparently torn to pieces for bearing the same name as one of the conspirators. The farce of mistaken identity is given a savage edge in this triumph of destructive unreason.

From this random victimisation we are turned to the cool but even more shocking scene (Act IV, Scene i) in which the three masters of the situation arrange in private the deaths of those who sympathise with their opponents. The grimly bargained proscriptions (Antony agrees to tick off his nephew's name – in Plutarch, an uncle's – in return for Lepidus's consent to the elimination of his own brother) convey immediately the energy and ruthlessness of the new government. Antony then sends Lepidus off to fetch Caesar's will so that they can misappropriate some of the funds which had been bequeathed, or so Antony had proclaimed, to the citizens (money-matters arise frequently from now on). As soon as Lepidus's back is turned, Antony falls to criticising him, not for 'the primal eldest curse' he has just earned, but for being unoriginal. He is an ass, a horse, a natural slave, and expendable. 'Do not talk of him / But as a property.' The triumvirs' alliance is purely an expedient, an affair of commodity, and already the time is anticipated when thieves will fall out. Antony assumes in himself too easily the qualities of leadership which he slights Lepidus for lacking. Octavius points out that Antony took Lepidus's opinion on the proscriptions and also 'he's a tried and valiant soldier', still the most relevant consideration at that juncture. Octavius has the last word in this scene, indicating by a calculating distrust how little he is convinced by Antony's showing. 'And some that smile have in their hearts, I fear, / Millions of mischiefs.' He gives expression here to an astuteness to match that of Cassius, which, together with his unusual self-command, constitutes his qualification for the leadership.

V

The real break in the structure of *Julius Caesar*, as most producers recognise,[11] occurs here, before the quarrel-scene between Brutus and Cassius. The shift of scene from Rome decisively ends the excitement and introduces a note of clipped pathos. The characters are men in uniform. In the vague place of Sardis, far from public buildings, on the outer edge of their world, the bleakness of the republicans' prospects is suggested, not only by the unfamiliar place-name, but also by the stiff military phrases which formerly articulate men are reduced to using for greetings: 'Stand ho! Speak the word along.' In the argument with Cassius, Brutus still insists on a guarantee of unimpeachable conduct.

> What, shall one of us,
> That struck the foremost man of all this world
> But for supporting robbers, shall we now
> Contaminate our fingers with base bribes,
> And sell the mighty space of our large honours
> For so much trash as may be grasped thus?

Caesar's support for robbers is adumbrated here for the first time in the play (it is found in Plutarch). Brutus does not necessarily mean that it was purposive support; much injustice is involved in a system tending to one-man rule, and Brutus possibly glances at Caesar's friends' conduct since his death to make the charge more plausible. But its straight dramatic point is to rebuke Cassius for venality. The emphasis falls on the gesture of grasping a contemptible handful of trash, with which Brutus contrasts 'the mighty space of our large honours'. His pleonasm is that of the false sublime. Their cause is near to inanity in their present predicament. Their language retains potency only in reference to the past. It is only remembrance of their former comradeship that lets Brutus drop his protests, as is demonstrated when Cassius invites him to strike at his breast, as he had done at Caesar's. Their common theme now is longing for the old Rome. The poetry takes on a tone of stern valediction. The twice-told report of Portia's death, unless it indicates authorial revision, points up Brutus's laconic endurance of sorrow. The uncertainty as to whether it was seventy or one hundred senators that the triumvirs had put to death is a kind of gruesome pedantry darkened further by the certainty that Cicero was one of them. The fatal decision to march to meet the enemy at Philippi is made as if it were their last chance. 'We, at the height, are ready to decline.' The melancholy mood comes into its own as Brutus bids everyone repeatedly, 'Good night', and Lucius plays his sleepy tune. Even Plutarch's 'horrible vision of a man', which showed plainly 'that the Gods were offended with the murther of Caesar', is toned down by Shakespeare into a dubious subjective apparition of Caesar himself shaped by the weakness of Brutus's eyes. Its message is fatalistically repeated by Brutus, but with calmness. If it is, as it says, Brutus's own 'evil spirit' (and it is heard by no one else), its relation to the Gods' opinions is left ambiguous. Brutus's subsequent behaviour is not that of a guilty man; it is not like Macbeth's after he has seen the ghost of Banquo. Caesar's ghost provides just another pointer to the unavoidable outcome; it signifies power rather than judgment. The definitive sense in which the spirit of Caesar is mighty yet is soon to be explained. The plot of the play turns, as Goethe says all Shakespeare's plots turn, upon the hidden point of conflict between 'the peculiarity of our *ego*, the pretended freedom of our will' and 'the necessary course of the *whole*' event. [12] The republican leaders quite foresee their defeat as probable, but remain patiently unrepentant. Brutus assures Cassius,

> think not, thou noble Roman,
> That ever Brutus will go bound to Rome;
> He bears too great a mind.

One may object to this self-estimate as somewhat vain without recoiling from the speaker. The context is one of solemn farewell and Brutus is refusing the alternative of survival as a prisoner. The ceremonial scene presented as they iterate their 'everlasting farewell' assures us that their parting is 'well made'. They have nothing to regret; their stand is not ultimately meaningless. In accordance with this attitude. Cassius in his last deed makes his servant Pindarus a freeman for assisting him in his suicide. Shakespeare gives to his bondman, whose soliloquy is entirely his own idea, a strangely exhilarating couplet, which breaks the slow monotony of sacrifice. He naïvely rebels against the whole Roman situation: he has known Rome enough.

> Far from this country Pindarus shall run,
> Where never Roman shall take note of him.

The audience cannot help responding to this healthy reaction. Pindarus's perfunctory dislike of Romans is perfectly natural, but we still feel that Cassius has deserved partly to be exempted. And Shakespeare has two magniloquent tributes in reserve for him; one from Titinius,

> The sun of Rome is set. Our day is gone;
> Clouds, dews, and dangers come; our deeds are done.

and then, from Brutus,

> The last of all the Romans, fare thee well!
> It is impossible that ever Rome
> Should breed thy fellow.

The idea that the tragedy marks the demise of a historical tradition could not be more obviously stated. Both Brutus and Cassius die with a mention of Caesar's posthumous revenge, but Brutus's resignation and his final recollection of the doubtful will with which he had killed Caesar do not mean crudely that he got what he deserved. More neutrally, he got what was coming to him.

Shakespeare's *Julius Caesar*, though far from biassed in favour of Caesar's assassins, no doubt contributed to republican sentiment in 17th-Century England. But the play is not a tract for those who need an unmistakeable commitment. The tone of the verse, often praised for its augustness, restraint and classical spirituality, is in fact predominantly one of hopelessness. The nobility it celebrates had become too shrunken for grandeur. But the conspiracy against Caesar is not shown merely as the mistake of men who did not understand politics well enough to bring off a complex success; it emerges as a last stroke of defiance in a society which had become impervious to political subtlety. *Julius Caesar* mourns the supercession of a political tradition by armed force. The conditions for the old politics cannot be re-established by assassination. As in *Hamlet*, free consciousness is confronted by a primitive demand and destroys itself in a revenge-feud. But there is nothing modern about *Julius Caesar*. There is no wasted future to lament, only an irrelevant past and a vacant centre. The city of Rome was no longer the real landscape of government, but on the perimeter of her world the ignorant armies clashed, sounding the prelude to empire. There the political dramatist, like the free Pindarus, nimbly gets out.

Notes

1   Robert B. Heilman, 'To know himself: an aspect of tragic structure', in *A Review of English Literature*, 5 (April 1964), p. 41.
2   John Anson has argued in his 'Caesar's stoic pride', in *Shakespeare: Julius Caesar* (Casebook, ed. P. Ure, 1969, p. 215), reprinted from *Shakespeare Studies*, 2 (1966), that in his whole presentation of Caesar's illness Shakespeare 'is attempting to represent the pathological constrictiveness of Stoic morality'.
3   In *The Massacre at Paris* Marlowe, or the actors, had made the wicked Guise talk of himself as Caesar. Elizabethan ambivalence with regard to Caesar is examined in G. Bullough's *Narrative and Dramatic Sources of Shakespeare*, 5 (1964).
4   See note to Act III, Scene i, pp. 47–8, in the Arden edition, p. 65, for a review of this controversy.
5   *Loc. cit.*, p. 218.
6   N. Rabkin, 'Structure, convention, and meaning in *Julius Caesar*', in *Journal of English and Germanic Philology*, 63 (1964), 244.
7   Mark Van Doren, in his 1939 essay on *Julius Caesar*, reprinted in L. Dean's *Twentieth Century Interpretations of Julius Caesar* (1968), pp. 8–16, argues that 'the music of monosyllables' is no one speaker's monopoly in the play, the purpose at all times being 'to pour into the ear an unimpeded stream of eloquence, a smooth current of artful sound' (p. 11). But Shakespeare uses it very discriminatingly in fact.
8   R. A. Foakes, in 'An approach to *Julius Caesar*', in *Shakespeare Quarterly* 5 (1954), 267–8, notes that the words 'Rome' and 'Roman' occur 72 times in the play and, after Act III until Antony's tribute to Brutus, 'only in the mouths of the rebels'. One could compare the way the words 'British Empire' occurred only in the mouths of certain politicians between, say, 1945 and 1955.
9   L. C. Knights, 'Personality and Politics in *Julius Caesar*', in *Further Explorations* (1965); reprinted in P. Ure's 'Casebook', p. 138.
10 Act II, Scene i, pp. 162–83; Brents Stirling, in his 'Ritual in *Julius Caesar*' (1956), reprinted in P. Ure's 'Casebook', p. 164, argues that Brutus is being evasive; he needs 'ceremony which will purify the violent act of all taint of butchery', but one must remember that the metaphors refer to keeping down the numbers likely to be killed by them, if carried away by anger.
11 Many critics, however, see the entrance of Antony's servant in Act III, Scene i as the turning point of the play; see L. Kirschbaum, in his 'Shakespeare's stage blood', in *PMLA*, 64 (1949), reprinted in P. Ure's 'Casebook', p. 157. But I believe the conspirators' discomfiture in Rome must follow the murder without a break.
12 G. H. Lewes, *The Life and Works of Goethe* (1855), 2, Ch. 6. Goethe's 'Oration on Shakespeare' (1771) is translated there by George Eliot evidently.

[1970]

DAVID PIRIE

Hamlet without the Prince

I

Perhaps Shakespeare was drunk, mused Voltaire, discussing the peculiarities of *Hamlet*. Certainly it is a bizarre work, though nowadays its real strangeness is seldom noticed. The tedious debate as to whether Hamlet is unnecessarily slow to kill the King and if so why seems to have distracted us from much more strikingly odd elements in the play. G. B. Harrison, for instance, devotes twenty pages of his essay to convincing himself 'that in the play which Shakespeare wrote there was no delay', and so leaves himself only one paragraph in which to acknowledge that Shakespeare seems to keep abandoning his play about Denmark to write about something else:

> for some reason he used *Hamlet* as a vessel into which he poured his thoughts on all kinds of matters which have very little to do with the action of the play. The interpolation on the siege of Ostend has already been noticed. The advice to the players on rant and clowning is likewise a topicality, and directed at two recognisable actors, Edward Alleyne and Will Kempe. There is a comment of forty lines on the Stage War then raging, and on the Children's Companies which were such dangerous rivals to the Chamberlain's Men in 1600 and 1601 ... Apart from these, some of the more famous of the set speeches are comments on general problems which neither help the plot nor greatly add to the characterisation. (*Shakespeare's Tragedies*, 109–10)

To Harrison these are irrelevancies too slight to damage the play's real power, which lies elsewhere. They merely 'give the play a certain leisurely air so that concentration of incident and speech is dissipated'. But surely the Prince's habit of chatting to the audience about matters which have nothing to do with his situation as a Danish courtier and often a great deal to do with theirs as people listening to him in an English theatre is crucial. Through it Hamlet tells the audience that his Elsinore existence seems to him a meaningless theatrical game. His view from the outset is that which Macbeth is eventually driven to:

> Life's but a walking shadow, a poor player
> That struts and frets his hour upon the stage,
> And then is heard no more. It is a tale
> Told by an idiot, full of sound and fury,
> Signifying nothing.

Hamlet's own fascination with actors who have 'strutted and bellowed' their way across a stage (III.ii.32) grows from his bitter appreciation of the analogy. The 'real' world of Elsinore is too vile to be comfortably believed in, too absurd to be taken seriously. It signifies nothing more than a number of bad plays. The ghost has cast Hamlet for the role of ruthless hero in a conventional revenge tragedy. Claudius expects him to pursue the plots of an ambitious claimant to the throne in a political drama. Polonius sees him playing Romeo to Ophelia's Juliet in a tragedy of star-crossed lovers parted by their fathers. Fortinbras – less consciously of course – challenges the Prince to accept the role of a Danish Henry V, and play out a military epic of the kind performed by old Fortinbras and old Hamlet. Hamlet's instinct is to reject all these scripts as morally and intellectually unworthy. The audience is asked to enjoy the tension created by the leading player's refusal to act in the play.

I I

The refusal often amounts to a comic detachment, though modern productions are usually too solemn to let the humour have free rein. It was not always so. In 1604 Anthony Scoloker defined the ideal play as one in which 'the Commedian rides, when the Tragedian stands on Tiptoe' so as to 'please all, like *Prince Hamlet*'. Even a critic as innocent of excessive levity as Doctor Johnson found that 'the pretended madness of Hamlet causes much mirth'; and Coleridge found it impossible to define the limits of the play's humour: 'In *Hamlet* the Fool is, as it were, divided into several parts, dispersed through the whole piece'. Certainly most of the important characters have their moments of unconscious comedy as they play out their insane games with pompous earnestness. But the professional comic of the play, the joke-spinner, the jig-maker, would have been quickly recognised by the contemporary audience as none other than the Prince. He admits it himself, reminding them why he has ended up treating life as a sick joke; he is: 'your only jig-maker. What should a man do but be merry, for look you how cheerfully my mother looks, and my father died within's two hours' (III.ii.124–6). Hamlet is the play's official punster, offering verbal wit where the plot demands action, evading the latent tragedy of his situation in grim jests. But the pun has gone out of fashion. We are still aware of the sombre appropriateness in Hamlet's word-play but ignorant of the genuine humour that used to accompany it. From his first line ('A little more than kin, and less than kind') Hamlet is established as determined to send up his own play with bitter jests. He maintains his role of comic until the end but what modern production reveals the humour with which he poisons the King? It is undoubtedly there. He has already stabbed Claudius with the envenomed sword. So when he insists that the dying man should drink the wine that killed Gertrude, Hamlet is being theatrical:

165

David Pirie

> Here, thou incestuous, murderous, damned Dane
> > (*He forces him to drink*)
> Drink off this potion. Is thy union here?
> Follow my mother. (V.ii.323–5)

The situation would seem too desperate to allow room for mere games of poetic justice. But Hamlet is lured on by the opportunities in that word 'union'. This can mean either the poisoned pearl that Claudius himself put in the wine; or it can mean the relationship between man and wife which has just ended a second time in murder. Even here where Hamlet has finally been tricked into a show-down, he cannot be merely pragmatic. The comedian in him is distracted by awareness of what will entertain the spectators: the people he describes in his next speech as 'mutes or audience to this act'.

Hamlet's jokes have not been wholly ignored by modern critics. But the response is normally to explain them away until they are no longer jokes at all. The easy assertion that their incongruity reinforces the tragedy without seriously complicating our attitude towards it, is still common. An unusually scholarly version of this paradox is offered by Lily B. Campbell who sees *Hamlet* as an exercise in pathology, the prince exemplifying the deterioration of a man of sanguine humour into a hopeless case of melancholy. She cites the grave-diggers' scene as one in which:

> Hamlet exhibits another accepted manifestation of his being the victim of melancholy adust as it is derived from the sanguine humour, for the sanguine adust turns tragedies into comedies as does Hamlet here while he jests with horrors. (*Shakespeare's Tragic Heroes*, 1930)

The Prince's effort to push his play towards comedy are immediately allowed by Miss Campbell to sink back beneath the dark waters of Elizabethan medical jargon. But it surely raises important questions. Harry Levin allows himself a slightly bolder flirtation with the idea, remarking that Hamlet 'becomes a court jester ... at the court where he cannot be king, must perforce be fool, an artificial fool pretending to be a natural' (*The Question of Hamlet*, 1959). Later on Levin quotes Erasmus' view of life as a kind of comedy in which 'men come forth disguised one in one array, another in another, each playing his part ... And all this is done under a certain veil or shadow, which taken away once, the play can no more be played'. Levin himself seems unruffled by the bizarre implications of Erasmus' remarks. But surely Hamlet as court jester is committed to rending the veil, and so threatens to make the Elsinore play unplayable. Levin's own conclusion is more cautious. Hamlet's irreverent wit is for him but one aspect of a character who remains safely within his play: 'Hamlet's complexity is compounded of many simples: the frustrated scholar, the unwilling courtier, the mourner who becomes a revenger, the lover whose imagination rages like that of the lunatic or the poet, and still others – not least the witty fool.' To me these roles seem more clearly interconnected: the scholarly mourner with a lover's imagination is asked to express himself in impossible terms: the scripts of court dialogue and the plots of revenge melodrama. He is compelled to resist either by becoming the poet and trying to rewrite the play or by playing the fool and laughing at it from the outside. Levin himself at one point seems to suggest that Hamlet, if not actually outside the play, is yet strangely intimate with the audience:

> Hamlet disapproves of comedians who attract attention by speaking 'more than is set down for them' (III.ii.38). Yet his own performance *ad libitum*, during the presentation of the play-within-the-play, is aptly compared by Francis Fergusson to the improvised antics of a 'night-club entertainer'. In his manic phase, after the success of the entertainment, Hamlet momentarily toys with the notion of turning actor; and he displays the showman's aplomb when, by acting out the object-lessons of the recorder and of the cloud, he tells off Rosencrantz, Guildenstern and Polonius . . . He indulges his own humour – and that of the audience.

Hamlet's relationship with the audience is distinctly odd. His disengagement from the dramatic actions of Elsinore leads him closer to the calm observations of the spectators in the Globe. His response to the Ghost's anguished revelations is to copy down in his tables or note-book his father's memorable exit line:

> My tables, meet it is I set it down   (*he writes*)
> That one may smile, and smile, and be a villain,
> At least I'm sure it may be so in Denmark . . .
> So, uncle, there you are. Now, to my Word,
> It is 'Adieu, adieu, remember me.'   (I.v.107–11)

In fact the original player of the Prince would at this moment be doing exactly what some members of the audience were doing: jotting down the best lines. In the First Quarto of *Hamlet* itself a clown is accused of being so unoriginal that 'gentlemen quote his jests down in their tables *before* they come to the play'. A character in Marston's *Malcontent* remarks: 'I am one that hath seen this play often. I have most of the jests here in my table-book'. At such moments – and they are frequent – Hamlet reminds the audience that they are watching a play. In the famous conversation about contemporary theatre he even goes so far as to remind them that they are watching specifically in the Globe theatre beneath the flag which pictures Hercules carrying the world:

> *Hamlet*   Do the boys carry it away?
> *Rosencrantz*   Ay, that they do my lord, Hercules and his load too.

David Pirie

Hamlet	It is not very strange, for my uncle is king of Denmark, and those that would make mows at him while my father lived, give twenty, forty, fifty, a hundred ducats apiece for his picture in little. (II.ii.363–9)

Hamlet has led Rosencrantz to explain the latest developments between the theatres which compete for the contemporary public. The audience is accused of being all to willing to take their custom off to the fashionable Children of the Chapel company. Suddenly he asks them to think of him as a despairing Danish prince. John Dover Wilson is typical of most commentators on this passage when he blandly remarks: 'The fickleness of popular favour brings Hamlet back from Shakespeare's London to Elsinore'. But surely his commuting so openly between the two needs explaining. A. P. Rossiter seems alone in trying to respond fully to the challenge:

> The 'factual' world of Elsinore is not *real*. It sugars o'er the devil himself. . . It is because of this confusion of worlds and realities – with the real most unreal and the ordinary business of Courts a most extraordinary and poisonous charade – that the Players ('incarnation of the unreal', as Granville-Barker calls them) enter into the play's second movement, and 'playing' becomes a main theme in the third. Nor is it disharmonious irrelevance, or forced topicality, which makes these players the Lord Chamberlain's, troubled about little eyases; and themselves troubling William Shakespeare by periwig-pated ear-splittings or clownish gaggings. It *is* disharmony, but relevant: since about illusion..

III

Rossiter's stimulating – if rather vague – hints seems to me worth developing.

Certainly for Hamlet the artificial stage of the Globe and the fraudulent trappings of the court world are all too similar. He says that the earth is no more meaningful than the bare boards of the apron stage, the sky no more heavenly than the painted stars and moon which decorate the ceiling of the Elizabethan inner stage:

> indeed it goes so heavily with my disposition, that this goodly frame the earth, seems to me a sterile promontory, this most excellent canopy the air, look you, this brave o'erhanging firmament, this majestical roof fretted with golden fire, why it appeareth nothing to me but a foul and pestilent congregation of vapours.   (II.ii.301–7)

The use of 'this' demands that the actor points but at what can he point in a modern theatre? Few have a stage shaped like a promontory running out into the audience. None have either the gaudy inlaid ceiling of the inner stage nor the real weather of an English sky above a roofless auditorium. But originally the point must have been clear. The prince explains his depressed withdrawal in terms of the audience's immediate experience. The earnest lunacies of Elsinore seem to him no more real, no more demanding of his participation than the play-acting seems to the audience. Later in the scene Hamlet points out that the analogy can be carried further. Not only is the ornate stage-sky a false idealisation of the real one, but the players will each in his own role deny the bitter truth of reality: 'He that plays the King shall be welcome, his majesty shall have tribute of me, the adventurous Knight shall use his foil and target, the Lover shall not sigh gratis, . . . and the Lady shall say her mind freely' (II.ii. 323–9). Only player-kings deserve honour. Only player-soldiers do not kill – the latest editor of *Hamlet* remarks that foil and target mean 'a light fencing sword and light shield; a real knight would have heavier weapons, but these light ones are enough for a player-knight'. Only in an idealised play will the sighs of a lover like Hamlet get their reward rather than be for nothing. Only in a play will Ophelia be allowed to express her love openly. Hamlet knows that *his* king is a usurper, that Claudius in spite of the sycopantic tributes of the court is unworthy of respect. He knows that Fortinbras who may look like a glamorous epic hero, an adventurous Knight, is inevitably a mass-murderer. He knows that his sighing letters to Ophelia will be read by his enemies. He knows that far from being able to speak her mind freely, Ophelia will allow apparently private conversations to be rigged by eavesdroppers. He knows in fact that every relationship, every activity that Elsinore offers him is a false script. In this same scene Rosencrantz claims that 'the world's grown honest', that he and Guildenstern are Hamlet's friends. They want him to relax and trustingly reveal any ambitions he may have to recover the crown from Claudius. But ambitious plots imply hope and Hamlet cannot express his insights in such cheery terms. He tells them merely that Denmark is a prison, and that the whole world is a prison 'in which there are many confines, wards, and dungeons'. Similarly he cannot follow the script of jolly courtliness offered by Polonius:

Polonius	How does my good Lord Hamlet?
Hamlet	Well, God-a-mercy.
Polonius	Do you know me, my lord?
Hamlet	Excellent well, you are a fishmonger.

A few lines later Polonius asks him what he is reading and Hamlet answers: 'Words, words, words'. This is a deflating comment not just on his book and on the fraudulence of Polonius. It questions the value of drama itself. Where in these plots and dialogues can Hamlet express his true self?

These moments of impatience in which Hamlet not only rejects the scripts offered him by other characters, but seems to be trying to lure them into a

David Pirie

new one of his own have led some critics off at a sentimental tangent. If Hamlet's attempts to be a playwright are not confined to his adapting *The Murder of Gonzago* into *The Mousetrap*, then perhaps we have here a portrait of Shakespeare. This misleading view was stated most bluntly by H. A. Taine who decided that 'Hamlet is Shakespeare'. Bradley more temperately observed that he is at least the only Shakespearean character whom we can conceive of as the author of Shakespeare's plays. Shakespeare, of course, called his son Hamnet and G. B. Harrison remarks that when Shakespeare was fifteen a girl called Katherine Hamlet 'of Tiddington, about a mile from Stratford, fell into the water and was drowned at a spot where the Avon's banks in summer are overhung by willows and thickly crowned with wild flowers'. But if the memory of this did inspire the dirge for Ophelia it obviously does not prove any autobiographical intention in the play. The essential distinction is surely between seeing Hamlet as Shakespeare's portrait of himself as an individual on the one hand, and on the other recognising the play as an analysis of drama, Shakespeare's own craft, which inevitably suggests some kind of portrait of the artist. The questions raised are not as personal as Harold C. Goddard suggests in asking: 'What if Shakespeare had turned from writing *Hamlets* and *King Lears* to go to war like Essex, or, like Hamlet to run his rapier through an old man behind a curtain!'. Such questions lead Goddard to bury all the humour of the play-scene in moralistic solemnity. To him *The Murder of Gonzago* is the pious alternative to murder:

> Why not make his art an instrument for finding out whether the King is guilty, an instrument not of revenge, but of revelation?
>
>> The spirit that I have seen
> May be the devil.
>
> The play's the thing wherein to discover whether it was the devil or not. It is an inspiration if Hamlet ever had one – no injunction from a dead man but an intimation from his own innermost genius. His evil spirit has told him to kill the King. His good angel tells him to show the King to himself by holding up the mirror of art before him. The dagger or the play? That is the question. It is God's Hamlet who chooses the play.

Goddard thus sees the *Murder of Gonzago* as the turning-point at which the hero is corrupted into joining the sordid world of violent action:

> Hamlet has an opportunity to act like Shakespeare . . . In so far as he regards *The Murder of Gonzago* as such a work and is willing to let it have its own way with the King, he is doing what his soul calls him to do. But in so far as he regards it as a trap, an engine for torturing a victim, for catching not the King's conscience but the King himself, the play is nothing but a contrivance for murder.
> (*The Meaning of Shakespeare*, 1951)

Wilson Knight in ' "Hamlet" Reconsidered' offers an equally earnest view. Hamlet's moral doubts force him to seek an alternative to bloodshed, and he finds 'the artists's solution' of the play before the King: 'It is approach, attack, and love, all in one. Hamlet becomes therefore a critic of society resembling Moliere, Voltaire, Swift, Ibsen, Shaw, using art . . . to awake conscience.' The fact that four of the five supposedly relevant writers are humorists should surely have led Wilson Knight to question his own view of Hamlet's solemnity as a dramatist. But he continues unabashed:

> He wants to bring truth to light:
> The play's the thing
> Wherein I'll catch the conscience of the King!   (II.ii.608–9)

> Let 'King' stand for government, for society, the world over and 'the play' for dramatic art, so consistently concerned with sin and conscience, at all times and places.
>
> *(The Wheel of Fire, 1949)*

But surely the truth is that Hamlet's amateur theatricals turn out to offer him further amusing opportunities to remind the audience that they, like the courtiers, are watching a play. His role here as dramatic critic makes it difficult for either the play within the play or the overall scene in which the court watches it to keep the serious involvement of the theatre audience. It embarrasses them until like 'guilty creatures sitting at a play' they question the value of responding to a fictional story's 'cue for passion'. In spite of Hamlet's writing 'a speech of some dozen or sixteen lines' for *The Mousetrap*, in spite of his re-scripting the plot of a letter so that Rosencrantz and Guildenstern have their roles changed from murderers into victims, Hamlet's most frequent response to his play is not an attempt to rewrite it into a moral work 'concerned with sin and conscience'. His most frequent response is an often disconcertingly humorous rejection.

IV

Hamlet rejects his play, insists it is only a play, undermines its tone with jokes, and frustrates its plot by inactivity because it is a bad play, untrue to him and untrue to life. It is populated by dishonest characters pursuing hollow crowns and faithless women. All their frenetic activity can achieve nothing more significant than the cardboard crown of a player-king or the lisped endearments of a boy-actor dressed in women's clothes. This rejection seems, oddly enough, to have been what T. S. Eliot dimly sensed:

> The only way of expressing emotion in the form of art is by finding an 'objective correlative'; in other words a set of objects, a situation, a chain of events which

> shall be the formula of that *particular* emotion . . . The artistic 'inevitability' lies
> in the complete adequacy of the external to the emotion; and this is precisely
> what is deficient in *Hamlet*.

Eliot then betrays this sound observation in the staggeringly obtuse
conclusion that Shakespeare here 'tackled a problem which proved too
much for him'. Actually Shakespeare has Hamlet himself begin the play by
bemoaning the lack of objective correlative. He complains that the weapons
of theatre – costume, gesture, facial expression – and the forms of court
ceremony – mourning and so on – are inadequate to express his profound
despair:

> Seems, madam! nay it is, I know not 'seems'.
> 'Tis not alone my inky cloak, good mother,
> Nor customary suits of solemn black,
> Nor windy suspiration of forced breath,
> No, nor the fruitful river in the eye,
> Nor the dejected 'haviour of the visage,
> Together with all forms, modes, shapes of grief,
> That can denote me truly. These indeed seem,
> For they are actions that a man might play,
> But I have that within which passes show,
> These but the trappings and the suits of woe.   (I.ii.76–86)

So Hamlet knows from the outset that his world offers him no 'set of objects'
which can accurately reflect his feelings. He knows that in Elsinore he cannot
find 'a situation, a chain of events which shall be the formula of that *particular*
emotion'. Consider Laertes as a contrast. When Laertes thinks that *his* father
has been killed by Claudius, his grief is specific enough to find adequate
expression in armed rebellion. But Hamlet's response is more sensitively
inclusive. For him *all* the uses of the world become 'weary, stale, flat, and
unprofitable' (I.ii.133–4). Anyway Hamlet knows that the kind of 'just' wars
that Laertes trusts to are really the sacrifice of 'Two thousand souls' in a
cause as ultimately trivial as an 'egg-shell'. It is slaughter for nothing more
than 'a fantasy and trick of fame' (IV.iv). The lack of objective correlative
which is Hamlet's problem is solved artistically by the theatrical metaphor.
His sense that action cannot faithfully reveal emotion is demonstrated by
reference to the limitations of the art-form of drama. What Hamlet cannot
define for the audience in deeds, he can show them through their own
detachment from a play they don't *really* believe in. According to the Second
Quarto there is a flourish of trumpets before two superficially very different
entries. One is when the King and his court come on in I.ii. The other is when
the chief player (who later plays the King) and his troupe march on in II.ii.
For Hamlet both are merely theatrical flourishes. Like the audience he can
find Claudius interesting enough for a play and is therefore prepared to

goad him with *The Mousetrap*. But when in the next scene he is invited to involve himself to the extent of killing the king, he opts out. His excuse is a dogmatic theory about the after-life which we know from the soliloquies is a source of endless doubt for him. The effect is that Hamlet, like the audience, does nothing. To admit the validity of action would be to deny his own sense of existence as meaningless. To him the world is a bad play for which he is willing to be 'as good as a chorus' (III.ii.245), but not as earnestly involved as an actor.

However Hamlet is, of course, sometimes tricked into action by the energy with which the other characters pursue the plot. So in blind anger when he thinks that Claudius has been placed by his mother to eavesdrop on their private talk, he stabs through the arras, only to find the wholly inappropriate object of a dead Polonius. Action is absurdly ineffectual, and yet characters like Claudius believe in it with the ignorant faith of children. Hamlet is forced to explode potential tragedy into farce:

> King   Now, Hamlet, where's Polonius?
> Hamlet At supper.
> King   At supper? where?
> Hamlet Not where he eats, but where a' is eaten – a certain convocation of
> politic worms are e'en at him: your worm is your only emperor for
> diet, we fat all creatures else to fat us, and we fat ourselves for
> maggots. Your fat king and your lean beggar is but variable service,
> two dishes, but to one table – that's the end.
> King   Alas! Alas!

Hamlet goes on with his jokes to show Claudius that the crown for which he struggled so feverishly is useless since 'a king may go a progress through the guts of a beggar'. Finally the exasperated Claudius shouts again 'Where is Polonius?' and Hamlet throws out his crushingly casual punchline: 'But if indeed you find him not within this month, you shall nose him as you go up the stairs into the lobby' (IV.iii.16–36). Now this is all meant to be funny as well as disturbing. I cannot share Wilson Knight's almost hysterical revulsion. Before he dares quote the passage, he warns the sensitive reader that these 'disgusting words' are 'even more horrible' than Hamlet's ungentlemanly remarks to his mother, and later apologises for having to shock the reader with such obscenities: 'A long and unpleasant quotation, I know. But it is necessary'. His later essay seems to me to be groping towards a healthier response: 'Like many a poet or dramatist (e.g. Byron, Shaw), Hamlet attacks society by wit and buffoonery, as well as by play-production.' Our response to Hamlet's buffoonery about Polonius, the archetype of Elsinore society, is clearly crucial. Of course Hamlet's attitude here does partly strike us as dangerously insensitive and to this I want to return later. But in at least two ways we recognise that his irreverence is wittily appropriate.

Firstly, there is the moralistic view that Polonius deserves no better. He is merely a puppet – not just because his strings are pulled by Claudius – but because he cannot see his fellow human beings as more than puppets. He has no respect for their privacy because he cannot identify with those intimate, intense emotions that privacy preserves. Having no heart himself, no secrets, nothing to declare but words, words, words, he can rummage without embarrassment in other people's lives. But the same emotional deficiency which allows him to do it without shame ensures that he does it without insight. He will learn no more about his son in using Reynaldo as agent provocateur than a list of puppet-actions: 'drinking, fencing, swearing, quarrelling, drabbing' (II.i.25). An audience's intellectual snobbery is bound to reinforce their moral distaste for Polonius and weaken his chances of sympathy. His stupidity as well as his nastiness ensures that we reject him in III.i. In instructing Ophelia in her part, he reveals himself as incapable of recognising either her complexity or her preciousness:

> Ophelia, walk you here – (To the King), Gracious, so please you,
> We will bestow ourselves – (To Ophelia) Read on this book
> That show of such an exercise may colour
> Your loneliness.

To Polonius, the producer of this wretched little play, she is no more than a performing doll. He continues into an admission which Claudius is forced more thoughtfully to share:

> We are oft to blame in this,
> 'Tis too much proved, that with devotion's visage
> And pious action we do sugar o'er
> The devil himself.
> King   O 'tis too true!
> How smart a lash that speech doth give my conscience.
> The harlot's cheek, beautied with plast'ring art,
> Is not more ugly to the thing that helps it,
> Than is my deed to my most painted word:

The two men are not only making a harlot of Ophelia in their politic stage-managing. They are also prostituting the noble roles of King and Chancellor. Claudius is at least aware of this. He may send Rosencrantz and Guildenstern into a drama of false friendship so that he can extract information from their old school chum. But he is painfully aware of the values that such devices seem to ignore. His aside here, together with his prayer-scene soliloquy, balance our impression of his shallowness which we form on the evidence of his speeches in dialogue and his deeds. Polonius on the other hand can see no difference between a true King and the one he has presumably created – the Chancellor must have had a large say in 'the election'. He does not comprehend the love that may lie behind the nunnery scene. He clearly has no real affection or understanding for either of the children to whom he so pompously acts the role of the concerned father. He is equally blind to the potential intensity of relationships between mothers and their sons. His plan for Gertrude's script in III.i is that it should provoke Hamlet to passionate revelation:

> Let his queen-mother all alone entreat him
> To show his grief, let her be round with him.   (III.i.185)

and he guarantees to Claudius the production of a rousing performance: 'I'll warrant she'll tax him home' (III.iii.29). In his last instructions to Gertrude he repeatedly demands that she should play boldly with the fire which leads to his own destruction:

> A' will come straight. Look you lay home to him,
> Tell him his pranks have been too broad to bear with,
> And that your grace hath screened and stood between
> Much heat and him. I'll silence me even here –
> Pray you be round with him.

Polonius dies because he has no comprehension of the feelings his last production will arouse. He himself has long ago died emotionally so that to him Hamlet's attempts to express his despairing detachment are merely 'pranks'. There is a kind of logic in Hamlet's regarding the removal of such a 'rash, intruding fool' as itself little more than a prank.

But there is a second way in which an audience can see the end of Polonius as the discarding of a puppet rather than the murder of a man: Polonius is after all only an actor on the stage of the Globe theatre. It is only make-belief as the insistent references to contemporary stage gossip keep stressing. In III.ii the actor playing Polonius has to say: 'I did enact Julius Caesar. I was killed i' the Capitol. / Brutus killed me.' To which the actor playing Hamlet replies: 'It was a brute part of him to kill so capital a calf there.' Now Shakespeare's company had put on his *Julius Caesar* just a few months before the first production of *Hamlet*. The male lead of Brutus had presumably been taken by the actor now pretending to be the Prince, and the older part of Caesar by the actor now playing Polonius. In both plays the same actor pushes the same wooden sword against the same colleague. The Globe audience were meant to notice this. Similarly they must have been meant to register the parody of contemporary play-bills in Polonius's 'tragical-comical-historical-pastoral' and so on; Dover Wilson suggests the Admiral's Men as a specific target here. Certainly when Hamlet in the next

David Pirie

line calls Polonius old Jephthah he must be pointing to that company's production in July 1601 of Dekker and Mundy's play, *Jephthah Judge of Israel*. Hamlet in thus deliberately reminding the audience how far they are from Elsinore does not persuade them to go all the way with him in dismissing Polonius as a trivial artefact. But he does through this theatre metaphor define for them his own disengagement from what by conventional assumptions would be 'enterprises of great pitch and moment'. (III.i.86)

Hamlet's disengagement amounts to more than a statement about his own situation. It constitutes a major criticism of conventional drama. Wordsworth in his only attempt at a tragedy discovered the paradox that drama works through deeds and conversation but the subject of tragedy is often passive and lonely suffering:

> Action is transitory – a step, a blow,
> The motion of a muscle – this way or that –
> 'Tis done, and in the after-vac...cy
> We wonder at ourselves like men betrayed:
> Suffering is permanent, obscure and dark,
> And shares the nature of infinity.   (*The Borderers*, 1538–43)

Throughout *Hamlet* action is clumsy and grotesque, continually failing to express the feelings or intentions of those who attempt it: Laertes, for instance, trying to kill his only ally against the real murderer of his father or trying to define his grief at his sister's death by a sordid punch-up at her grave; Claudius accidentally poisoning his wife; Hamlet driving the girl he loves to suicide. These are men whose transitory actions leave them wondering at themselves as if betrayed, baffled by the permanence of the havoc they have wrought. Macbeth's tale of sound and fury signifying nothing becomes in *Hamlet* a chaotic anthology:

> Of accidental judgements, casual slaughters,
> Of deaths put on by cunning and forced cause,
> And, in this upshot, purposes mistook
> Fall'n on the inventors' heads.   (V.ii.380–3)

It is little wonder that Hamlet regards the plot of his play as an unreliable vehicle for his feelings. The gulf between his sense of suffering as obscure and dark on the one hand and the plot's manic pace is total. This gulf baffled Voltaire who complained that though the 'vulgar and barbarous' plot was absurd, the play contained 'some sublime passages worthy of the greatest genius'. G. H. Lewes too found *Hamlet* a bewildering juxtaposition 'of reflection with tumult, of high and delicate poetry with broad, palpable, theatrical effects. The machinery is a machinery of horrors ... by which moves the highest, the grandest, and the most philosophic of tragedies'. But

176

this juxtaposition is the essence of the play's form and meaning, and the core of Hamlet's problem. Wondering whether to be or not to be, musing on 'the dread of something after death', probing the nature of infinity cannot be expressed in specific choices of plot or in the dialogue which is nearly always some sort of sparring match with *agents provocateurs*. So Hamlet has to opt out of the genre to explain himself. He offers the audience a number of poems – the soliloquies – and a few digressive conversations with characters irrelevant to the play proper: the players, Horatio, the gravediggers. The most moving speech about death in the play has as its subject none of those corpses stranded by the plot on stage at the end. It is about a court-jester who never appears and was dead long before the play got under way.

V

Hamlet's retreat into the private monologue is as telling a rejection of the Elsinore play as his jokes. John Holloway argues that 'the stress on delay in the soliloquies' can be seen as 'showing how the protagonist is preoccupied with his role, in order to stress that it *is* a role: a recognisable "part".' But the innate antithesis between the freedom of soliloquy and the tyranny of role in plot is not explored. For Holloway, Hamlet is too much the victim of fate to use the soliloquies as any effective escape from the pressures they discuss. Harry Levin probes further in reminding us that the very style stresses the gulf between the trivial remarks which Hamlet is confined to within the play proper and the amount he can explain in soliloquy. Levin shows that the transitions from fraudulent court dialogue to revealing soliloquy are pointed by a shift from prose to verse:

> his medium for dialogue is his own kind of antic prose. The exceptions to this rule are consistent: the soliloquies and his confidential interviews with Horatio and the Queen. Characteristically he shifts into verse when the others leave the stage:

> Ay, so, God bye you.
> > *Exeunt Rosencrantz and Guildenstern*
> Now I am alone.
> O, what a rogue and peasant slave am I! . . .   (II.ii.552–3)

> Conversely, when he and Horatio are joined by the others, he manoeuvers a quick change into prose: . . . The main effect is to isolate Hamlet from everyone whose discourse runs in the expected rhythms, so that we are continually and painfully reminded of his predicament.

The same soliloquy suggests to A. P. Rossiter that Hamlet's private monologues threaten our ability to concentrate on the public play. He feels

David Pirie

that it 'is only partly "about" the story: much more about "What is it that happens to me when I see an actor act and am moved?".' To Rossiter this suggests an unusually subjective play in which we are supposed to be as interested in what goes on in Hamlet's mind as we are in the events occurring externally around him. To me it seems that Hamlet's questions are addressed as much to the audience as to himself: what do *they* think about their ability to be moved when they see an actor feigning emotion? They have just seen the First Player in tears as he recounts Hecuba's grief at the murder of her husband. The Elsinore play is less straightforwardly stimulating. There is no sign that Gertrude's reaction to being widowed was to:

> Run barefoot up and down, threatening the flames
> With bissom rheum, a clout upon that head
> Where late the diadem stood.   (II.ii.509–12)

Nor is Hamlet's present inactivity of the same gigantic ominousness as that of Pyrrhus:

> So as a painted tyrant, Pyrrhus stood,
> And like a neutral to his will and matter,
> Did nothing:
> But as we often see, against some storm,
> A silence in the heavens, the rack stand still,
> The bold winds speechless, and the orb below
> As hush as death, anon the dreadful thunder
> Doth rend the region; so after Pyrrhus' pause,
> Aroused vengeance sets him new a-work;   (II.ii.484–92)

Hamlet has been a neutral to his own melodrama in a rather different way during the past two hundred lines which he has devoted to the latest London theatre gossip, dramatic criticism, and enjoying this performance by the Players. Nor has this leisurely episode seemed like the lull of an epic simile before the thunder-clap of a climax. The audience will not be surprised to find that when Hamlet's own 'aroused vengeance' does eventually set him new a-work at the end of the scene it is to the planning of amateur theatricals. What Hamlet is stressing to the audience in the II.ii soliloquy is that theatre can be more emotive than 'real life', the converse of this discovery that 'real life', if it is as heartlessly fraudulent as Elsinore, can seem as tangential to oneself as a play about fictional characters. The player's speech about murdered kings and mourning widows has whipped up more hatred of Claudius than the chilling fact of his uncle's sin. But how real is that hatred? Do emotions generated in the theatre really change us? The hatred sounds convincing enough in ranting language inspired by the Pyrrhus speech:

178

> I should ha' fatted all the region kites
> With this slave's offal. Bloody, bawdy villain!
> Remorseless, treacherous, lecherous, kindless villain!
> O, vengeance! (II.ii.582–5)

But Hamlet is himself immediately suspicious of this verbal posturing:

> Why, what an ass am I! This is most brave,
> That I, the son of a dear father murdered,
> Prompted to my revenge by heaven and hell,
> Must like a whore, unpack my heart with words,
> And fall a-cursing, like a very drab. (II.ii.586–91)

Hamlet's brief flirtation with the Pyrrhus style is rejected as a kind of self-prostitution. The 'silence in the heavens', merely a literary self-indulgence to the First Player, a man of shallow words for all theatrical seasons, is to Hamlet an echo of the sterility of earth. 'The motive and the cue for passion' given him by the Ghost falls on deaf ears. He shows as little interest in gaining the throne as his father seems to have shown in anything other than extending its sway. Old Hamlet wearing armour from head to toe can return demanding a plot of revenge. His son is too busy telling the audience of his

> dread of something after death,
> The undiscovered country, from whose bourn
> No traveller returns. (III.i.78–80)

The inconsistency is intentionally obtrusive. The audience cannot hope to find an easy consistency between the soliloquies and the play to which Hamlet is repeatedly summoned. It has been prepared for in the disconcerting farce which cuts across I.v, where the audience could reasonably have expected a solemn episode of Hamlet's dedication to revenge. There the ubiquitous noise of the Ghost popping up repeatedly beneath Hamlet's feet led to some of his most relaxed humour: 'Well said, old mole! canst work i'the'earth so fast? / A worthy pioneer!' Dover Wilson's airy explanation of Hamlet's belief that no traveller returns from death seems woefully incomplete: 'in this mood of deep dejection Hamlet has given up all belief in the "honesty" of the Ghost, and . . . Shakespeare wrote the lines to make this clear to the audience.' The audience is in fact reminded of Hamlet's constant reluctance to give his most serious attention to the kind of dramatic action which the Ghost recalls from the past and requires of Hamlet in the future. Indeed in the bedroom scene there is open conflict between the Ghost's demand that Hamlet get on with the plot and Hamlet's own instinct which is to talk about the frailty of women. Hamlet's real worry about the Ghost is not as Dover Wilson claims that it may be telling lies about its own past. Hamlet is more disturbed by the possibility that the future to which it calls him may be one in which he is unable to tell the audience the truth about himself. His real doubts concern not so much the Ghost's 'honesty' as its relevance and the value of its genre. It may have returned from the undiscovered land but it has no language in which to answer Hamlet's questions. For all that it can tell someone wondering whether to be or not to be it might as well have stayed where it was. The soliloquies can question the value of the plots and dialogues that the Ghost's return sets in action. But those plots and dialogues have no answers to the soliloquies. The audience is asked to accept that only in personal poems, usually recited alone, will they glimpse the truth about the hero; that in conversation and action he will – sometimes intentionally – misrepresent himself. It amounts almost to their being told to stop wasting their time, go home and read the sonnets.

VI

All this might suggest that the Prince is bound to have exclusive rights on the audience's sympathy and respect at the expense of other characters still struggling to attract the audience through the unreliable means of plot and dialogue. But Shakespeare allows a soliloquy to at least one other character, Claudius. This may at first seem a distinctly odd choice. The King too has his lonely meditation – in the prayer-scene. He struggles to repent but is unwilling to surrender either the power or the love he gained by his crime. His speech is as long and as honest as Hamlet's own soliloquies. Claudius reveals to the audience a sensitivity and complexity in his personality which the other characters – judging him only by deeds and public words – cannot know. Now Hamlet is in this respect as ignorant as anybody else. He assumes that the kneeling King is in the kind of simplified mood in which his soul might wing straight to heaven. So for the rest of the play we are aware of a mutual ignorance in the two characters. Just as Hamlet remains in Claudius's eyes the ambitious heir to the throne, a theatrical stereotype, so to Hamlet himself Claudius is the straightforward caricature of evil found in old-fashioned morality plays: 'a vice of kings', 'a king of shreds and patches'. Thus Hamlet in III.iv describes him to Gertrude. The original audience would be aware of the contemporary transition of the Vice, from a simplistic emblem of evil into a clown wearing the traditional costume of different coloured scraps and patches of cloth. In Hamlet's descriptions of Claudius they would see the theatrical metaphor taking a new turn. Hamlet's arrogant rejection of his world as a clumsy play may lead him to culpable ignorance. Elsewhere he identifies 'our monarchs' with 'outstretched heroes' (the latter meaning bombastic stage-players) and this clearly points to the same simplification of Claudius, a simplification which the audience is led to reject as inadequate. But they have the advantage over both men. They can hear the soliloquies. They have been led to see that the play without the prince's soliloquies would be as false and clumsily simple as *The Murder of Gonzago*. But it is in terms of that melodramatic little piece that Hamlet and Claudius try to understand each other. To the King the crucial fact about Hamlet is that he offers the threat of the *Mousetrap* in which as Hamlet stresses 'Lucianus, nephew to the king' gets the crown from his uncle. To Hamlet, Claudius is nothing more than the same stage-enemy in the same play, straightforwardly 'A murderer and a villain' (III.iv.96). Hamlet is too clever to join in the Elsinore play, and allow his own subtle feeling to be travestied as merely a series of plot facts. But he is stupid enough to understand other characters by reference only to those facts. He claims that the purpose of plays is 'to hold as 'twere the mirror up to nature', but he goes on to define the theatre's mirror as satirical and moralistic: 'to show virtue her own feature, scorn her own image, and the very age and body of the time his form and pressure'. (III.ii.20–4.) When Hamlet puts this into practice his mirror is as superficial in its insights as the worst of plays. He promises Gertrude in III.iv:

> You go not till I set you up a glass
> Where you may see the inmost part of you.

But the Hamlet mirror offers only an obsessional reduction of her relationship with Claudius:

> In the rank sweat of an enseamed bed,
> Stewed in corruption, honeying and making love
> Over the nasty sty –

For Hamlet it is all Vice or Virtue, Hyperion to a satyr. Of course he has been shocked into these unthinkingly extreme attitudes. What he says of Rosencrantz and Guildenstern is true of the whole cast:

> Ere I could make a prologue to my brains,
> They had begun the play. (V.ii.30–2)

But though the causes of his extreme attitudes may attract sympathy in the early scenes, the damage caused is bound to chill it in later ones.

The most important casualty of this approach is clearly Ophelia. For Hamlet she must belong in one kind of nunnery or another; she is either the spotless virgin or the tart. It is of course as the latter – partly because he identifies her with his mother, partly because of her manipulation by Polonius – that Hamlet pigeon-holes her. This is understandable. As

David Pirie

Dover Wilson points out (though coming to different conclusions) she does set up a situation in the nunnery scene which is so innately theatrical that Hamlet is likely to judge her as a theatrical stereotype:

> The unhappy girl has sadly overplayed her part. Her little speech, ending with a sententious couplet, as Dowden notes, 'has an air of being prepared'. Worse than that, she, the jilt, is accusing him of coldness towards her. Worst of all, Hamlet who has been 'sent for', who meets her in the lobby 'by accident', finds her prepared not only with a speech but with the gifts also. She means no harm; she has romantically arranged a little play-scene . . . But the effect upon Hamlet is disastrous . . . For play-acting has completed her downfall in his eyes.

If Ophelia will join in the fraudulent plots of Elsinore, if she agrees to play her part in dialogues scripted to conceal the truth, then Hamlet is likely to reject her claims to be a real and precious human being along with those of the rest of the cast. But the audience cannot join in that rejection. They recognise in her, as much as they do in Claudius, a person capable of genuine feeling. Her speeches and songs in IV.v have the same validity as soliloquies. She speaks in the isolation of madness, so there is no sense of dialogue. She is about to kill herself so there is no possibility of plotting. Thoughts of death lead her to exactly the same conclusion as Hamlet reaches in the 'To be or not to be' soliloquy: 'Lord, we know what we are, but not what we may be.' (IV.v.41-2.) So the emotions she here verbalises (significantly enough mostly in lyric verse) have the value of the personal poem rather than the clumsily public play. On the point of death, freed from the demands of transitory action, she explores that suffering which shares the nature of infinity. This suffering revolves for her around the two obsessions of death as she mourns her father and love as she sings of betrayal by her lover. For both Hamlet is directly responsible. Moreover because the loss of Polonius is to Ophelia the loss of a real person, it is partly so to the audience. Many of the people whom Hamlet dismisses as a cast of professional illusionists keep at least one foot in reality by being cared for by somebody else. In Ophelia's love for her father, in Claudius's love for his wife, the audience is shown that Polonius was to somebody more than guts to be lugged into the next room, that Gertrude can be real outside the limits of Hamlet's stereotyped alternatives: loyal widow or whore. Hamlet in disengaging himself from the court and from the play also cuts himself off from the possibility of human relationship. Deeds and dialogue may be innately imprecise metaphors for emotion. But for the emotions of tenderness and mutual need, of friendship and love, they are the only metaphors. The soliloquy is an implied denial of the pointfulness of trying to share oneself or one's life with another person. The audience will obviously understand why Hamlet failed to see Ophelia in time as someone worth more concern than a character in a play. But they will be led by her mad scene, as much as by the king's soliloquy, to see that Hamlet's withdrawal though at first amusing is ultimately pathetic. His disengagement is based not only on a despairing knowledge, but also on a tragic ignorance. *Hamlet* without the prince is not only a comedy of intellectual detachment. It is also a tragedy of waste.

VII

The audience of course want and get both. It amuses them to see the rules of the game they have come to watch so shamelessly flouted. Hamlet's detachment gives them a range of intellectual stimulation that no conventional hero could offer. It mocks their expectations and they relish the novelty. On the other hand they have paid to see a noble tragedy and they have been cheated. An audience's mood on thus being surprised and challenged is bound to be ambivalent. It should be the perfect mood in which to see *Hamlet* as uniquely amusing and uniquely depressing. Perhaps the audience is meant to shift the emphasis of their conflicting sympathies as the play proceeds. At first they will side with the daring young prince flouting all the conventions of theatre. Towards the end they will be more concerned with the destruction which has been brought about by this moral holiday: both in Elsinore in as much as they still believe that Ophelia was more than an actress; and in their own values in as much as they still need some positive faith by which to live, still want to suspend their disbelief in both the reality of plays and the pointfulness of life. The real oddity of *Hamlet* then is that it is not only about 'life' but also about plays, and that it asks each of these two discussions to illuminate the other. If our most powerful thoughts and feelings are always travestied when carried into social talk or public action, is loneliness the only truth, and relationship merely a variety of deceit? If the theatre relies on social talk and public action as its traditional means of articulating human feeling, is it an innately falsifying medium? For the producer both questions depend on a more specific one raised by Lamb over a century and a half ago:

> Nine parts in ten of what Hamlet does are transactions between himself and his moral sense; they are the effusions of his solitary musings, which he retires to holes and corners and the most sequestered parts of the palace to pour forth . . . These profound sorrows, these light-and-noise-abhorring ruminations, which the tongue scarce dares utter to deaf walls, and chambers, how can they be represented by a gesticulating actor, who comes and mouths them out before an audience, making four hundred people his confidants at once?

David Pirie

The answer is that the text *demands* that Hamlet should explain himself as a gesticulating actor who thinks he has no-one to confide in but the audience, as a man whose transactions between himself and his moral sense have reduced him to being closer to the audience watching Elsinore as a play than to those busy actors who still think it worthwhile to enact its plots. The play has to stagger through its five acts without the prince becoming responsibly involved. The price at one level is Ophelia, at another it is one's own faith in the pointfulness of dramatic art. But like *Tristram Shandy*, that other defiant masterpiece which bullies its own genre, it stands as its author's most moving and most popular work. Modern productions which try to force the Prince back in the play, which try to turn *Hamlet* into a consistent 'realistic' drama inevitably obliterate its structure and baffle us. The original production must have been more hilarious, more harrowing, and certainly a great deal more interesting. T. S. Eliot in a remarkably unpleasant piece of snobbery dismissed the people who 'have thought *Hamlet* a work of art because they found it interesting' on the basis that the proper attitude is to find it 'interesting because it is a work of art'. He then went on to conclude that it was a bad play. My own instinct is to trust the judgement of people who go to the theatre with the healthy desire to be interested. I wish some producer would be bold enough to show them *Hamlet* in all its fascinating oddity.

[1972]

PETER MERCER

Othello and the form
of heroic tragedy

Dr Leavis' celebrated de-sentimentalising of *Othello* in the essay 'Diabolic
Intellect and the Noble Hero' was, no doubt, a useful and timely reaction
against the simplistic mystifications of Bradley, even if it didn't succeed in
finding the 'critical centre' quite as accurately as Leavis suggested. It did
plausibly locate the reason for the tragic collapse within Othello himself and
so avoided the necessity for an Iago of stupifying ability. Dr Leavis' attempt
to identify this reason, however, displays assumptions about the nature of
Shakespearean drama surprisingly little different from Bradley's. His resort,
after all, is to the familiar 'fatal flaw', some crippling psychological and moral
deficiency. Dr Leavis is decently apologetic about the need to call on so
antiquated a concept, but finds it inescapable.

> . . . even *Othello* (it will be necessary to insist) is poetic drama, a dramatic poem,
> and not a psychological novel written in dramatic form and draped in poetry,
> but relevant discussion of its tragic significance will nevertheless be mainly a
> matter of character-analysis.

His analysis in fact takes as its starting point the observation that Othello
displays a singular readiness to respond to Iago's suggestions and goes on to
establish a concept of Othello as a man whose admitted martial virtues
are decisively outweighed by tendencies towards self-approval,
self-dramatisation, sentimentality, self-ignorance, and plain stupidity. The
most obvious, if unsatisfactory, objection to such a view is that it simply fails
to account for our continuing interest in the play. Dr Leavis makes gestures
at its 'marvellously sure and adroit . . . workmanship', but testimonials to
craftsmanship seem hardly adequate. The specific inadequacy of such a
view has, in fact, to do with inappropriate assumptions about the tragic
mode, about the functioning of poetic drama (not 'dramatic poem'), and
about the relationship of concepts like 'character' to verbal texture and
process. Dr Leavis' criticism is founded upon an idea of character and action
as abstractions arising easily and immediately from a general sense of the
drama. He moves, for example, from the perception of Othello's rapid
capitulation to speculation about his psychological and moral deficiencies.
He does not, at any time, investigate the processes involved in this
capitulation, the arguments employed, the responses misunderstood, the
deceptions practised, in order to discover why, exactly, so self-sufficient and
competent a character should suffer so total a defeat. He does not investigate

the qualities of Othello's distinctive rhetoric in relation to the verbal contexts it opposes and inhabits. For all his professed attention to the 'evidence' and the 'plain facts', Leavis seems to be working along speculative lines perhaps more appropriate to his hypothetical 'psychological novel' than to poetic drama. There is no attempt to secure awareness of the play as a coherent poetic structure; in consequence the play is deprived of significance and reduced to a rather arbitrary intrigue against a self-deceiving egotist.

It is, of course, the simplest of matters to reduce the central situation of any tragedy to such banal proportions, which may, in itself, suggest that significance and effect is going to be located in interrelations more complex than the psychological abstractions we call characters. However, even when attention to these elements is a declared critical effort – as it is, for example, in the work of D. Traversi and L. C. Knights – there is a pervasive reluctance to accept what appear to be the obvious claims of tragic heroes. So Dr Leavis' reduction of Bradley's Othello to more fallibly human proportions may be due to something more than inadequate investigatory methods; it seems finally to have to do with a general, historically identifiable, distaste for the tragic mode itself. Such a distaste, with all the consequent re-interpreting and re-emphasising, is at its most obvious in L. C. Knights' essay, 'How many children had Lady Macbeth.' Having traced the basic patterns of imagery in the play with due New Critical zeal, Knights displays a distinct discomfort with the Macbeth of the last act – a man so sunk in sin and despair that by 'normal' naturalistic standards he should be quite lost to compassion. So he attempts to shift our attention to Malcolm and Macduff, to 'the tendency of the last Act (order emerging from disorder, truth emerging from behind deceit)' and away from the apparently dominant rhetoric of the doomed Macbeth. Knights even goes so far as to warn us against the danger of misinterpreting the seductively impressive 'Tomorrow' speech.' . . . The poetry is so fine that we are almost bullied into accepting an essential ambiguity in the final statement of the play.' However he contrives to resist such unfair pressure. The assumptions are clear enough. A play is a 'statement' (Macbeth is a 'statement of evil'), ideally unambiguous, having some moral, social, political or philosophical significance. And in a tragedy 'conventional "sympathy for the hero" [must not be] allowed to distort the pattern of the whole.'

The same assumptions are evident in D. A. Traversi's essay on *Macbeth* though here the distorting effect of a familiar kind of political enthusiasm is more starkly obvious. We are invited to see the play as enacting an inversion of values inherent in ordered society followed by the welcome rectification of the situation by 'the rightful successor to Duncan: a king, in short, to whom the loyalty of free men is properly due, and from whom royal bounty may again be expected to flow'. So that we may applaud unhampered this cheering conclusion the dramatist so contrives it that Macbeth himself 'shrinks to something small and rather absurd as his fall becomes inevitable . . . Before the advancing powers of healing good, evil has shrunk to insignificance. Macbeth is seen to be a puny figure dressed up in a usurped greatness, a dignity not of his own, and we are ready for the final bravado flourish with which he dies'. It seems Othello isn't the only one to get himself disliked. It is not of course in dispute that the 'powers of order and good' and so on do re-establish themselves in Scotland; the question is simply whether it is this process that so wholly captures our interest in the last Act of the play, whether it isn't what is happening to Macbeth that constitutes the core and significance of the drama here as throughout. The Aristotelian idea of the tragic action, a process involving the hero in a sequential pattern of hamartia, peripetetia, anagnorisis and catharsis, and inducing in the spectator mixed, if not ambiguous, emotions of pity and fear, has been replaced in these essays by an idea of 'social' drama, in which a disrupted society is 'purged' (a favourite metaphor) of the infected hero, the disruptive influence, and authority (or more romantically 'harmony' and 'order') is restored. The sins of the hero may be various: Hamlet's perversity and morbidity, Othello's stupidity and impetuosity, Lear's folly, Antony's lust, Macbeth's ambition – but they all have inevitably the characteristic of 'excess', and in the social and moral order acknowledged or aspired to by these critics it is excess that is most deplored.

It would be possible to explore the social, political and historical sources and influences that lie behind such a view of tragedy – presumably a mixture of theoretical egalitarianism, dislike of the hero concept of the imperialist myth, and a rather disturbing, though hardly surprising enthusiasm for authority and stability. This last, of course, finds a dubious respectability in Elizabethan apologies for dictatorship and Ulysses' hypocritical hymn to order in *Troilus and Cressida*. Such speculations are however of little relevance to the critical problem involved in re-adjusting our expectations of tragedy. In specifically critical terms the readings of these critics imply nothing less than a shift of the emotional centre of tragedy from the hero or protagonist to what may be identified archetypally as the choric element. The love of reasonableness and order, the fear and dislike of excess (either of vice or of virtue), the advocacy of the moral norm that inform these essays provide almost a definition of a Sophoclean chorus. In *Oedipus Rex* and *Antigone* perhaps the most clearly diagrammatic of tragedies, the troubled chorus views an action of deep moral ambiguity certain only of the fatal excessiveness of the hero's commitment, his rigour, his consistency, and probably of his rhetoric. They remain, to heal the wounds or to witness the healing, but our interest in their final platitudes is only ironic. If general definitions of tragedy are notoriously elusive it can at least be asserted that it remains a defining characteristic of tragedy that we are left with an overwhelming sense of the gap, the veritable chasm, between the 'quality' of the hero and his action and the 'quality' of those left to pick up the moral and political pieces. And this quality is not moral – morality is for the chorus and ends where tragedy begins – but has to do with a total realisation and affirmation of identity in the face of failure and destruction, a forcible re-imposition of form on a disintegrating personal universe. And it follows, of course, that this supreme effort, this uniquely tragic effect, is largely a matter of rhetoric. In Shakespearean tragedy above all, it is this rediscovery of rhetorical form that characterises the final movement and so perplexes and irritates the moralistic critic.

It is just such an irritation that T. S. Eliot is registering in his famously fastidious remark about Othello simply 'cheering himself up' in his final speech. One would hesitate to include Eliot in the same moral/political critical camp as Leavis, Knights or Traversi, but, beneath all the differences of belief and technique, we find the same antipathy to the tragic mode, or at least to the quality that distinguishes the mode. The trouble, at bottom, seems to arise from a combination of earnest rationalism and emotional fastidiousness; these critics feel far more at home with the 'second men' of tragedy – with Horatio, Banquo, Gloucester, Enobarbus, Cassio, and their philosophies of reason. Eliot's remark is, in a way, central to the problem in its blithe refusal to recognise the claims of heroic rhetoric and its central function in Elizabethan tragedy. In plays with a relatively simple moral scheme this function is too obvious to ignore. The 'quality' of, for example, Tamburlaine, Richard III, or, in a different tone, Richard II, is clearly a matter of linguistic vitality; rhetoric is the essence of their superiority. It is the complex moral and symbolic structures of Shakespeare's major tragedies that may tend to obscure this simple truth. Perhaps the simplest cursory demonstration of this proposition is made by considering Eliot's censure against the final movement of any of the 'heroic' tragedies (*Lear* and *Troilus and Cressida*, for example, are more plausibly classed as 'ironic' tragedies).

Othello's notorious final speech may indeed seem, from a moral or psychological standpoint, the ultimate gesture of egotism, but its remarkable similarity in form to the equivalent speeches of Macbeth, Cleopatra, Coriolanus or Hamlet suggest a function more directly involved with the nature of heroic tragedy than with the psychological peculiarities of Othello. It would seem more useful to consider it, and similar speeches, as concluding a symbolism of rhetoric rather than as exposing psychological or moral facts. These speeches, in fact, are attempts to rise above the muddle and death that fill the action, to declare, establish, from a state beyond hope or judgement, the lost quality, the virtue of the hero. They are, as their declaratory form suggests, bids for immortality.

> I pray you, in your letters,
> When you shall these unlucky deeds relate,
> Speak of me as I am; nothing extenuate,
> Nor set down ought in malice. Then must you speak . . .   (*Othello* V.ii)

The concern is wholly for identity – 'As I am' not 'As I miserably and destructively have been'; the concept of tragedy is Aristotelian rather than moral – 'unlucky deeds'; and the demand is not for judgment but, essentially, for recognition. The authority is total – 'Then must you speak'. Of course it is possible to see this as arrogance or egotism, but such a response, at the least, makes nonsense of a climactic moment. More importantly it ignores the entire rhetorical strategy of the play.

We may compare the final speeches of Cleopatra

> Give me my robe, put on my crown; I have
> Immortal longings in me . . .
>   . . . Husband, I come.
> Now to that name my courage prove my title!
> I am fire and air; my other elements
> I give to baser life.   (V.ii)

and of Coriolanus

> Your judgments, my grave lords,
> Must give this cur the lie . . .
>   . . . 'Boy'! False hound!
> If you have writ your annals true, 'tis there
> That, like an eagle in a dove-cote, I
> Fluttered your Volscians in Corioli.
> Alone I did it. 'Boy'!   (V.vi)

It is indeed the final irony suffered by Hamlet, the actor searching for a tragic role, that he misses his cue for this crucial speech and is obliged to delegate the responsibility to Horatio.

> You that look pale and tremble at this chance,
> That are but mutes or audience to this act,
> Had I but time, as this fell sergeant Death
> Is strict in his arrest, O, I could tell you –
> But let it be. Horatio, I am dead:
> Thou livest; report me and my cause aright
> To the unsatisfied.   (V.ii)

But, irony aside, the concern for reputation is common to all. Explanations involving terms like 'egotism' suggest a resort to irrelevant psychological categories. The total concern for 'self', for identity, is a defining characteristic of the tragic hero. And it is clear that in all these moments of self-assertion the view of events advanced by the hero and by the attendant characters is traditionally Aristotelian. It is a question not of moral deficiency but of 'unlucky deeds', 'carnal, bloody, and unnatural acts', 'plots and errors'. Our interest in Shakespearean tragedy is not then primarily moral; psychology and morality do not provide the elements of dramatic articulation. It might be tentatively suggested that such drama is essentially a spectacular action, involving psychology and morality, but functioning above all in the ineluctable progress towards disaster. It is the process of language and action, the fearful coherence of elements, that is the reality and meaning of the drama. Psychological qualities such as Oedipus' irascibility and obstinacy, Othello's credulity and ignorance, Coriolanus' pride, Hamlet's 'miscasting' are only données for the significant action.

Thus in the tragedy of *Othello* the executive causes of the action have far more to do with problems of cognition and semantics than with given psychological conditions. The central action is essentially a progress from an heroic certainty to total unbearable uncertainty, and this shift is engineered by Iago's exploitation of inherent, and ultimately insoluble, problems of identity, of cognition, and of the relationship of language to object. The play turns upon the suggested discrepancy between the linguistic and the existential worlds.

Othello begins in a deliberately stimulated chaos, a confusion of contradictions and lies and a barrage of questions. Iago creates a totally unreliable context in which motives and judgments are arbitrary and interchangeable. He moves effortlessly from his own complaint of non-promotion to Roderigo's jealousy – they are merely different dimensions of a will to chaos. His sarcastic assessment of Cassio, 'mere prattle, without practice, Is all his soldiership', is as arbitrary as his later declaration to Montano that Cassio is 'a soldier fit to stand by Caesar And give direction'. Iago's identification speech – 'I am not what I am' – declares his pose as a caricature Vice figure or Machiavel but more importantly insists on his identification with this shifting surface of false appearances. He is a genius of the scene. His insistence on a total disparity between appearance and reality –

> For when my outward action doth demonstrate
> The native act and figure of my heart
> In compliment extern, 'tis not long after
> But I will wear my heart upon my sleeve
> For daws to peck at. (I.i)

establishes a norm of deceit against which Othello's massive certainty and integrity will, when it comes, make so stark a contrast. This disruption extends outwards from the Iago/Roderigo dialogue to the rousing of Brabantio and from this outward again with the dispatching of the servants to wake the city. Throughout the confrontation with Brabantio, which Iago handles as a malicious but vigorously obscene joke, there is a complex pattern of questions and declarations about knowledge and identity. 'What are you? . . . what profound wretch art thou? . . . Thou art a villain. You are – a Senator . . . If this be known to you . . . But if you know not this . . . Belief of it oppresses me already' (I.i). This scene is of course a rehearsal in miniature of the main action. Brabantio is told his daughter has eloped and is freely supplied with highly emotional terms in which to view the matter.

> You'll have your daughter cover'd with a Barbary horse . . .
> Your daughter and the Moor are now making the beast with two backs . . .
> Your daughter . . . hath made a gross revolt.

It is a simple but powerful demonstration of the power of rhetoric to impose a selected value upon reality – or at least upon reported events. And it is one of the assumptions of this play that there cannot, in the nature of things, be a direct confrontation with reality. Language always mediates between observer and fact, Iago is always there to interpret the visual show. And when Othello gives his version of the elopement before the council, it is no less of a highly specialised rhetorical interpretation. Unlike Iago, of course, he does not intend to confuse or mislead, but he is nonetheless offering a version of reality. It is validated for the moment, by the fact that Desdemona concurs in it.

Before Iago's devastating onslaught Brabantio, crying for more light, dissolves into a pathetic confusion that might almost be a parodic anticipation of Othello's agony.

> It is too true an evil. Gone she is;
> And what's to come of my despised time
> Is nought but bitterness. Now, Roderigo,
> Where dids't thou see her? – O unhappy girl! –
> With the Moor, says't thou? – Who would be a father? –
> How dids't thou know 'twas she? – O, thou deceivest me
> Past thought! – What said she to you? –
> Get more tapers;   (I.i)

Brabantio's struggle to release himself from this confusion is essentially an effort to suggest the improbable probable. He too is enmeshed with the elusive vocabulary of cognition. His accusation of magic contains a paradoxical appeal to 'sense'.

> For I'll refer me to all things of sense . . .
> Judge me the world, if 'tis not gross in sense . . .

> ... I'll have't disputed on;
> 'Tis probable and palpable to thinking. (I.ii)

Brabantio's accusation is, of course, more than simply abusive; in a sense, language and rhetoric is magic in this play, in that it has power to transform and pervert experience. Iago will use this magic of language on Othello just as he uses the magic of alcohol on Cassio. But the important thing for the coherence of the play is that magic, or language, is not necessarily evil – Othello's seduction of Desdemona by the rhetoric of romance is felt as good because it is consistent with their mutual responses and feelings. But his is not simply saying what is 'true'. The relationship between language and fact is not that simple.

The debate about the size and direction of the Turkish fleet that opens the third scene is a further extension of confusion into the political world. Again the problem is the unreliability of evidence – 'There is no composition in these news / That gives them credit' – and the exchanges are cluttered with verbs of cognition. This, however, is a council, practised in debate, and in the speech of the First Senator, we have a timely example of one way of choosing between alternative possibilities – reason:

> This cannot be,
> By no assay of reason. 'Tis a pageant
> To keep us in false gaze. (I.iii)

And this process is immediately vindicated by the entrance of a messenger to confirm the diagnosis. The Duke too is cautiously and firmly analytical when faced with Brabantio's 'vouching':

> To vouch this is no proof –
> Without more wider and more overt test
> Than these thin habits and poor likelihoods
> Of modern seeming do prefer against him. (I.iii)

His conclusion on this more difficult question, after exposure to Othello's magnificently romantic speech, is however singularly subjective: 'I think this tale would win my daughter too' (I.iii). The situation is only resolved by a direct appeal to Desdemona herself, and it might not be merely pedantic to suggest that the discovery of witchcraft is not likely to be expedited by consulting the supposedly bewitched. So we see that, even among those who are aware of the dangerous gap between language and reality, reason is a tool of limited power. It is, in the end, only a choice of probabilities. For those who do not recognise this gap, like Othello, an evidential situation of real complexity and stress will prove disastrous.

It is of course the central irony of the tragic situation that Othello's peculiar virtue should be so essentially involved with this ultimately disabling ignorance. For the essence of his heroic claim is his personal integrity, his wholeness and consistency. And these qualities are constantly verbalised in terms which declare the identity of language and reality. His belief in the irresistible, almost magical, powers of language is recognisably primitive. The very texture of his language declines distinctions between existential and verbal realities:

> Let him do his spite.
> My services that I have done the signiory
> Shall out-tongue his complaints
>
> . . . and my demerits
> May speak unbonneted to as proud a fortune
> As this that I have reached.
>
> Not I, I must be found,
> My parts, my title, and my perfect soul
> Shall manifest me rightly. Is it they?

Iago By Janus, I think no.   (I.ii)

Located as it is in a context of deception and doubt the clarity and assurance of these statements are startling enough. But, more significantly, Othello is appealing not to reason or evidence, as the senator does, but to himself. Othello's concept of reality is his own identity; consequently he counters accusation not with argument but with self-display. It is a magnificently primitive response wholly consistent with his origin, his history, and his profession. And it is this certainty in himself that accounts for the detached and elegant formality of his rhetoric. It is not primarily a means of communication but of self-projection. The famous line 'Keep up your bright swords, for the dew will rust them' is characteristically more expressive of Othello's image than relevant to the situation. It seems clear that the response invited by the play here does not involve moral judgement. In reality, of course, a person of Othello's certitude would be intolerable; in the play this quality stands out against the pervasive uncertainty as a clear and persuasive heroic claim.

This claim is symbolically proved by his performance before the senate. Othello's disclaimers of subtlety – 'Rude am I in my speech', 'a round unvarnished tale' – are not ironic but accurate. His rhetoric is elegant and picturesque but never logically or syntactically complex. A comparison with the tortuous speeches of Iago that end the first Act makes evident Othello's rhetorical simplicity. But if Othello's range, intellectually and verbally, is narrow, his intensity is beyond question. The highly developed specialisation of his language is a correlative of his highly specialised social position. Indeed he exists almost outside society – hence his alien origin –

and serves it without participating in it. In a sense, Othello's first mistake is to attempt to involve himself in society in the most symbolically central manner – by marrying. His heroic simplicity and certainty, his self-sufficiency, are irrelevant if not dangerous in a social relationship as complex and hazardous as marriage. This movement out of his element (the sea) is implied by Iago's comment on his elopement: 'Faith, he hath tonight boarded a land carrack.'

But in the council scene his triumph seems complete. He articulates his value, his identity, and receives the traditional reward of the hero – the symbolic princess. Desdemona is Brabantio's 'jewel' and ultimately Othello's lost 'pearl'. She declares herself and is accepted as the central symbol of Othello's faith. Before the Duke she asserts, beyond concepts of morality or emotion, her symbolic role.

> My heart's subdu'd
> Even to the very quality of my lord:
> I saw Othello's visage in his mind;
> And to his honours and his valiant parts
> Did I my soul and fortunes consecrate.　　　　　　　　　(I.iii)

She represents Othello's bid for perfection as hero *and* lover; she is integrated into Othello's self-created myth as the ultimate expression and extension of his identity. It is not a 'relationship' in any morally or psychologically comprehensible form. Othello confirms her significance and function unequivocally: 'My life upon her faith.'

The council scene ends with a very formal exchange – 'a sentence' – between the Duke and Brabantio. In couplets they agree that, in common-sense terms, it is better to grin and bear it: 'To mourn a mischief that is past and gone / Is the next way to draw new mischief on' (I.iii). This spells out the reasonable response to misfortune, the will to accommodation that makes social life possible, the lowly sanity that proves wholly impossible for Othello. They admit the imperfection of this response, the inherent equivocation, but can tolerate this because they do not aspire to the heroic condition, whose very meaning is its coherence and homogeneity; it is a specialised perfection and cannot admit incongruity. And when that incongruity appears to be corruption in the central symbol of Othello's life the result is the disintegration of the heroic world into an obscene nightmare. Aptly and ironically Brabantio shuffles off the dilemma with a simple denial of the powers of rhetoric. 'But words are words: I never yet did hear / That the bruis'd heart was pierced through the ear.'

The final scene of the first Act, between Iago and Roderigo, makes more specific the threat to Othello's new harmony. Iago's corrosive cynicism declares itself as fundamentally antagonistic to Othello's idealism. Its potential for destruction is inherent in the ultimate dependence of idealism upon faith. The world of suggestion, evidence and proof to which Iago proposes to seduce Othello is alien to the Moor's ideal certainties, and despite its victory no more real. Iago's strength lies in his recognition of the subjectivity of value – 'Virtue? A fig! 'tis in ourselves that we are thus or thus' – and in his consequent ability to confuse and deceive those who locate their values in the 'objective' world, or fail to recognise the distinction. When he suggests to Othello a total discontinuity between subjective and objective reality, a flat contradiction between value and fact, the Moor is quite unable to keep the categories distinct. In symbolically objectifying his value in a wife he has, to his own sense, collapsed the distinction. And since Desdemona belongs in essence, if not in significance, to the external world and is therefore necessarily finally unknowable, Iago is enabled to introduce doubt and suspicion into the elements of Othello's world. There is no need, therefore, to search for psychological or moral deficiencies as offering explanations for the effectiveness of Iago's attack.

This is further evident in the powerful reassertion of the symbolic value of Othello and Desdemona upon their arrival in Cyprus. It is, as Othello acknowledges, their moment of perfection and it affirms, on the brink of the abyss, the reality of the ideal that will be destroyed. If Othello was an alien in Venice it becomes clear that Cyprus is his symbolic home: a besieged garrison island which the play shows him delivering from the enemy single-handed. The ready co-operation of the elements that so effectively destroys the Turkish fleet, the enemy from outside, insists on Othello's symbolic role. He comes out of his element, the sea, to save the island. Cassio articulates the significances.

> Great Jove, Othello guard,
> And swell his sail with thine own powerful breath,
> That he may bless this bay with his tall ship.
> Make love's quick pants in Desdemona's arms,
> Give renew'd fire to our extinced spirits,
> And bring all Cyprus comfort. (II.i)

But Cyprus is not just a Venetian garrison, it is the island of Aphrodite. And Cassio's sequence of references to Desdemona, culminating in his speech of welcome, and despite his self-conscious gallantry, does associate her with the mythical birth of Venus.

> Tempests themselves, high seas, and howling winds,
> The gutter'd rocks, and congregated sands,
> Traitors ensteep'd, to clog the guiltless keel,
> As having sense of beauty, do omit
> Their common natures, letting go safely by
> The divine Desdemona. (II.i)

Peter Mercer

So the familiar abstractions of love and war organise the scene, and, as Othello and Desdemona embrace, the storm, already structurally symbolic, takes on a further significance. It becomes the symbolic consummation of their love.

> If it were now to die,
> 'Twere now to be most happy, for I fear
> My soul hath her content so absolute,
> That not another comfort, like to this
> Succeeds in unknown fate.   (II.i)

The irony, of course, is grim enough, and Desdemona protests at this absolutism. But it is wholly appropriate that Othello is absorbed in the ideal quality of the moment; it is a seizure of perfection not easily compatible, for all his acquiescence, with Desdemona's hopes for steadily increasing 'loves and comfort'.

Throughout this spectacular scene, however, the interruptive presence of Iago reminds us that he too has turned up inside this extension of Othello's world. As the obviously external enemy, the Turk, is so effortlessly repelled Iago begins his infusion of cynicism into the situation. In his dialogue with Desdemona he counters the idealistic quality of the moment with 'old fond paradoxes'. In a series of obscene epigrams he exposes a possible reality that he will attempt to introduce into Othello's consciousness – a reality in which every woman is a whore. And because of the necessary idiosyncrasies of Othello's attitude to language and reality, he will be unable to see that this proposed alien reality is neither more nor less possible than his own, and in a steadily encouraged confusion will submit to it as irrationally as he previously clung to his idealism.

The vulnerability of an idealism as undiluted as Othello's is first dramatically demonstrated in his dismissal of Cassio. This is obviously a symbolic rehearsal for the rejection of Desdemona on a morally simpler level. The reality of the offence and the contingencies of a military situation excuse the absolutism and the finality. But Othello has been tricked and when the same characteristics operate in the infinitely more complex circumstances of the main action the consequences will be disastrous.

It is not possible here to describe in detail the way in which Othello moves, or is led, from the first induced suspicion to insane certainty. It has, in any case, received the attention of many critics. What I am concerned with is the reason why Iago is able to begin and continue the process, the element in the situation that provides him with his chance and his success. It is relevant, however, to note that Othello's first step into doubt turns upon an ambiguity and a non-sequitur that he fails to notice. Iago has suggested that Desdemona deceived her father in eloping – a rather negative suggestion

196

already dealt with in the senate – and Othello, worried by this, ponders on its implications: 'And yet how nature erring from itself – '. Iago immediately takes this up and uses it to suggest that Desdemona 'erred' in marrying Othello, that it was perverse in her

> Not to affect many proposed matches,
> Of her own clime, complexion, and degree,
> Whereto we see in all things nature tends;
> Fie, we may smell in such a will most rank
> Foul disproportion, thoughts unnatural. (III.iii)

This is a much more provocative accusation, carrying the inference that it would be 'natural' for Desdemona to revert to Cassio, but Othello does not notice that it is not a continuation of the previous suggestion but a contradiction of it. Confusion at the evidential and logical level is central to Iago's process.

However the fundamental point about Othello's rapid conversion to doubt is that it is impressed upon him that there is no possibility of certainty as to the reality of his wife's faith. He is introduced to suspicions that, in the nature of the case, it is simply not possible to allay conclusively. The failure to find evidence doesn't remove the possibility of infidelity. The corollary of this – that evidence of infidelity is equally elusive – is simply used by Iago to inflame Othello's imagination.

> And may, but, how, how satisfied, my lord?
> Would you, the supervisor, grossly gape on,
> Behold her topp'd?

Othello's disintegration follows upon his frenzied attempts to restore certitude – either of guilt or innocence – at any cost, an operation he thinks at first will be easy.

> No, Iago;
> I'll see before I doubt; when I doubt, prove;
> And, on the proof, there is no more but this –
> Away at once with love or jealousy! (III.iii)

The impossibility of such a simple rationalistic procedure is the fact upon which Iago can work. Once doubt has been introduced, Othello has begun upon a spiral of emotional and moral collapse. Ironically, Iago warns him precisely of this danger.

> O, beware, my lord, of jealousy;
> It is the green-eyed monster which doth mock
> The meat it feeds on.

It is in response to this warning that Othello cries, 'O misery' – a world, or rather anti-world, has suddenly been conjured up to him. It seems beside the point to attempt the familiar critical distinction between Othello as idealist and Othello as jealousy incarnate. The two roles are at this point ironically and necessarily interdependent. Jealousy, in its self-propagating fashion, makes it impossible for him to cease doubting, while his idealism, his intense need for coherence and unity if he is to continue to signify, makes it impossible for him to halt the cycle by refusing to explore further. What would save him is an act of Venetian compromise or accommodation – an acknowledgement that truth was finally unknowable and a consequent refusal to be precipitated into action by doubt. But that, in the context that the play has established, is an unthinkable procedure in an effort so purely heroic as Othello's.

What happens then in the third Act is that the play becomes a horrifying articulation of sexual jealousy. All Othello's virtues and capacities, his idealism and his rhetoric, co-operate in the process of his self-destruction. But the effect of this is surely not to remove him from the reach of our moral comprehension; the whole effort of the play here is towards overwhelming us with the agony and the inescapability of his jealousy. Othello tries repeatedly to cling to some certainty, to some sense of his own value, but he has involved his identity so intimately with his wife's 'faith' that he can save no part of it. His attempts morally and emotionally to separate himself continually collapse into spasms of uncontrolled emotion.

> She's gone, I am abus'd, and my relief
> Must be to loathe her: O curse of marriage,
> That we can call these delicate creatures ours,
> And not their appetites.   (III.iii)

And the efforts to reassert his rhetoric, to find a balance in a kind of stoic acceptance, prove equally fruitless.

>   O, now for ever
> Farewell the tranquil mind! farewell content!
> Farewell the plumed troops, and the big wars
> That makes ambition virtue . . .
> Farewell! Othello's occupation's gone.
> Iago   Is't possible, my lord?
> Othello Villain, be sure thou prove my love a whore – '   (III.iii)

Othello's certainties, under the pressure of Iago's sophistry and suggestions, have become contradictions,

> I think my wife be honest, and think she is not;
> I think that thou art just, and think thou art not.   (III.iii)

and it is upon such logical and emotional chaos that Othello finally achieves the perverse stasis of will that ends this phase.

> Like to the Pontic sea,
> Whose icy current and compulsive course
> Ne'er feels retiring ebb, but keeps due on
> To the Propontic and the Hellespont;
> Even so my bloody thoughts, with violent pace,
> Shall ne'er look back, ne'er ebb to humble love,   (III.iii)

The perversity of this temporary triumph of will and rhetoric is insisted upon by the spectacle of Iago and Othello kneeling together to make their insane vow.

The real depth of this insanity is, of course, revealed in Act Four. The impossibility of knowledge and the torments of jealousy unhinge Othello's mind, and he desperately seizes upon the trivial handkerchief as a symbol of his life and proof of his wife's faith. It has, after all, the virtue of being a material object – its existence cannot be disputed – and Othello once again fails to distinguish between fact and significance. His rhetorical disintegration becomes one with his emotional and physical collapse and he falls into a trance. This total dislocation is the condition upon which will and rhetoric are precariously founded in the movement that culminates in the murder of Desdemona, and it is constantly evident in Othello's pathetic vacillations between tenderness and savagery. But throughout this process we are reminded of the real significance of her presumed adultery for Othello. He shows himself still conscious, beyond the insanity, the dislocation of illusion and reality that enables him to believe her adulterous, of the emotional and moral capital he has invested in her.

> Yet I could bear that too; well, very well;
> But there, where I have garner'd up my heart,
> Where either I must live or bear no life,
> The fountain from the which my current runs,
> Or else dries up – to be discarded thence!   (IV.ii)

What is horrifying, then, is the distance and yet the easy proximity of this anguish for a lost life and the perverse control that Othello attempts to impose upon it. The translation of emotion into action produces the grotesque parody of heroic nobility and certitude that informs the speech before the murder.

> It is the cause, it is the cause, my soul –
> Let me not name it to you, you chaste stars –
> It is the cause. Yet I'll not shed her blood,
> Nor scar that whiter skin of hers than snow,
> And smooth as monumental alabaster.
> Yet she must die, else she'll betray more men.   (V.ii)

199

Peter Mercer

This is indeed recognisable as a version of Othello's heroic rhetoric but it is disturbingly invalidated by its catastrophic irrelevance to the truth of the situation as perceived by the audience, and by the internal evidence of the precariousness of its consistency. Even without resort to psychological speculations about Othello's motives or 'sincerity' it can be asserted that the effect of this speech is of a parade of cold sensuality and irrelevant motive. Given the circumstances, horrifyingly clear to the audience, if not to Othello, the appeal of 'Justice' suggests a total breakdown between Othello's life-style and rhetoric and the realities and values that gave this manner substance and significance. And it is precisely this dislocation, this perversion of the relationship between Othello's hitherto self-sustaining romantic view of reality and real or potential 'actualities', that Iago has devoted his efforts to achieving. The discrepancy is objectified by Desdemona's awakening; she presents too strong a reality for the idealisation of murder.

> Mak'st me call what I intend to do
> A murder, which I thought a sacrifice. (V.ii)

This disastrous irrelevance of the relationship between rhetoric and situation is 'proved' by the squalid violence of the actual murder and Emilia's uncompromising intrusion of reality.

After this emotional crux, after Othello at his most profoundly deceived as to fact and motive, we may define two concluding movements. The first, comprising the revelation of the truth and of Othello's remorse in response to it, is usefully identifiable as the Aristotelian 'recognition'. Othello, despite his sword, is paralysed by his loss of motive; like Macbeth in the 'Tomorrow' speech he discovers he has destroyed the basis of his moral life. His self-accusations collapse into inarticulate groans.

> Whip me, ye devils,
> From the possession of this heavenly sight.
> Blow me about in winds, roast me in sulphur,
> Wash me in steep-down gulfs of liquid fire.
> O Desdemona! Dead! Desdemona! Dead!
> O! O! (V.ii)

The rapid sequence of minor relevations that follow – discovered papers, the explanation of the handkerchief – clears the way for the final movement. And this is Othello's attempt at heroic reassertion. The appeal is to a personal value that the play has shown perverted and destroyed. In the manner of heroic tragedy, we witness his symbolic rediscovery, in the face of this paralysing loss of motive and honour, of his rhetorical form. And it is this rhetoric that affirms his heroic identity and provides the context and the impetus for the significant action of suicide.

200

It would seem not unreasonable to identify this movement as having to do with Aristotle's sublimely vague 'catharsis'. The etymological and historical debates on this topic having proved continually inconclusive, it may perhaps be possible to appropriate the term for a dramatic process that is at least identifiable. Traditional speculation about the effects of tragedy on the audience seems, in any case, to offer more possibilities to the psychologist than to the critic. In fact, the process of rhetorical reassertion that I have claimed as an element in heroic tragedy and attempted to demonstrate in 'Othello', has much in common with Professor G. Else's persuasive analysis of the concept of 'catharsis' in his reading of the 'Poetics'. His suggestion that the term refers to the concluding movement in a tragic drama during which the protagonist becomes aware of the moral significance of the action and of his own responsibility, and the audience, thus aware of his awareness, is enabled to go beyond judgement to an emotion that may, however inadequately, be identified as 'awe', has an obvious relevance to the observations I have been making on tragic form. It is not inappropriate to consider the process whereby Othello moves from the repulsive self-deception of 'It is the cause, it is the cause, my soul – ' to the curiously effective mixture of humility and pride with which he asserts his nobility in his final speech as essentially purgative. The protagonist loses his delusions and his hopes, and in the privileged moment before death, defines himself with oracular certainty; the audience, observing this change, is released from antipathy and made able to react to the hero's demands for what is essentially sympathy (in the proper sense) without the distracting necessity for moral judgement. Whatever the inadequacies of such an abstraction, it does provide an idea of tragic form that avoids the inevitable distortions of our felt response that the attempt to explicate tragedy in wholly moralistic terms has been seen to produce. Such criticism has been unhappy with tragedy because finally it had no way of explaining or of registering pathos; it had no terms in which to articulate the implications of Cassio's final comment: 'For he was great of heart.'

[1969]

DAVID PIRIE

Lear as King

Critics tend to muffle the tough-minded conclusion reached at the end of *King Lear*. Jan Kott, for instance, superimposes a soothingly amoral world in which we need seek no meanings: 'All that remains at the end of this gigantic pantomime is the earth – empty and bleeding. On this earth, through which tempest has passed leaving only stones, the King, the Fool, the Blind Man and the Madman carry on their distracted Dialogue.[1] In fact, at the moment in question, three of the specified characters are silenced by death, and the fourth has appeared sufficiently undistracted to get himself elected King. Christian critics on the other hand tidy away the corpses by exalting them into intimations of immortality. For Helen Gardner the tableau of Lear holding his dead daughter in his arms recalls the image of Mary holding the body of Jesus.[2] O. J. Campbell goes even further, assuring us that Cordelia is finally 'hanged as Christ was crucified, so mankind might be saved'.[3] Campbell calls his article 'The Salvation of Lear', while a book by Paul A. Jorgensen is entitled *Lear's Self-Discovery*.[4] This interest in Lear's supposed progress to self-knowledge is still the most popular means of evading the story and its painful ending. Some modern critics may take a gloomy view of the *Lear* universe but Lear himself is usually seen as learning, if not about God, at least about the modern verities of humility and personal affection. By these contemporary standards, R. C. Sharma as recently as 1975 is able to conclude that 'Lear has been regenerated by suffering'.[5] Such approaches are so keen to find movements in Lear's mind that the intractable stasis of the corpse he finally carries tends to lose its palpability. Richard II does indeed call for a mirror to find out what the surrender of the crown has done to his own sense of identity (*Richard II*, IV.i). But Lear's use of a mirror has no interest in self-discovery, or in the implications of ceasing to be a King. For him it is only a device by which to find any surviving life in the person he loves. His urgent search with mirror and feather for a sign – not of moral worth or philosophical illumination, but of breath – has an absolute physicality. Our immediate response to that search should be no more noisily cerebral than a lump in the throat: a response which evokes the preciousness – and the precariousness – of that bodily life without which we can learn nothing.

Lamb found the clumsy physicality of *King Lear* in performance 'disgusting'. 'On the stage we see nothing but corporal infirmities and weakness' whereas 'the greatness of Lear is not in corporal dimension, but in intellectual'. He protested that 'to see an old man tottering about the stage with a walking-stick, turned out of doors by his daughters in a rainy night' merely makes us 'want to take him into shelter and relieve him'.[6] But surely this is one valid, even necessary, reaction. It may be complicated by our identification with Lear's pride in rejecting Regan's humiliating terms. It may be counterbalanced by curiosity as to how the mental drama will develop under such physical strain. But the play, even in its most loquaciously thoughtful passages, insists on the innate importance of the body and its vulnerability. Caroline Spurgeon traces the torrent of images which evoke: 'a human body in anguished movement, tugged, wrenched, beaten, pierced, stung, scourged, dislocated, flayed, gashed, scalded, tortured and finally broken on the rack'.[7] But the play's view of the human body is also very often sexual. Lear matures belatedly into an awareness of the adult world's complexity. But he does so only to panic back into a regressively simple-minded horror of the post-pubertal body. His rage at Goneril takes shape as a prayer for her sterility (I.iv.284–90). Fearing that his officials may not dispense justice fairly, he imagines a beadle who 'hotly lusts' to use 'the whore he lashes' (IV.vi.162–5). He soon forgets the notion that it is only those who 'lack soldiers' who need to resign themselves to defeat in a revolted vision of an invincible nymphomaniac. Her lecherously 'riotous appetite' centres on the 'stench' of her loins' 'sulphurous pit' (IV.vi.119–31). This is immediately followed by Gloucester wishing to kiss his King's hand. The ashamed sense of no longer being worthy to receive such respect from his subjects is given a sensual self-disgust in Lear's 'Let me wipe it first; it smells of mortality' (IV.vi.135). Such references make Lear's childish retreat from responsibility powerfully tangible. The maturity demanded by supreme office seems always to have been a strain for him. In I.i. he wishes to be 'unburthen'd' and become, not the father, but the child in Cordelia's 'kind nursery' (I.i.41, I.i.124). What he gets by this attempted role-reversal is, of course, only a bullying step-mother. Goneril, observing that 'old fools are babes again' (I.iii.20), ticks him off for his 'pranks' (I.iv.246). This rash pursuit of helplessness draws a typically physical gibe from the Fool: 'thou gav'st them the rod, / And pull'st down thine own breeches' (I.iv.179–81).

So Lamb seems to me to pose a false dichotomy in saying that it is Lear's 'mind which is laid bare. This case of flesh and blood seems too insignificant to be thought on'. Surely the play insists on mind and body being interdependent. Lear's physical suffering clearly contributes to his mental collapse, and what his 'mind laid bare' finally reveals is a chaos in which his only certainty is the need to find signs of life in Cordelia's 'case of flesh and blood'. The unyielding stance adopted by Lear's mind condemns his body to the storm – a storm which is primarily a cold, wet reality, and only secondarily a symbol of more intellectual discomforts. Mason argues that the gale is 'there above all to make one point: that an old man's daughters and his faithful servant could lock him out at night in such weather'.[8] But its reality as a natural phenomenon has at least one function since the old man is also the King. Lear's Canute-like discovery that 'the thunder would not peace at my bidding' (Iv.vi.104) is often mistakenly seen as teaching him useful truths about the impotence of kings. Critics admire his deduction that he is no more than 'A poor, infirm, weak and despis'd old man' (III.ii.19–24). But the unreliability of such an experiment can be guessed from Lear's wandering immediately into the compulsive fantasy in which the storm is in league with his 'two pernicious daughters' (III.ii.19–24). In fact the trial of strength with the storm is the same self-pamperingly dotty nonsense as Richard II's deduction that if God won't send him angels he has no means to fight Bolingbroke for his throne (*Richard II*, III.ii). Lear may be 'infirm' (though a day's hunting followed by a night's exposure on the moors seems to leave him a remarkable amount of energy). But he is 'despis'd' only by England's enemies who are arrogantly enjoying his throne. England's friends who seek to dislodge them treat Lear with consistent respect. Even when faced by his rejection, Cordelia addresses Lear as 'Your Majesty' (I.i.92; I.i.223) and Kent calls him 'Royal Lear, . . . ever honour'd as my King' (I.i.139–40). For both he is still explicitly the King as late as IV.vii (13. 77). Lear has chosen to be 'weak'. His inevitable powerlessness against the storm provides a rationale for a far from inevitable feebleness towards his more mortal enemies. A defiant attitude of mind is held with more consistency and more physical cost by his suffering subjects. Kent's refusal to compromise may only temporarily deprive him of the use of his legs in Cornwall's stocks. But Gloucester loses his eyesight for ever.

'The opaque, irreducible brutality' of Gloucester's blinding is rightly said by S. L. Goldberg to define 'the world's power to really hurt. As such it prevents us from thinking that there was nothing for Lear to get worked up about' and that his madness is 'merely a pathological condition'.[9] But most critics are too committed to the paradox that Lear's mental suffering does him a power of good to view his derangement as anything but a nobler kind of sanity. For them the blunt physicality of Gloucester's torment has little place. Bradley objects to its presentation on the stage because only in reading can its 'physical horror' be 'so far deadened' as to function properly.[10] Heilman tidies it away as but one element in a safely intellectual pattern:

> The blinding of Gloucester might well be gratuitous melodrama but for its being embedded in the concept of *seeing*: references, whether literal or figurative, to the act of seeing, to things seen (sights) to the conditions of seeing (darkness and light), and to the means of seeing (eyes) persist throughout the play . . . and what is always implied is that the problem is one of insight, of the values which determine how one sees.[11]

But the problem for Gloucester is both simpler and greater than that. Such critical cowardice seems to me forgivable. We all want Gloucester's agony to be about something smaller and less hideously simple than it is. But moralists who accept that real flesh has been torn and then see it as proper punishment for fleshly sin do alarm me. Traversi says that 'the "dark and vicious place" in which Edmund was "unnaturally begot" brought the father in due course to blindness and his bastard son, in the very moment that should have been that of his triumph to his fall'.[12] If human beings can see that as a moral pattern, I join Edmund in saying 'Now, gods, stand up for bastards' (I.ii.22). The story in fact tells us that Edmund has enough faults of his own to make Edgar's destruction of him perfectly just. Gloucester's own case is infinitely more marginal. His role in the exposing of Lear to the heath is equivocal. So there may be a kind of excessively rough justice in the disaster he suffers at the hands of those with whom he has perhaps, however unconsciously, chosen to ally himself. But his role in changing back so firmly to the right side is heroic.

Gloucester is punished by the ruling regime for seeking to overthrow it. He rashly tells Edmund that he is aiding Cordelia's attempted coup on behalf of the rightful monarch: 'there is part of a power already footed; we must incline to the King . . . If I die for it, as no less is threatened me, the King, my old master, must be relieved' (III.iii.12–20). He has sent his own retainers with Lear's knights to join a rising of 'well-armed friends' in Dover (III.vii.15–19). He is therefore not only in correspondence but also in military alliance with those whom Cornwall calls 'The traitors / Late footed in the kingdom' (III.vii.43–4). Gloucester is not some independent-minded social worker trying to rescue an old man from domestic violence. He has got Lear to the Dover rallying point because he wants him to be King again in power as well as name. Being joined by their King would be of enormous value to the insurgents' morale. Cornwall presumably hopes partly to counterbalance this by releasing a blinded conspirator to 'smell / His way to Dover' (III.vii.92–3). His tormentors four times in the blinding scene call Gloucester a 'traitor' and they allow him to live on as an example to other so-called rebels. The device back-fires, of course, since the brutality revealed through Gloucester's blinding does not intimidate but enrage potential royalists. Regan complains that 'where he arrives he moves / All hearts against us' (IV.v.10–11). But essentially Gloucester suffers for a political stance, and it is that right-minded stance not his terrible suffering which the play approves.

The good characters argue throughout the play that the abdication should be revoked and England again be ruled by its rightful King. At the outset we have Kent's outraged insistence that Lear keep the crown: 'Reserve thy state; / And, in thy best consideration, check / This hideous rashness'

David Pirie

(I.i.149–51). At the end there is the reformed Albany's commitment to 'resign, / During the life of this old Majesty, / To him our absolute power:' (V.iii.298–300). But Lear himself is on both occasions looking away. At the end he can see nothing but his murdered child: 'Look on her, look, her lips, / Look there, look there!' (V.iii.310–11). At the beginning he must be glowering at Cordelia and blind to the crown he hands to Cornwall and Albany. Otherwise he would see not only the intellectual inconsistency but also the practical absurdity of 'This coronet part between you' (I.i.139). If he had even noticed the physical fact of what he was doing he would have had to hand them a hack-saw with the crown, a point made by the Fool: 'When thou clov'st thy crown i' th' middle and gav'st away both parts, thou bor'st thine ass on thy back o'er the dirt: thou hadst little wit in thy bald crown when thou gav'st thy gold one away' (I.iv.167–71). The embarrassment of two men trying to accept one crown is but one of the play's crucially visual moments. The political lunacy seen in physical action by an audience can be missed by a reader on such occasions. Another is the map with which Lear shows Goneril and Regan their own sections of dismantled England (I.i.63–67; I.i.79–82). He introduces it with ominous words as soon as he enters:

> Meantime we shall express our darker purpose.
> Give me the map there. Know that we have divided
> In three our Kingdom. (I.i.36–8)

Early productions may well have made this map large enough for the audience to be able to recognise the shape of their own recently and precariously united kingdom. Kenneth Muir notes: 'If *King Lear* was written in the winter of 1604–5 the date would fit in with the political situation, for between 1604 and 1607 James was trying to get Parliament to approve of the union of England and Scotland, and referring in speech after speech to the misfortunes that division brought to early Britain'.[13] M. C. Bradbrook quotes the Bishop of Bristol arguing in 1606 'for the existent utility and urgent necessity of the desired happy Union'. The Bishop preached that its political opponents should be killed rather than allow the unity of the kingdom to be put at risk. The division of the realm would be as unnatural as the disintegration of 'the firmament of heaven which God hath adorned'.[14] Muir only cites the political situation as a means of dating the play and Bradbrook dismisses it as 'subsidiary', but it may well not have seemed so to Shakespeare. In *Henry IV* it is the rebels who gather round a map of England divided 'Into three limits very equally'. They immediately start squabbling about the relative worth of the territorial booty each intends to gain if their coup against the King is successful (Part I, III.i.). In *King Lear* too the divided kingdom is shown to collapse inevitably into conflict between competing shareholders.

As early as II.i Edmund and Curran discuss the news that rivalry between Cornwall and Albany is likely to lead to war. Bradley, like so many critics since, treats the bloodshed of civil war with a chilling blandness. Lear's surrender of the throne, unlike his rejection of Cordelia, 'was not a "hideous rashness" or incredible folly . . . It would probably have led quickly to war, but not to the agony which culminated in the storm upon the heath'.[15] But the play explores more than the mental agony of Lear as a man. It also documents the physical torment to which as an abdicating king he exposes his subjects. Gloucester's servant dies trying to stop one English nobleman from blinding another. The Old Man is advised that to be caught comforting Gloucester will put his own life in jeopardy (IV.i.16–17). Albany confesses that the brutality of the regime has been widespread: an army of 'others whom the rigour of our state / Forc'd to cry out' has rallied to the old King (V.i.21–3). They have 'Most just and heavy causes' for their opposition to the junta (V.i.27). As the climactic horror of civil war looms nearer, we are told that the battle is 'like to be bloody' (IV.vii.97). Later, grim confirmation comes from the victorious Edmund complaining: 'We sweat and bleed; the friend hath lost his friend' (V.iii.56).

Bradley anyway seems to me mistaken in thinking that Lear's own 'agony . . . upon the heath' is not made almost inevitable by his equivocal abdication. Much of the indignity suffered by Lear derives from his nonsensical attempt to stop being, and yet go on being, King. He gives away 'all the large effects / That troop with majesty' and yet somehow retains 'all th'addition to a king' (I.i.130–9). If the abdication is valid Mason is right to describe Cornwall's putting Kent in the stocks as 'an exercise of proper authority . . . that became his by Lear's own act.' Kent has indeed behaved towards Oswald 'as if Lear were still fully King and Oswald were the servant of a rebel'.[16] But then Kent believes just that, since the abdication has always seemed to him sheer nonsense. It is Lear himself who equivocates as to how far he is still 'The King' and how far what Oswald suggests, merely a father whose reception must depend on how 'dear' he is to his daughters (II.iv.101–2). So Goneril may be justified in complaining at a Fool who has been insulting her courtiers as if he were still all-licensed by a reigning monarch. A. L. French argues that she and Regan behave reasonably at first and that there is then a 'radical change in their presentation' beginning in III.iii. There, he says, Gloucester reports them as banning in 'a quasi-regal way' any contact with Lear, and indeed that they are plotting to assassinate him.[17] We need not accept French's view that here Shakespeare is just offering a cheeky inconsistency. As the impossibility of Lear's remaining merely an ex-king dawns on everyone, the present rulers move from thinking him a nuisance to recognising him as a danger. In I.iv. it is but one of Goneril's objections to the

David Pirie

retention of an armed escort that Lear might use them in an attempt to regain power 'And hold our lives in mercy' (I.iv.337). But by II.iv., Regan is beginning to see the inherent threat of Lear's Janus-like status:

> How, in one house,
> Should many people, under two commands,
> Hold amity? 'Tis hard; almost impossible.   (II.iv.242–4)

What is true of one house may well be true of one country, and Regan insists that Lear commit himself to full abdication: 'I pray you, father, being weak, seem so' (II.iv.203). Lear's stubbornly unexplained resolve to keep his armed men leads her to 'spy a danger' (II.iv.249). Once he has stormed off with his followers, Regan (with Cornwall's explicit approval) orders that the doors be shut against the possibility that Lear's 'desperate train' should 'incense him' into attempting a night attack (II.iv.304–11). It is hardly surprising that Regan should already be adopting Edmund's later view that Lear as a potential rallying-point for rebellion is too dangerous to live: 'for my state / Stands on me to defend, not to debate' (V.ii.68–9). What is surprising perhaps is that Lear's own attitude is so different. Far from mounting the feared attack he does indeed debate and leaves his undefended state to a political nightmare.

All this is, of course, a vulgar distraction for those who see the play as a spiritual striptease in which one old man lays bare his soul. To them Lear's deranged debate is all-important: 'it is no accident that the drama of self-discovery is made far more intense, more painful, and more exhausting by the hero's madness. For even we that are young see the whole journey through Lear's aged and bewitched eyes'.[18] But surely to do so is a wilful misreading of what is, after all, a play and not a dramatic monologue. Lear does admittedly discover – however belatedly for a head of state – that society is cruelly unfair to the poor, and that the dispensation of justice by a fallible human being is exceedingly difficult. But he remains incapable of relating these insights either to his own responsibilities as King or to the immediate situation. Having decided that he has 'ta'en too little care of' his kingdom's 'poor naked wretches', Lear finds his party frightened by just such a figure in Poor Tom. The Fool panics shouting 'Help me! Help me!' but it is Kent, not Lear, who takes the Fool's hand and asks Poor Tom who he is. All Lear can offer is the obsessive egotism of 'didst thou give all to thy daughters? And art thou come to this?' Within a dozen lines of admitting responsibility for his subjects' poverty, he has persuaded himself that it is all the fault of the Gonerils and Regans (III.iv.28–49). There is an oddly similar gulf between apparently thoughtful generalisation and unthinkingly ignored example in Act IV. There he tells the wealthy Duke of Gloucester who has just been blinded that in an unjust society the rich are invulnerable:

> Robes and furr'd gowns hide all. Plate sin with gold
> And the strong lance of justice hurtless breaks;
> Arm it in rags, a pigmy's straw does pierce it.
> None does offend, none, I say, none. (IV. vi. 167–70)

Lear in eventually discovering the difficulty of making sound distinctions decides not to make any. Either even those who have blinded Gloucester have not committed an offence or, as in the last scene, all have offended, Edgar and Kent being as guilty as the usurpers who killed his daughter:

> *Edgar* 'Tis noble Kent, your friend.
> *Lear* A plague upon you, murderers, traitors all! (V. iii. 267–70)

Indeed the only distinction Lear learns to make is that which validates Cordelia as more precious to him than his other daughters and (by the end) than anything else in the universe. Even this discovery is made slowly. As late as II. iv. he thinks he could not accept shelter in Cordelia's home if it meant humbling himself. It would, he says, be as bad as returning to Goneril, or even being 'slave and sumpter' to a man like Oswald (209–19). He does not mention Cordelia in the storm scenes or even in IV. vi. where he lectures Gloucester for more than a hundred lines about what he has learnt from his suffering. These ramblings are more concerned with trying to remember the other great obligation he tried to deny at the outset.

He may show no sign in this scene of wanting again to be Cordelia's father, but he does try to remember the other vital role which he initially tried to discard. He enters saying 'they cannot touch me for coining; I am the King himself'. He is right to see all other aspirants to the throne as counterfeits but he seems still uncomprehending of the fact that it was he himself who minted their bogus royalty in I. i. Pathetically confused attempts to reassert his status continue when Gloucester calls him King and Lear replies: 'Ay, every inch a King: / When I do stare, see how the subject quakes' (IV. vi. 109–11). Gloucester of course is not quaking with respect because Lear no longer looks like a King as he did to Kent in I. iv. 30 ('you have that in your countenance which I would fain call master'). On the contrary his subjects now quake because the one man who must be King is mad. Lear, 'fantastically dressed with wild flowers' and announcing as his 'great image of Authority' a yapping dog (IV. vi. 159–60), is to Edgar a 'side-piercing sight' (Iv. vi. 85). To the Gentleman this is: 'A sight most pitiful in the meanest wretch, / Past speaking of in a King!' (IV. vi. 205–6). Lear's own wearied brain insists on the fact: 'I am a king, masters, know you that?' and it is without irony that his abandoned but loyal subjects manage to reply: 'You are a royal one, and we obey you' (IV. vi. 201–2). Jorgensen rightly sees so many references in one scene as 'surely significant', but they suggest to him only the 'insecurity of identity' and 'anxiety of guilt' of an archetypal human being, not a precariously confused attempt by Lear to accept again his peculiar responsibilities as a king. [19]

The almost immediate failure of that attempt in the next scene where he awakes to Cordelia is welcomed by critics as a triumph. Jorgensen says that Lear at last 'faces the full truth of who he is: one still not in his perfect mind, old and a *man*. Significantly he no longer mentions his being King.'[20] But would the 'full' truth not have included a memory of *both* the great values he denied in I.i? Indeed a 'full' understanding even of the importance of human love might have led him to identify with Cordelia's interest in saving his kingdom. But Lear's re-established love of Cordelia, as we shall see, does not involve accepting the truth about her. He can credit her giving him houseroom as a private person in her new French home. He cannot believe that she is so different from him as to be mounting a military campaign to restore him to the English throne:

> Lear   Am I in France?
> Kent   In your own Kingdom, Sir.
> Lear   Do not abuse me.   (IV.vii.76–8)

Lear is led away by his doctors, mumbling resignedly that he is 'old and foolish', asking only that Cordelia and the rest 'forget and forgive' (IV.viii.84). He leaves on the stage Kent and the Gentleman who have more urgent things to discuss than an ex-politician who wants to see himself only as 'a very foolish, fond old man' (IV.viii.60). They do not exchange a syllable about Lear. Kent for instance needs to know who commands the enemy forces now that Cornwall is dead. The Gentleman is anxious about news that potential allies are absent abroad. As 'the powers of the kingdom approach apace', Kent says that what he has stood for all his life will turn out 'well or ill, as this day's battle's fought' (IV.vii.93–6). He exits to risk his neck in a conflict which neither his King nor most modern criticism seems to care about. Neither seem to grasp the awesome physicalities by which power is lost and gained.

Bradley will not stoop to concern himself with the fight for England. He complains that 'There is something almost ludicrous in the insignificance of this battle . . . Even if Cordelia had won . . . Shakespeare would probably have hesitated to concentrate interest on it, for her victory would have been a British defeat'.[21] This is absurd. Would Kent or Edgar or Gloucester or the peasantry represented by his martyred servant or the loyal gentry (characterised by that thoroughly civilised Gentleman of III.i. and IV.iii.) have seen the defeat of Cordelia as a British triumph? As for the King of France, he is conveniently absent. So we know that he has no more selfish motive than support for his wife's desire to see her father back on the throne of her original country. In engineering the absence, Shakespeare economically provides an example of a king to contrast with Lear. France does accept direct responsibility for his subjects' welfare. He has to return 'so suddenly' because his own kingdom is in 'so much fear and danger that his personal return' is 'most requir'd and necessary' (IV.iii.1–7). One bewildered critic complains: 'No-one would notice the King's absence if our attention hadn't been drawn to it in this clumsy way'.[22] But our attention is surely being drawn – however clumsily – to the fact that the presence of a true ruler, especially when his people are in 'fear and danger', is absolutely 'required and necessary'. Lear's less fortunate subjects are abandoned by their King and must seek what help they can. Obviously an English audience would think it an embarrassing measure of the chaos of the divided kingdom that its patriots have to resort to an alliance with the French of all people if it is to be saved. But saved the audience must wish it to be.

Critics who are unduly concerned with Lear take little notice of Cordelia's attempt to win back his throne. They might at least observe that her defeat in battle ensures that she, and her father, will be killed. At a relatively early stage we hear of a plot to assassinate Lear (III.vi.92). He must seem to Goneril and Regan as likely a focus for rebellion as Mary Queen of Scots seemed to Elizabeth. Cordelia's ability to substitute for her raving father and successfully raise an insurrection must make her too an unacceptable threat to the Junta. The adventurer, Edmund, at first aiming only at his brother's lands, finds himself in the political vacuum created by Lear's abdication able to go for the throne itself. He is thus clear-headed enough to dismiss Albany's delusion that they can have secure power while the rightful king and his heir survive:

> As for the mercy
> Which he intends to Lear and Cordelia,
> The battle done, and they within our power,
> Shall never see his pardon; (V.ii.65–9)

Muir explains that at this point: 'Edmund hopes that Goneril will kill Albany, and kill, or be killed by, Regan, leaving him free to marry the survivor. The survival of Lear and Cordelia would prejudice his chances of becoming King of the united kingdom.'[23] Thus Edmund's machiavellian shrewdness and Kent's traditional wisdom strangely unite into a shared common sense. Both know that the divided kingdom is a temporary nonsense which, in the order of things, must resolve itself again to monarchical government; and that the emerging ruler will have to have a genealogical claim.

The contemporary audience would probably agree with them. Certainly they would be able to predict that Edmund will think his victory fragile until it is underpinned by regicide. The much publicised trials of the Gunpowder

David Pirie

Plotters took place in the January of 1606 when the play may well have been written. Some of these would-be regicides had been implicated in Essex's rebellion four and a half years earlier. Then a production of Shakespeare's Elizabethan drama of abdication – *Richard II* – had been banned as too sensitively relevant. In his Jacobean play on the topic it seems likely that he could anticipate an audience which would think little had changed in the interval. The revulsion and terror caused by the news of the November 5th plot made the English eager to listen to endless sermons about the sanctity of hereditary Kings and the unnaturalness of rebellion. I am not suggesting that *King Lear* is any such simplistic sermon. But its first audience in December 1606 were still so earnestly congratulating each other on their own miraculous escape from a political Armageddon that they are not likely to have ignored the play's plot of a murderous struggle for power.

Cordelia herself explicitly fears 'the worst' as they are being led off to prison. Perhaps her anticipation that they will be killed is what nerves her to want a final confrontation in which to denounce her sisters:

> We are not the first
> Who, with best meaning, have incurred the worst.
> For thee, oppressed King, am I cast down;
> Myself could else out-frown false Fortune's frown.
> Shall we not see these daughters and these sisters? (V.iii.3–7)

This plucky suggestion is Cordelia's last statement in the play. It is immediately crushed by Lear's quadruple rejection:

> No, no, no, no! Come, let's away to prison;
> We two alone will sing like birds i'th' cage:
> When thou dost ask me blessing, I'll kneel down,
> And ask of thee forgiveness: so we'll live,
> And pray, and sing, and tell old tales, and laugh
> At gilded butterflies, and hear poor rogues
> Talk of court news; and we'll talk with them too,
> Who loses and who wins; who's in, who's out. (V.iii.8–15)

This appallingly insensitive response to his daughter's question reduces her to tears. She has told him that she is ready to curse her enemies, and he hears only the murmuring fantasy in which she asks for his blessing. She has selflessly thought of one way in which he, as an 'oppressed King', deserves more pity than she does. He shows no understanding of the way in which she as a young bride will feel more deprivation in prison than he can. She has brought an army from France because of her conviction that it matters desperately 'who's in, who's out'. He regards such court news as merely entertaining gossip comparable to laughing at butterflies or swapping old stories. Bradley puts the popular view in describing Lear's 'serene renuncia-

212

tion of the world' as a sign of his 'recovery'.[24] But the world Lear so scorn-fully seeks to escape is his own kingdom. Nahum Tate, adapting the play in 1681 for a happy ending, did have Lear retiring from active politics. But he knew that no audience would then approve an ex-king who was so uncon-cerned about 'who's in, who's out'. So Tate's Lear looks forward to taking a proper interest in the way his surviving child and her consort will run the country, making him 'Cheered with Relation of the prosperous Reign / Of this celestial Pair'. But Shakespeare's Lear is not likely to have a surviving child to compete with those aspirants who are still at liberty to fight it out. A king who is so dismissive of the power-struggle for his country may become vulnerably unimportant to those urgently resolving 'Who loses and who wins'.

Lear is dimly aware that the retreat represents a sacrifice of Cordelia's own instincts. He almost admits the possessive selfishness which delights in finally having 'caught' her:

Upon such sacrifices, my Cordelia,
The Gods themselves throw incense. Have I caught thee?
He that parts us shall bring a brand from heaven,
And fire us hence like foxes.   (V.iii.20–3)

Edmund's gaol functions also as Lear's bird-cage or foxhole in which Cordelia – unless there is supernatural interference 'from heaven' – can no longer escape him. The moral confusion of all this is nicely pointed by the imagery. He had once railed at his two unloving daughters as being sub-human 'she-foxes' (III.vi.24). Now in his sweepingly inclusive acceptance that 'None does offend', he serenely sees himself and Cordelia as foxes. Similarly 'birds i' the cage' may appear to celebrate their helpless confine-ment but the weeping Cordelia cannot rejoice in it, and a defeated King should not. Lear's haziness about any peculiarly human needs and values here recalls earlier images of birds. One had expressed his anarchic delusion that people are indistinguishable from the creatures whose sexuality dis-gusts him:

die for adultery! No:
The wren goes to't, and the small gilded fly
Does lecher in my sight.
Let copulation thrive . . .   (IV.vi.114–16)

If Cordelia has no more demands than a caged bird in Lear's tired brain, he has not fully grasped the gulf between her and his other 'pelican daughters' (III.iv.75), one of whom he describes as both a 'kite' and a 'vulture' (I.iv.271, II.iv.136). The pattern has incidentally been reinforced by the Fool telling Lear that Goneril is both a 'cuckoo' and 'A fox' (I.iv.224, I.iv.326). Cordelia presents herself in her last speech as an essentially human face, wishing to 'out-frown' her sisters, and, when prevented, collapsing into tears. But Lear dotes on her, one fears, for much the same confused reasons that he will laugh at his faceless gilded butterflies.

Lear's last denial of Cordelia's reality is to tell her – even while she is weeping – that it is impossible for her to be reduced to tears:

> Wipe thine eyes;
> The good years shall devour them, flesh and fell,
> Ere they shall make us weep; we'll see 'em starved first.
> Come.
> *(Exeunt Lear and Cordelia, guarded.)* (V.iii.23–5)

So Lear leads her away into the vulnerable irrelevance he has chosen for himself. Those who remain in the accelerating plots of the play (and of the world it images) are too busy to remember the drop-outs until too late. Many critics have complained that the delay in discovering what has happened to Lear and Cordelia is inexplicable. But the text is frank enough. When Kent comes 'To bid my King and master aye good night', he simply jogs memories which had been preoccupied. Albany piously calls it a 'great thing of us forgot' (V.iii.234–7). But in fact so many more urgent matters have been being resolved that the audience itself may have been similarly forgetful. Regan announcing her plan to marry Edmund, the latter's arrest for high treason, Regan's departure to die of poison, the crucial battle between the brothers and the reported deaths of Gloucester and Goneril flood the mind until, perhaps, as Harrison suggests, we find: 'In the fury and confusion of these crowded moments, we had forgotten the old King'.[25] Albany does solemnly suggest that 'this old Majesty' should again take power, but he has made it clear half a dozen lines earlier that the idea is impractical: 'He knows not what he says, and vain is it / That we present us to him' (V.iii.292–300). Albany now knows what the audience has known at least since the 'birds i' the cage' speech: Lear's second abdication is irrevocable. He had serenely welcomed Edmund's prison bars as finally cutting him off for ever from the values he gave away with the crown. He hoped by this to get back the rejected daughter who is now by a brutal logic made equally unreachable.[26] But though this is the end of Lear, and an end so potently moving that it seems impertinent to offer commentary on his last shattered and shattering speeches, it is not the end of *King Lear*. Edgar agrees with Albany that it is 'Very bootless' to try to interest Lear again in affairs of state (V.iii.294). Yet it is Edgar who makes the last appeal to him. Edgar, who understands all that the old men have learnt about the suffering of 'poor, naked wretches' but rejected the escape-routes of suicide and madness, biding his time until he could strike down the tyrants with a sword of justice, is the last to try and win Lear back to the world. 'Look there, look there' cries the dying Lear, clutching the corpse which is beyond all human aid. 'Look up, my Lord' says Edgar who stands amongst the survivors of Lear's holocaust: survivors who desperately need their new King to 'Rule in this realm, and the gor'd state sustain' (V.iii.312–20).

We should respond to both claims on our attention. With Edgar we look up at the dangerous and demanding world. There we see those who suffered through Lear's forgetting them, and who have now unwittingly wrought their terrible revenge by themselves forgetting until it is too late the only person he loves. With Lear we look down towards the lifeless remains of one who had become all that Lear wanted and whose death leaves him with literally nothing in which he can take interest: 'No, no, no life!' (V.iii.305). The power of Lear's intolerably frustrated love for Cordelia lies not in any moral quality but in its anguished intensity. The Lear who in I.i. found it so outrageous that his daughter should love her husband as well as himself is still recognisable in the old man who expects her to find happiness with him alone in prison. But the love which develops so little in terms of imaginativeness about the beloved's separate nature still grows enormously in stature. It is only the guilt-ridden Lear himself who wrongly thinks that love from someone who is morally flawed cannot impress:

> If you have poison for me, I will drink it.
> I know you do not love me; for your sisters
> Have, as I do remember, done me wrong;
> You have some cause, they have not.   (IV.vii.72–4)

But for Cordelia – and presumably for Shakespeare – love is more absolute than this. However clumsily selfish Lear's need of her may seem, its strength moves us. In extreme old age he stumbles towards a person he will never understand, offering her with idiotic confidence his paradise which we must expect to be for her a veritable hell. But she loves him for it. Through her, Shakespeare challenges us to value Lear's love as the blundering but passionate thing it is. It makes him no cleverer as a philosopher. It makes him no nicer to other people, not even his best friend, Kent. It probably makes him even more irresponsibly determined to forget his subjects. It leaves him no better informed about the qualities in Cordelia that make it reasonable to love her. But because of, not in spite of, all these things his final heart-break voices with supreme clarity the logic-defying certainty of love's importance.

While we look with Lear at the unspeakable lifelessness which eventually overtakes everyone we love, love's preciousness is paradoxically asserted. To the extent that we can turn away and look up with Edgar at a community wounded by civil war, the courage of those who strive to hold the community together is given a sober dignity. By such painfully discovered positives

215

David Pirie

tragedy achieves its equipoise. But in *King Lear* we are also offered an overall equivocation in two apparently different assertions being made through the story of one man. Lear's love is torn by death to reveal his need of Cordelia. His country is ripped open by anarchy to show its need of a king. The fact that Cordelia perishes at the hand of a politican assassin while the country is fought for by those who have forgotten her does not mean that Lear is punished for valuing private love to the exclusion of public duty. It merely records the fact that the world in which we live is one and indivisible. There is no escape from it into any Utopian gilded cage. But equally Edmund is deluded in trying to play out his game of power politics as if personal relationship existed only in a quite different world. It is his love-affair with the sisters that causes his arrest for treason by one of their husbands and it is the resulting trial by combat that kills him.

Ripeness is all to the ubiquitous Edgar. He knows when to comfort his father, when to leave him to do just battle, and when to return – once it is clear that 'King Lear hath lost' – to ensure his father gets away safely. This dangerously unified world through which Edgar so deftly threads his way is the world of the play. The story insists that Lear and the daughter he loves cannot escape it except in death. Perhaps criticism too should now try to see Lear not only in the confused ways he sees himself but also in the daunting but inescapably integrated world portrayed as *King Lear*.

Notes

All references to the play are to the Arden edition.

1 *Shakespeare Our Contemporary* (Methuen, 1964), 118.
2 *King Lear, The John Coffin Memorial Lecture* (The Athlone Press, 1966), 27–8.
3 'The salvation of Lear', *ELH*, XV: 2, 93–109.
4 University of California Press, 1967.
5 *Lear's Self-Discovery* (Macmillan, 1975), 263.
6 *On the Tragedies of Shakespeare*.
7 *Shakespeare's Imagery* (1935), 339.
8 H. A. Mason, *Shakespeare's Tragedies of Love* (Chatto & Windus, 1970), 195.
9 *An Essay on 'King Lear'* (Cambridge, 1973), 88–9.
10 *Shakespearean Tragedy*, 205.
11 R. B. Heilman, *This Great Stage* (University of Washington Press, 1948), 25.
12 'King Lear', *Scrutiny* vol. XIX, 1952–3.
13 Introduction to Arden edition, xxiv.
14 *The Living Monument* Cambridge University Press, 1976), 155.
15 *Shakespearean Tragedy* (1904), 205.
16 *Shakespeare's Tragedies of Love* (Chatto & Windus, 1970), 190–1.
17 *Shakespeare and the Critics* (Cambridge University Press, 1972), 163–5.
18 Paul A. Jorgensen, *Lear's Self-Discovery* (Macmillan, 1975), 82.

19   *Ibid.*, 109.
20   *Ibid.*, 110.
21   *Op. cit.*, 209.
22   A. L. French, *Shakespeare and the Critics* (Cambridge University Press, 1972), 151.
23   Arden edition, 197, note to lines 68–9.
24   *Op. cit.*, 239.
25   G. B. Harrison, *Shakespeare's Tragedies* (Routledge & Kegan Paul, 1951), 182.
26   William Empson, in a brilliant review of Maynard Mack's *King Lear in Our Time,* writes: 'A man within earshot of an army advancing to kill himself and his daughter says 'Let us become beatniks; we will enter peace together', and she weeps; after the enemy has killed her, he naturally decides that it wasn't much good being a beatnik' (*Essays in Criticism*, vol. XVII, No. 1, January 1967).

[1980]

W. HUTCHINGS

Beast or god: the *Coriolanus* controversy

Coriolanus is one of Shakespeare's most controversial plays. While critics disagree fundamentally about its politics, meaning and status, it has often flaunted its theatrical vitality. A French performance at the time of the Stavisky affair provoked riots, a German translation by Hans Rothe was suppressed by the Nazis, the Americans banned performances in Germany after the Second World War, and the Berliner Ensemble prepared a celebrated version based on Brecht's uncompleted adaptation (in which tribunes and plebeians were vindicated, and Martius degraded). Critical uncertainty about its standing may, indeed, owe much to its provocative nature: a play which sets authoritarianism against democracy, ruler against ruled, the shedding of blood against the ties of blood, is likely to be the object of constant, committed, re-assessment.

Coriolanus may have begun its life in controversy. E. C. Pettet (*Shakespeare Survey*, 1950) has argued that the play alludes to riots which occurred in the Midlands in 1607, caused by anti-enclosure feeling and fears of a corn shortage. Though limited in extent and effect, this popular uprising may have spurred Shakespeare to make the issue of famine more prominent than in Plutarch. Whether or not Pettet's speculation is correct that the play's depiction of the plebeians displays 'the natural reactions of a man of substance to a recent mob rising in his country' (Shakespeare by then owned land in Warwickshire), its initial topicality is clear. The state of the world today ensures its continued topicality.

All critics would agree that politics is important in the play; but not all see politics as central. A primary division exists between those who would have Martius taking his place within Shakespeare's analysis of the state of Roman society, and those who would have Martius as standing out against a political background. Is *Coriolanus* about a society or about one great man? Since it is Martius who connects diverse elements of the play (Volumnia and Virgilia, the patricians, the battle, Aufidius and the Volscians) and who gives it its title, it is not surprising that many writers have concentrated their attention on him. Historically, though, emphasis on tragedy as character can be seen as a legacy of a tendency, prevalent in the late nineteenth and early twentieth centuries, to treat plays as if they were novels without a narrator. So Edward Dowden and A. C. Swinburne, writing in 1875 and 1880 respectively, very firmly put Coriolanus at the centre. For Dowden, 'the central and vivifying element in the play is not a political problem, but an individual character and life'; while Swinburne asserts that the play 'is from first to last, for all its turmoil of battle and clamour of contentious factions, rather a private and domestic than a public or historical tragedy'. These Victorian judgements contrast with the stress which William Hazlitt had laid on the political issues, even in the context of a study of Shakespeare's characters. Writing as a radical himself, Hazlitt detected Shakespeare's sympathies as, alas, lying on 'the arbitrary side of the question': the bitter moral is 'that those who have little shall have less, and that those who have much shall take all that others have left'.

Character and politics can be regarded as complementary rather than antithetical in the structure of *Coriolanus*. Shakespeare himself points the way by the scrupulous care with which he opens the very first scene. The plebeians who begin the play talk about their grievance, that they are suffering from famine while the patricians have more food than they need, but spend an almost exactly equal time on Martius: in the Arden text, the first forty-five lines divide roughly into twenty-eight about Martius and twenty-seven about the famine. Further, Shakespeare quietly relates the two topics through his language; as when the First Citizen asks that the patricians would 'yield us but the superfluity' of their corn, and goes on to remark that Martius 'hath faults, with surplus'. Menenius's entry concentrates attention on the famine, his fable of the belly relating individual hunger to the organisation of the state by moving from 'body' to a metaphorical 'body politic' (on which concept see Andrew Gurr, *Shakespeare Survey*, 1975). The forceful entry of Martius then demonstrates class strife in violent operation in the attitude of one dominating figure. Shakespeare sustains the notion of excess when Martius responds to the news that the Volscians are in arms with the wry comment that war will 'vent / Our musty superfluity'. If the plebeians think that the patricians have too much food, Martius thinks that there are too many plebeians.

The effect of such careful ordering is to keep before the audience both the current state of Rome and the pre-eminent Roman. The two are inextricably involved with each other. The play's crisis occurs when the great Roman quits Rome. Coriolanus's cry of 'I banish you!' (III. iii. 123) raises the question of whether Rome can still be properly Roman when the great exemplar of Roman military prowess departs; or, from the other point of view, the question of whether a man with such an attitude can properly be regarded as Roman. From either angle our attention must be on the state and Caius Martius Coriolanus, for our attitude to the one affects our attitude to the other.

Emphasis on the politics of the play has a further problem to deal with. While Hazlitt thought that *Coriolanus* betrayed Shakespeare's bias,

W. Hutchings

Coleridge praised the 'wonderful philosophic impartiality in Shakespeare's politics'. Whether or not it be the result of a desire not to convict Shakespeare of views generally unacceptable in the West today, modern criticism tends to agree with Coleridge, claiming that the two sides of society receive comparable praise and blame. Even such a critic as O. J. Campbell (*Shakespeare's Satire*, 1943), who, daringly for the date of publication, openly takes the Hazlitt line, is very careful to hedge with qualification and even excuse. He sets Shakespeare in his age, pointing out that political theory of the time saw in what we call democracy the 'absence of all government – a form of organized disorder'. On the other hand, Campbell convicts Coriolanus of being a bad ruler, so that the situation is one in which 'no civil group performs its prescribed duties properly'. This careful, historically-aware approach has the merit of preventing us from jumping to indefensible conclusions, but rather smooths over a rough-edged play. *Coriolanus* is, in language and action, violent and painful; and any conclusion which fails to take account of this is out of tune with the drama.

Those familiar with the writing of Jan Kott will not be surprised to find his view of the play highly disturbing. His essay (*Shakespeare Our Contemporary*, 1965) gives greater intensity and precision to the idea of antagonistic social groups. His *Coriolanus* is a history of class struggle with Shakespeare unflinchingly bringing into confrontation three conflicting systems: egalitarianism, hierarchy and 'solidaritism', the last being represented by Menenius's statement of the organic nature of society. Kott's argument is that, by refusing to opt openly for any of these systems, Shakespeare ruthlessly exposes the limitations of each. The people's cowardly behaviour in the war confirms Coriolanus's view of their inferiority: he calls them 'curs', 'hares' and 'geese' when he first enters, and by scene four they seem to have proved that they have 'souls of geese'. In contrast, Coriolanus is the archetypal warrior-hero; but his system of values is implicitly called into question when he describes what the victor in war does:

> Condemning some to death, and some to exile,
> Ransoming him, or pitying, threat'ning th'other;
> Holding Corioles in the name of Rome,
> Even like a fawning greyhound in the leash,
> To let him slip at will. (I. vi. 35–9)

Shakespeare here objectifies a set of values so that an audience is forced to judge. Who performs the more admirably, cowardly plebeians or ruthless patricians? Kott provides one of the darkest views: the world lacks all cohesion, and resolves no contradictions. This is typified in the figure of a man who wants to destroy the world because it rejects his 'absurd system of values'.

220

It may be significant that the one essay which rivals Kott's for gloom also concentrates on politics and also constitutes one of the four or five really indispensable pieces on *Coriolanus*. The key to A. P. Rossiter's view (*Angel With Horns*, 1961) is Act III scene i, where Coriolanus berates the two tribunes for upholding the rights of a rabble and the patricians for not taking drastic action to halt mutiny:

> Purpose so barr'd, it follows
> Nothing is done to purpose. Therefore beseech you –
> You that will be less fearful than discreet,
> That love the fundamental part of state
> More than you doubt the change on't; that prefer
> A noble life before a long, and wish
> To jump a body with a dangerous physic
> That's sure of death without it – at once pluck out
> The multitudinous tongue: let them not lick
> The sweet which is their poison. Your dishonour
> Mangles true judgement, and bereaves the state
> Of that integrity which should becom't,
> Not having the power to do the good it would
> For th'ill which doth control't.   (III. i. 147–60)

Central to the play are social order and disruptive forces which deprive the state of such integrity. Like Kott, Rossiter rejects simple interpretations, seeing Shakespeare as concerned with the 'conflict and uncertainty in human minds, confronted with the complexities and uncertainties of human events'. The tragic essence lies in the clash between rigid beliefs and the shifting nature of reality. Coriolanus's convinced determination is out of touch with social movement; whereas a Menenius is always prepared to adjust to new circumstances.

Again, the idea can be tested against Shakespeare's careful organisation of his play. After Martius's courageous, foolhardy exploits at Corioles, the scene switches to another part of the battle where Cominius is conducting matters in an altogether different manner:

> Breathe you, my friends; well fought; we are come off
> Like Romans, neither foolish in our stands
> Nor cowardly in retire.   (I. vi. 1–3)

Such a contrast between rash bravery and calculating caution acts as a military exemplar of Rossiter's point. As Kott would say, Shakespeare pursues logic to its remorseless end by making Act V repeat Act I: Coriolanus meets his death alone, surrounded by enemies, just as he entered Corioles alone to do battle with enemies. Coriolanus's nature does not change, but the situation does, turning triumph into defeat. For Rossiter, the play is a history, in which constancy is shown as inadequate before the forces of historical process. There is no factitious re-establishment of order: we are left with Aufidius as survivor, and the class warfare in Rome is unresolved. The play, like history itself, does not end neatly, but with proof that 'all is change, nothing absolute', as Rossiter puts it.

Such bleak interpretations are not the only possible result of seeing the play as essentially political; but it is true that the more hopeful critics tend to be those who focus more on Coriolanus as tragic hero. L. C. Knights (*Sewanee Review*, 1953) neatly shows how you can effect a transition from politics to character. He argues that perennial political issues are rendered in human terms. The prominence of the fable of the belly, and of the chain of imagery which it initiates, is important to Knights's view, since 'disruption in the state – the body politic – is related to individual disharmony by something more palpable than an Elizabethan trick of metaphor': social issues are manifested and made significant in human beings. From this, Knights extracts the moral that we must never lose 'our sense of the *person* on the other side of the dividing line of class or party or nation'. The gap between such fine, liberal sentiments and more radical critics may be gauged by comparing Knights with Kott's conclusion that 'Coriolanus did not love the people. But this does not mean that Coriolanus should be condemned. In that sentence there is contained in a nutshell the bitter drama of renaissance humanism; of any humanism, in fact'. The lesson found by Knights depends on the very humanism which Kott sees as exposed in its contradictions.

The most influential statement of humanism on *Coriolanus* is G. Wilson Knight's *The Imperial Theme* (1931). For him the play's conflict is between war and love, the former being revealed as essentially flawed through its exclusion of the latter. Coriolanus himself is, naturally, the embodiment of war, a figure with all the rounded perfection of a piece of mechanism. As Menenius puts it, 'When he walks, he moves like an engine and the ground shrinks before his treading' (V. iv. 18–20). Or as Wilson Knight, ever more colourful and outrageously anachronistic, expresses it, 'He is rather like a finely-modelled motor-cycle, flashing in bright paint and steel, every line suggesting power and speed, standing among a row of drab pedal-cycles'. For all its attractiveness, such a machine is loveless and therefore deadly. In this analysis, the crisis of the play, and the point where Shakespeare reveals his true faith, comes when, faced by mother, wife and child before the gates of·Rome, Coriolanus must acknowledge the overriding power of love. Coriolanus goes off to his death, but all is well as love has been triumphant.

Criticism is often a display of the critic's world-view: impartiality is seldom detectable, especially with a text like this one. Wilson Knight is honest enough to declare that he believes that 'any world-value divorced from love' is ultimately 'a destruction, a death-phantom masquerading as life'; and he is happy to find Shakespeare agreeing with him. A Kott, on the other hand, would find such humanistic beliefs questioned by the action. Kott's taut bitterness and Wilson Knight's dithyrambic enthusiasm – so ironically unlike the play's bareness of style – are the poles between which other interpretations lie.

Coriolanus the man gets an almost universal bad press, except for those who, like Wilson Knight, have him seeing the light at the end. F. N. Lees (*RES*, 1950) appositely quotes E. M. Forster's phrase 'the undeveloped heart' as a summary of Coriolanus's lack of the 'vital power of sympathy'. Wyndham Lewis's splenetic attack on Coriolanus as 'the incarnation of violent snobbery' (*The Lion and the Fox*, 1927) represents the intemperate extreme of the Coriolanus-haters, and serves only to show how the play arouses violent reactions. Most other critics are, fortunately, more constructive.

Willard Farnham, for example, argues that he represents a development from Shakespeare's major tragic heroes, combining, like Antony, deep human flaws with nobility (*Shakespeare's Tragic Frontier*, 1950). His flaw, that of pride, is the source of all that is bad in him, but also of all that is good in him. Farnham is here approaching the question that Coriolanus's detractors must answer: if he is so monstrously unsympathetic, why should we be interested enough in him to sit through three hours of boorish behaviour? When Volumnia contradicts all her teaching by begging her son to set aside his loathing for the plebeians and feign humility to them, he replies:

> I will not do't,
> Lest I surcease to honour mine own truth,
> And by my body's action teach my mind
> A most inherent baseness. (III. ii. 120–3)

A good test of our reaction to Coriolanus is the extent to which we find this assertion of personal honour and integrity attractive and convincing. The scene is full of irony, as his very next speech will actually yield to his mother, thus dramatising the conflict of determination and personal pressure. This pattern is repeated, of course, in Act V scene iii, as Coriolanus again changes his mind under extreme prompting. This may be love triumphant over violence; but may also be integrity (remember how important that word is at III. i. 158) crumbling before insidious, unfair pressure.

Farnham is helpful in correcting over-simple views of Coriolanus which want to extract from him those very qualities that render him so impressive. Some other critics, though, have gone further to explain how an apparently loud-mouthed bigot can be fascinating, perhaps even admirable. I. R. Browning (*EC*, 1955) contributes a sensitive consideration of the mother/son relationship which is crucial to any estimation of the play.

223

W. Hutchings

Browning investigates the irony (a word which crops up quite regularly in writing on *Coriolanus*) of a boy who depends solely on his mother for affection finding that, because of her teaching, he can only earn affection through warfare. But his fame, which he feels his deeds merit, depends on the favour of the very people whom his mother has taught him to despise. The culmination of such ironies is, again, Act V scene iii, where Volumnia 'condemns a course of action to which everything she has done in the past has rigidly conduced'. A problem with Browning's argument is that it relies on a free interpretation of a relationship whose nature is to be restrained and unexpressed: how far can we render explicit what the play leaves teasingly implicit? It may be significant that, even before we see Coriolanus on stage, Shakespeare, following Plutarch, has a citizen comment that his deeds were performed 'to please his mother' (I. i. 38). But, as with so much in this strangely unyielding play, we are actually confronted by a surface, not a depth: soliloquies are infrequent and the few that there are hardly explore the mysteries of the mind.

Reuben Brower's analysis of the specifically Roman nature of the hero (*Hero and Saint*, 1971) helps to explain this quality, as when Brower shows how Cominius's praise of Coriolanus in Act II scene ii expresses through its 'august and at times coldly Latin style' the nobility of Coriolanus's virtue. 'Virtue' here must be taken as the Latin 'virtus', a complex word which relates moral qualities to physical prowess: as Cominius says, 'It is held / That valour is the chiefest virtue and / Most dignifies the haver' (II. ii. 83–5). Or as North translates Plutarch, 'in those dayes, valliantnes was honoured in ROME above all other vertues: which they called *Virtus*, by the name of vertue selfe, as including in that generall name, all other speciall vertues besides'.

It is because she takes this aspect of the play into full account that Una Ellis-Fermor's essay is the subtlest and best on Coriolanus (*Shakespeare the Dramatist*, 1961). She argues that an audience is forced to trace his real nature by means of a series of 'secret impressions'. It is only by careful attention to such signs as his hypersensitive modesty that we can make sense of his progress from heroic noble to vengeful soldier of fortune. Even early in the play, she argues, he is not simply the confident hero. An unease lies deep within him, caused by an inherent conflict between the ideal of Rome to which he dedicates himself and the apparent reality of Rome. The latter is not just a matter of cowardly plebeians and vacillating patricians, but even affects Volumnia. Most people find something repulsive, even ludicrous, in the scene where she and Menenius count up Coriolanus's wounds. Their gloating pleasure seems all the more excessive for the presence of poor Virgilia, who, as usual, keeps a pained silence. When the patricians, including Volumnia, press Coriolanus to beg the favour of the hated plebeians, the two Romes confront each other, and something has to give. Coriolanus from that point can no longer hold on to his ideal, but is obliged to play a series of roles. That he is aware of this himself is apparent from such lines as 'Like a dull actor now / I have forgot my part' (V. iii. 40–1).

In Ellis-Fermor's reading, Coriolanus's bizarre decision to join Aufidius is (as it is not often in criticism) properly explained: in the face of Rome's failure to be Roman, Coriolanus searches for his 'ideal objective' in his mirror-image. Once again, Shakespeare gives us the clue by linking his hero with Aufidius right from the beginning, as he gives to Coriolanus this remark as soon as he hears that the Volscians are in arms:

> They have a leader,
> Tullus Aufidius, that will put you to't.
> I sin in envying his nobility;
> And were I anything but what I am,
> I would wish me only he.   (I. i. 227–31)

It's worth adding that a further irony is that the ideal of Aufidius is to let Coriolanus down as surely as Rome does. That word 'envy' soon eats away the new concord between the mighty opposites.

The most convincing aspect of Ellis-Fermor's essay is the way in which she produces a coherent relationship between character and state, rather than concentrate on one to the detriment of the other. Also, she makes out a good case for the play as genuinely tragic in its depiction of an appalling, wasteful gap separating ideal and reality. For one of the most curious aspects of the critical controversy is that *Coriolanus*'s very status as tragedy is in doubt. The problem can be tested in that giant of Shakespearian criticism, A. C. Bradley, whose remarks on this play (*Shakespearian Tragedy*, 1904; *PBA*, 1911–12) insist on its limitations as compared with the 'great' tragedies. There is a want of the 'peculiar *imaginative* effect' which gives a play like *Hamlet* its mystery and sense of forces existing beyond the characters themselves. Bradley's reading of the end of the play indicates his concern to distinguish it from full tragedy. As in the case of *Antony and Cleopatra*, the finale is not tragic because such feeling is mingled with reconciliation. When Coriolanus yields to his natural ties as son, husband and father, he loses his life but 'we care little for that: he has saved his soul'. This triumph of love reveals Shakespeare at the end of his tragic period, on the way to his vision of forgiveness in the late plays.

Here, then, are the seeds of the humanistic views of Wilson Knight and others; and it is a direct line to the most determined modern attempt to downgrade *Coriolanus*, that by D. J. Enright (*EC*, 1954). He accepts the humanistic thesis that the play lacks sympathy: 'its final impression of aridness and waste might well be considered a warning against that petrifaction of humanity which occurs when people think only in terms of parties and movements and manifestoes'. So far this is L. C. Knights, but Enright goes further in arguing that a play so designed must be of inferior status. Through observing that the characters are all the time coming out with judgements of one another, he concludes that the audience is left as detached observers, witnessing a debate which exercises intellectual curiosity, but no more (not that imaginative response invoked by Bradley).

Enright's article provoked I. R. Browning's reply, where he makes out a case for *Coriolanus* as tragedy. The feeling does, however, persist that this play is different in kind from the great tragedies, even among critics who would not agree with Enright's frank demotion. For example, O. J. Campbell's remarks on its political nature are made in the service of suggesting that *Coriolanus* is not a conventional tragedy, but partakes more of the nature of satire. This depends on seeing the hero as deliberately alienated from the audience, set up for ridicule. With such views, the play is simply destroyed: if we end up with feelings of contempt, we are failing to recognize that the play dramatises vital issues and centres those issues in the figure of Coriolanus.

For other reasons, Derek Traversi's approach (*Shakespeare: the Roman Plays*, 1963) also fails to meet the tone and level of its subject. He is the most thoroughgoing of the detectors of irony, emphasising how the results of actions differ from what the agents intend. So, in the final confrontation scene, Coriolanus, a believer in honour, finds himself dedicated to ignoble revenge; while Volumnia is faced with the prospect of her world being destroyed by the son whose life she has moulded. Such observations are true enough, but they remain peripheral to the really serious concerns of the play. Irony is certainly one quality, but to select it as the 'key to the play's peculiar effect', as Traversi does, confuses part with whole. Such confusion emerges when, for example, Traversi claims that the end is both truly tragic because the simplicity of Coriolanus's code is dramatically convincing, and also ironic because 'his own perverse choices lead him irrevocably to deny' that code. Surely the point of the end is that Coriolanus denies the code under pressure, only to re-assert it (for what it's worth) in the final scene. A surprising number of critics, from Bradley on, think that the play really ends at Act V scene iii, rather than Act V scene vi.

To say that *Coriolanus* is different in kind from the great tragedies is not necessarily to admit its inferiority, but perhaps only to attest to its individuality. Willard Farnham is most interesting when he suggests that paradox makes it a work beyond (rather than beneath) tragedy. For him, Coriolanus is 'supremely guilty of pride the vice and at the same time supremely noble in pride the virtue'. His idea that we are taken beyond the conventional Aristotelian tragic responses into 'an area of paradox beyond the effective reach of merely human pity' is both an attempt to solve the problem of 'placing' the play and an indication that humanistic responses may be inappropriate. The uneasy feeling that *Coriolanus* does not fit comfortably into the Shakespearian canon is often to be detected when the play's language is discussed. Both Wilson Knight and Traversi comment on the narrowness of the range of imagery, its mechanistic or metallic tone. Maurice Charney (*Shakespeare's Roman Plays*, 1961) develops this idea most fully, concluding that, even in comparison with that of the other Roman plays, the style here is restricted, creative of 'a curiously cold, aloof, and objective world'. He relates the style to the hero being an unreflective man of action, so that the style bespeaks the man.

On this topic Charney's remarks can be usefully compared with those of Brower: where the latter sees august nobility, the former sees cold objectivity. These are different responses to a verse which seems less rich, less resonant than that of *Hamlet* or *Macbeth*; and yet which contains its own individual power. Here is part of Cominius's praise of Coriolanus:

> He stopp'd the fliers,
> And by his rare example made the coward
> Turn terror into sport; as weeds before
> A vessel under sail, so men obey'd
> And fell below his stem: his sword, death's stamp,
> Where it did mark, it took; from face to foot
> He was a thing of blood, whose every motion
> Was tim'd with dying cries: alone he enter'd
> The mortal gate of th'city, which he painted
> With shunless destiny, aidless came off,
> And with a sudden reinforcement struck
> Corioles like a planet. (II. ii. 103–14)

The crucial quality of such lines is their decorum, their fitting of language to subject. Images are honed to a point at which they solely represent the idea, rather than taking off into their own areas of resonance or implication. Sentences are generally restricted to the simplicity of main clauses and a few, straightforward subordinate clauses. The lines are usually not end-stopped and shun rhythmic grandeur, so that phrases like 'dying cries' seem facts, not fancies, statements, not rhetoric. This is certainly not the luxuriant style of Hamlet's soliloquies, but is vibrantly expressive verse in its own, perfectly valid, manner.

It is through an examination of Shakespeare's language that some of the most fruitful approaches to *Coriolanus* have come. Spade-work was usefully carried out by Caroline Spurgeon (*Shakespeare's Imagery*, 1935), whose

227

particular emphasis on metaphors of body and disease is also to be found in Wilson Knight; and by J. C. Maxwell (*MLR*, 1947) who drew attention to the animal imagery, commenting that 'the tone is often that of the beast-fable'. But it is one thing to point to the presence of imagery, another to apply one's findings to a satisfactory view of the whole play. The body metaphor, for example, owes its vitality to the way in which Shakespeare creates for it an early, emphatic statement in Menenius's fable of the belly, and at the same time establishes its real significance by making the setting for that fable a dramatic riot over famine. The metaphor thereby gains in reverberation and calls attention to its importance, for quite clearly the 'belly' of Rome (the ruling class) is not sending grain 'through the rivers of your blood' (I. i. 134). The neat, plausible model which Menenius advances to keep the people quiet is out of step with reality. We are thus prepared for a developing conflict between the forces of order and destruction, the ideal and the actual, the body politic and internal dissension.

Ralph Berry (*SEL*, 1973) provides an instance of an interesting idea that remains just that because of a failure to apply it convincingly to the whole play. He rightly notes an undercurrent of sexual images, but proceeds to claim that 'the interrelation of war and sex is the underlying statement of the play'. Now it would be difficult to think of a Shakespeare play which doesn't have an undercurrent of sexual imagery (and often the current isn't so far beneath the surface). In *Coriolanus* the mother/son relationship does express itself in fighting, and the language in which Coriolanus and Aufidius, rivals and co-mates in war, talk about each other is noticeably more passionate than that accorded to Coriolanus and Virgilia, his 'gracious silence'. But if war is, as Berry puts it, a sexual displacement-activity, it is also a lot more. He is right to draw attention to the possible significance of the Coriolanus/Aufidius relationship, but the idea needs to be explored in its relevance to the rest of the play (the politics of Rome, for example) before it can radically affect our responses to *Coriolanus*.

To point out a fundamentally relevant idea is precisely the quality of F. N. Lees's essay, one of the pieces of essential reading. He takes up Maxwell's observation of animal imagery, concludes that an atmosphere of animality clings to Coriolanus, and then gives the idea real profundity by adducing passages from Aristotle's *Politics* (in a 1598 translation) which have at their core the belief that 'He that is incapable of living in a society is a god or a beast'. These are not just of historical interest: Aristotle's political and social ideas were current at the time (Bacon quotes this very *dictum* in his essay *Of Friendship*), and the opening section of the *Politics* seems highly relevant to Shakespeare's depiction of both the state of Rome and Coriolanus's actions within it. Aristotle emphasises in the *Politics* and the *Ethics* that man is a social, civil being who remains essentially inseparable from his fellow human beings. The values of the *polis* (the Greek word for a city-state, from which we significantly derive the word 'politics') are intrinsic to human existence. So, when Coriolanus likens himself to 'a lonely dragon that his fen / Makes fear'd and talk'd of more than seen' (IV. i. 30–1), he is confessing, even revelling in, his profoundly unsocial and therefore inhuman behaviour.

This attitude is adopted by Terry Eagleton (*Shakespeare and Society*, 1967) who convincingly makes man's social being central to the play. '*Coriolanus* is about the conflict of authentic life and social responsibility, the tension between the way a man conceives of himself and the social character which is offered for him to make his own.' Eagleton suggests that Coriolanus represents adherence to the self, divorced from all consideration of social duties: hence his constant refusal to accept what others say, whether this be praise from his fellow-patricians or critical scrutiny from the plebeians. It follows that Coriolanus is out of place in the life of the city, only at home on the battlefield where, freed from social pressure, he can define himself solely through his own unaided actions. He is marked by 'a self-conferment of value', a rejection of 'the need for social verification, the evaluations of others'. His integrity – that word again – is so complete as to create a life 'enclosed and therefore self-consuming'.

Integrity is central to a recent essay by John Bayley (*Shakespeare and Tragedy*, 1981), who sees Coriolanus as refusing to play along with 'the complex comedy of public behaviour' acted out by the rest of Rome. Bayley, refreshing and perverse in equal proportions (perhaps one is a consequence of the other), contradicts nearly everybody by describing the play as a domestic comedy rather than an ideological tragedy. Coriolanus 'cannot bear to look at himself and accept there the absurdity of being ordinarily human'; but the climax of Act V scene iii – once again we see a critic emphasising the end which isn't the end – demonstrates that even he is, after all, only human. Eagleton and Bayley together constitute a fine instance of how much common ground can produce strikingly different fruit. While Eagleton defines the play's tragic value as lying in 'the intensity of energy with which a human position is held and maintained, even though the position is intolerable', Bayley thinks that Coriolanus ends up more like a Malvolio, excluded from the play's happy ending: Act V scene iii shows how society's instincts for comic processes defeat the tragic figure, and the rest of the play is simply a 'tragic postscript' which doesn't really alter the comic climax.

Judgement between Eagleton and Bayley (a judgement which is allied to the basic decision we have to make between the radical critics and the humanist critics) is partly a matter of testing their views against the play's theatrical effect: does the final scene come across as a postscript or a searing murder-scene? But even out of the heat of the theatre, there are some clear indications: for example, Coriolanus does not exit from the gates of Rome to leave them and the stage to the rest of the cast, but is the centre of the action right to the end. Further, Shakespeare's careful structural organisation, whereby Coriolanus's situation at the end recalls the moment of his greatest triumph at Corioles, would suggest that the last scene is to be significant.

The way to approach it is by more consideration of the language of the play. Language is the medium of the social life, of the *polis*. Coriolanus is very good at breaking into cities, but is not so good with words, at communicating with people who live in cities. As ever, Shakespeare draws our attention right away to this, as early as Martius's first entrance:

Menenius	Hail, noble Martius.
Martius	Thanks. What's the matter, you dissentious rogues That, rubbing the poor itch of your opinion, Make yourselves scabs? (I. i. 162–5)

His curtness with Menenius amounts to a break in mutual communication: how different if his reply had been 'Hail, noble Menenius' rather than 'Thanks'. Immediately he wishes to taunt the citizens, not to talk to them. His question (a normal method of setting up communication) is not one which seriously invites an answer. His language to both classes is unsocial, divisive. It is significant that Coriolanus's major moment of communication occurs when Shakespeare adopts North's phrase, 'holding her by the right hande', but with his own addition so that the actor is told that he must hold Volumnia 'by the hand silent' (S.D. V. iii. 182). Communication, real communication, comes through silence. This is why Virgilia's almost speechless role is such an important one, for it establishes a core of silent suffering in the midst of the clamorous sounds of war, insults and self-assertion.

James L. Calderwood (*SEL*, 1966) goes further by saying that customs and words in Rome have become utterly meaningless. So the gown of humility ritual is a sham, and when the people need food they are fobbed off with Menenius's soothing words which have little to do with the real state of affairs. The result, for Calderwood, is chaos: 'The bond between what is meant and what is understood by words, the common ground between speaker and listener which makes dialogue possible, is the whole social structure from which language issues. If this structure breaks down, as it does in *Coriolanus*, language breaks down with it'. Coriolanus is unable to adjust to the nuances of words, and this reflects his lack of sensitivity for human feelings. It is only fair to Coriolanus to interject here that his adherence to words' singleness of meaning has a positive side to it: one result is his inability to dissemble before the people, even when pressed to do so on all sides. The central distinction is certainly that between Coriolanus and the rest of Rome, and we might usefully recall Rossiter's argument about Coriolanus being out of step with the shifting nature of historical process. But there may be two points of view about such a situation: one man's intractable rigidity is another man's firm adherence to principle.

A specific example of language is one's own name. A particularly striking incident in the play occurs after the battle, when Coriolanus wishes to free a man who had treated him kindly, but forgets his name. Calderwood comments that this incident illustrates 'the futility of private meanings that cannot be translated into a public language'. It is ironic that his inability to put a name to a human being follows immediately after Martius has acquired a new name, the *agnomen* of Coriolanus. Later, when the banished Coriolanus confronts Aufidius, he refers to this name:

> My name is Caius Martius, who hath done
> To thee particularly, and to all the Volsces,
> Great hurt and mischief: thereto witness may
> My surname, Coriolanus. The painful service,
> The extreme dangers, and the drops of blood
> Shed for my thankless country, are requited
> But with that surname: a good memory
> And witness of the malice and displeasure
> Which thou should'st bear me. Only that name remains.   (IV. v. 66–74)

As Calderwood says, an honourable name has become divorced from reality, so that it has become just breath devoid of meaning. Names mean nothing because they are not supported by true actions.

The heart of *Coriolanus* lies in a conjunction of its concern with social cohesion and its stress on appropriate language; or, from the other point of view, it lies in how the problem of relating language to truth expresses social division. Cominius's language when he praises Coriolanus is superbly fitting, but only for a depiction of the warrior-hero: the problem comes when 'Coriolanus' (and it is Cominius who gives him that name) has to live and act in the city-state of Rome. On this issue the central article is that by D. J. Gordon (*Papers Mainly Shakespearian*, 1964). He brilliantly combines Lees's emphasis on the social nature of the state with consideration of the relationship between action and language in that state. Rational human life 'is defined by the walls of the city: it is the life of *conversazione civile*, civil intercourse, *civil conversation* – and our meaning for that word was separated out of the first. The bond is language'. Save Virgilia alone, the civil life of *Coriolanus* is marked by broken, perverted relationships between word and subject, man and fellow-man. Coriolanus's heroic exploits deserve, demand fame. But that fame is dependent upon the 'voices', the votes of the people. In the process of transference from action to word, something happens to change, to spoil, to complicate those actions. Actions may speak louder than words, but this is a play in which words radically affect actions.

The implications of the kind of argument advanced by Gordon are as bleak as those of a Kott or a Rossiter. The life of the *polis* will continue after Coriolanus's death, unchanged by it, just as the historical process will continue, ignoring the death of one man. The humanist view that love has triumphed is simply wrong: by not destroying Rome, Coriolanus avoids gaining 'such a name / Whose repetition will be dogg'd with curses' (V. iii. 143–4), and instead receives the name of 'traitor' from Aufidius. Rome, meanwhile, is unchanged from the loveless, class-divided state it was at the start. If Rome exhibits no trace of the ideal it should be, at least one man takes a part, if only a part, of that ideal with him. Coriolanus's death comes with a re-assertion of his Roman nature and his individuality:

> Cut me to pieces, Volsces, men and lads,
> Stain all your edges on me. Boy! False hound!
> If you have writ your annals true, 'tis there,
> That like an eagle in a dove-cote, I
> Flutter'd your Volscians in Corioles.
> Alone I did it. (V. vi. 111–16)

He asserts his identity at the moment that identity is to be snuffed out with the cry of 'Kill, kill, kill, kill, kill him!' Language here is reduced to its lowest form, a base repetition of a bestial noise. Aristotle's *Politics* is again pertinent: 'The reason why man is a being meant for political association, in a higher degree than bees or other gregarious animals can ever associate, is evident . . . man alone of the animals is furnished with the faculty of language'. Moreover, 'Man, when perfected, is the best of animals; but if he be isolated from law and justice he is the worst of all'. (I quote from book I, chapter ii of the Ernest Barker translation.) At the end it is not just Coriolanus who is so isolated: the conspirators' cry is symptomatic of the unregenerate animality into which the state, Roman and Volscian, has lapsed. Rome is saved, but what is it worth? Its future greatness, when the figure of Coriolanus will have a mythic value, is a historical fact. As for the Coriolanus dramatized by Shakespeare, we might recall Brutus's words to him, 'You speak o'th'people / As if you were a god to punish, not / A man of their infirmity' (III. i. 79–81); and then note again Aristotle's careful alternatives: 'The man who is isolated – who is unable to share in the benefits of political association, or has no need to share because he is already self-sufficient – is no part of the polis, and must therefore be either a beast or a god.'

Suggested reading

A selected list of the most valuable criticism on *Coriolanus*.
Essential essays are marked *

John Bayley, 'The thing I am: Coriolanus' in *Shakespeare and Tragedy* (1981)
Ralph Berry, 'Sexual imagery in *Coriolanus*', *Studies in English Literature 1500–1900*, 13 (1973)
A. C. Bradley, *Shakespearian Tragedy* (1904); and '*Coriolanus*', *Proceedings of the British Academy*, 5 (1911–12)
Reuben A. Brower, 'The Deeds of Coriolanus' in *Hero and Saint: Shakespeare and the Graeco-Roman Heroic Tradition* (1971)
I. R. Browning, '*Coriolanus*: boy of tears', *Essays in Criticism*, 5 (1955)
James L. Calderwood, '*Coriolanus*: wordless meanings and meaningless words', *Studies in English Literature 1500–1900*, 6 (1966)
O. J. Campbell, '*Coriolanus*' in *Shakespeare's Satire* (1943)
Maurice Charney, *Shakespeare's Roman Plays: the Function of Imagery in the Drama* (1961)
*Terence Eagleton, *Shakespeare and Society* (1967)
*Una Ellis-Fermor, '*Coriolanus*' in *Shakespeare the Dramatist* (1961)
D. J. Enright, '*Coriolanus*: tragedy or debate', *Essays in Criticism*, 4 (1954)
Willard Farnham, *Shakespeare's Tragic Frontier* (1950)
*D. J. Gordon, 'Name and fame: Shakespeare's Coriolanus' in *Papers Mainly Shakespearian*, ed. G. I. Duthie (1964)
G. Wilson Knight, *The Imperial Theme* (1931)
L. C. Knights, 'Shakespeare and political wisdom: a note on the personalism of *Julius Caesar* and *Coriolanus*', *Sewanee Review*, 61 (1953)
*Jan Kott, *Shakespeare Our Contemporary*, trans. Boleslaw Taborski (1965)
*F. N. Lees, '*Coriolanus*, Aristotle and Bacon', *Review of English Studies*, new series, 1 (1950)
*A. P. Rossiter, *Angel with Horns* (1961)
Derek Traversi, *Shakespeare: the Roman Plays* (1963)

In addition, Philip Brockbank writes a stimulating introduction to the Arden Shakespeare edition (1976), the edition from which I quote. There is a useful Casebook, edited by B. A. Brockman, which includes some of the above, though only Ellis-Fermor and Rossiter of the starred items.

[1982]